The Ultimate Writer's Guide to Hollywood

THE ULTIMATE WRITER'S GUIDE TO HOLLYWOOD

SKIP PRESS

BARNES & NOBLE BOOKS
NEW YORK

Academy Award® and Oscar® are registered trademarks of the Academy of Motion
Picture Arts and Sciences.
Emmy is the trademark property of Academy of Television Arts & Sciences/National
Academy of Television Arts & Sciences.
Nickelodeon® is a trademark of Viacom International Inc.
QuickTime® is a registered trademark of Apple Computer, Inc.

Library of Congress Cataloging-in-Publication Data
Available upon request

2004 Barnes & Noble Books

Book designed and text composition by HRoberts Design

ISBN 0-7607-6110-8

Printed and bound in the United States of America

04 05 06 07 08 09 M 9 8 7 6 5 4 3 2 1

This book is dedicated to my

readers and students everywhere;

I sincerely hope they achieve

their Hollywood dreams.

C O N T E N T S

ACKNOWLEDGMENTS

First and foremost, I owe Susan Miller of astrologyzone.com a great debt for introducing me to Laura Nolan at Barnes & Noble Books. I thank Susan for being such a great friend, and I thank Laura for being such a kind and fair editor. I also thank Laura for handing me to editor Heather Rodino, with whom I shared a lot of laughs and owe many thanks for working with me through unexpected ups and downs to get this book done. Thank you, Heather.

Acknowledgments

In Hollywood, I thank my friends Paul Mason, Rona Edwards, Gary Shusett, Jennie Lew Tugend, and scores of others (too many to list), for picking up the phone whenever I call. Hollywood catches a lot of heat, not all of it undeserved, but it still delivers the majority of the world's entertainment. I still love the place and the great people I know here.

To special clients James Ossi and Ted Gasowski, thank you for your stories and support. It's people like you who make it worth the effort.

I thank new Hollywood friends like Peter McHugh and The Gotham Group, and old friends I don't see often such as Joel Gotler for making the town a lot more interesting. I thank Craig Power of EducationToGo.com for helping me get my screenwriting course into hundreds of schools. I thank professional publishing friends Paula Munier, Craig Nelson, and Sol Stein for always offering great advice when I need it.

I thank Debbie Press for all her support over the years and her protection of my space as I've written my books, including this one. I thank our children, Haley Alexander and Holly Olivia, for giving me reason to marvel each day, as they grow into their own Hollywood dreams.

And of course, I thank my mother, Bettie Davidson, who took me to the movie matinees when I was the only kid in the family and helped fire my endless imagination. From Woody Woodpecker to *To Kill A Mockingbird* (1962) it was great sitting there with you, Mom.

INTRODUCTION

This book is a road map for anyone who wants to sell a "property" to Hollywood. I'm not referring to real estate. Although the film capital of the world derived its name from a housing development called "Hollywoodland," a property can be a true story, an article in a newspaper or magazine, a book (nonfiction), a novel (fiction), a stage play, an original screenplay, an old TV show or movie reworked, or even a simple commercial idea that is proposed to a Hollywood production company or television network.

In short, a property is anything that Hollywood can turn into a viewable product for public consumption.

I begin this book in such practical terms because the term "Hollywood" refers to the entertainment *business*. In southern California, where I've lived and worked for over two decades, the term "show biz" could refer to the film business, the television networks, video game production, or even adult entertainment. Each of which, I should add, earns billion of dollars each year. (And you might be surprised which ones earn most.) Do you see why you might need a road map?

While you're considering this journey, allow me to introduce myself. Skip Press is my real name, believe it or not. I've been working in Hollywood a long time. My first script sale was to a nationally syndicated radio show based in L.A. My first movie sale was negotiated by a fellow who is currently president of the Writers Guild of America, west. I've written more entertainment business articles than I can count, edited a Los Angeles entertainment business magazine, sold screenplays and had them "optioned" (a down payment toward a sale), written for television, made "how-to" videos, and "a whole lot more."

Since 1993, I've been in the Hollywood advice business while maintaining a screenwriting career. I've had scripts optioned and TV shows made. If you recognized my name, you may have read one of the three editions of my *Writer's Guide to Hollywood Producers, Directors and Screenwriters' Agents* or one of the two editions of my *Complete Idiot's Guide to Screenwriting*. You may also have taken one of my screenwriting courses, either online or in the classroom. More likely, you're simply someone with something to sell to Hollywood. Wherever you fit in, I think I can help you. If not, I probably can find someone who can, because I know "the business" and the people in it.

And that's very important. All too many creative people who approach Hollywood fail to realize that business value repeatedly trumps aesthetic value in this entertainment capital of the world. Could it be otherwise? Without due consideration to the bottom line, Hollywood would go out of business.

Thus, this is a book of facts, not academic speculation. That does not mean you should not work with passion, your muse at your side as your original voice floods onto the page or screen. You should still strive to be that "original voice" that echoes across the Hollywood Hills all too rarely. Do not think, however, that you can—to paraphrase a line from an unlikely box office success called *Field of Dreams* (1989)—simply write, and they will come.

Don't hold your breath waiting for Hollywood to discover you. To succeed in selling here, you will need talent, direction, persistence, vision, and a little luck. In short, all the elements that go into making a great motion picture.

If you have written a "spec screenplay"—a screenplay written on your own time with the speculation that you will at some point sell it—congratulations on completing it. I hope this book will help you sell it, or at least get you hired to write another screenplay. So get started on your next screenplay, and show yourself that you're serious about a screenwriting career. The great screenwriters, just like all great writers, are in it for the long haul. They cannot *not* write. Working writers in Hollywood are filled with ideas and constantly laboring to improve their craft. They know that their Hollywood customers may not like the first thing they see, but could like the writer, or the writing. So when the question, "What else you got?" (which will probably sound just like that) comes, they have something else ready to show and sell.

I repeatedly tell writers that most great screenplays become that way by being rewritten over and over. "Finished" scripts are often purchased only to have other writers brought in immediately to start rewriting that script. New works are read aloud in "staged readings" or "read-throughs" to get a sense of how the script will play on screen. If a joke doesn't work or dialogue doesn't make sense, changes are made. Even when a film is in production, scenes may be rewritten, dropped, or added daily.

All of this happens because even a "low-budget" studio feature film might cost $20 million to put on screen, and the public relations cost might equal that. A network television episode—even a thirty-minute situation comedy—might cost $1 million or more to produce. Many people are employed, and much is at stake. Collaboration is the key in Hollywood, and careers are on the line every single day.

That's where you come in, with this Hollywood road map in your hands. Got the talent? We'll provide the direction. By "we" I mean myself and all the other contributors to this book, people with decades

This is a terrific script. It just needs a complete rewrite.

—**Peter Bogdanovich**

of Hollywood experience. You're certain you have the persistence? Well then, what's your vision? That's what we really want to know. With a little luck, we'll help you find the right people to share that vision—those who will champion your project all the way through to completion.

And please understand this—the discovery of a great property or writer spreads through the rumor mills of Hollywood quicker than a brush fire in high wind conditions.

Even so, you'll probably need a champion to light your fire in this business. You will certainly need someone who will treat you fairly. If you don't know what it means to be treated fairly in Hollywood, you'll learn it in this book. And you'll learn how and where to find your champion(s).

I began writing about selling to Hollywood almost a decade ago. Many books, articles, and speaking engagements later, a great deal has changed, but the principles remain the same. The most notable difference in "the business" is the leveled playing field that resulted from the digital filmmaking revolution. For example, in 2004, a $7,000 film named *Primer* won the Sundance Film Festival. Spike Lee made his movie *Bamboozled* (2000) with a consumer model digital camera. And I'm sure you've heard about the massive success of *The Blair Witch Project* (1999). There are many other examples of people who did whatever it took to get noticed by Hollywood by making their own movie. So that might be your ticket.

If you're not ready to do that, no problem. I can teach you to write a saleable screenplay. I've written a couple of books on the subject and offer a course called "Your Screenwriting Career" at www.screenwritingcourse.com. And if you need to know where to learn filmmaking, keep reading.

If you'd rather just find an agent or a literary manager, some of the best are covered herein. If you need help with writer's block or want to find a writer's psychologist, we have those, too. From places to hang out to people who won't hang up on you, we've done our best to give you as complete a tour of the literary landscape of Hollywood as has ever existed.

And before I forget, allow me to define "Hollywood." It's not just a truncated sign left over from a real estate development. Hollywood is not only the film business, or even all the entertainment concerns in southern California. These days, thanks to the Internet and great filmmakers all over the planet, "Hollywood" now belongs to the world. It's all the creators of viewable product, wherever they reside. If you don't believe me, you weren't watching the Oscars in 2004 as Peter Jackson and his fellow filmmakers from New Zealand swept the Oscars.

Toward the new Hollywood reality, my purpose in writing this book is to show you the ultimate in possibilities, to answer all your questions, even those you didn't know you had. And if you do not find what you are looking for herein, you can always ask me a question. I respond to emails by the hundreds on a weekly basis, because I believe in a Hollywood principle known as "giving back."

When I began in this town, very successful people interested in giving back were very generous with their advice. They bought me lunch, told me what I was doing wrong, and explained how the business worked. I have enjoyed this generosity of strangers throughout my career. When I found out my wife's favorite film was *The Sound of Music* (1965), I bought a poster of the movie and started making calls. Superstar Julie Andrews signed it first, followed by screenwriter Ernest Lehman (a truly great writer), and legendary producer/director Robert Wise. All of them were more than happy to help thrill a person they didn't even know.

And isn't that really what this business is all about?

Over the years, I've found that the nicest people in Hollywood are almost invariably those at the top. That's where I hope you end up, and nothing would please me more than helping you get there.

Skip Press
July 2004
www.skippress.com

CHAPTER

1

Hollywood
Rules

Let me tell you about the very rich. They are different from you and me. They possess and enjoy early, and it does something to them, makes them soft where we are hard, and cynical where we are trustful, in a way that, unless you were born rich, it is very difficult to understand. They think, deep in their hearts, that they are better than we are because we had to discover the compensations and refuges of life for ourselves. Even when they enter deep into our world or sink below us, they still think that they are better than we are. They are different.

—F. Scott Fitzgerald

Francis Scott Key Fitzgerald's short story "The Rich Boy," excerpted above, was serialized in the January and February 1926 issues of *Redbook* magazine. It was written at the Hotel Tiberio on the isle of Capri as the author awaited the publication of what would become his most famous novel, *The Great Gatsby*. Fitzgerald commanded $4,000 for a short story in those days; adjusted for inflation, that would total more than $42,000 today. His observation that the rich are different became so famous that ten years later his friend Ernest Hemingway

commented on it in his own short story, "The Snows of Kilimanjaro":
"Yes, they have more money."

What does this have to do with today's Hollywood? Almost eight decades after its publication, the opening lines of Fitzgerald's story could just as easily have been written now about the rich and powerful in the world's film capital; those financiers and creators of celluloid dreams who influence the lives of billions.

If you hope to do business with such people, you must understand them. Good or bad, Hollywood movers and shakers are probably different than you, and you should never be shocked if their motivations for making a movie do not match your own.

And yes, they probably do have more money than you or me.

"The Rich Boy" was about a magnetic, immoral young man named Anson Hunter. To deal with Hunter, said the narrator, he had "to approach him as if he were a foreigner and cling stubbornly to my point of view. If I accept his for a moment I am lost—I have nothing to show but a preposterous movie." The protagonist felt no need to apologize for anything, whether he was being a drunk, taking advantage of women, or wreaking emotional havoc among relatives and friends. In short, Hunter was as sociopathic as some of the movie business people dissected in tell-all books such as *You'll Never Eat Lunch in This Town Again* by Julia Phillips, *Hello, He Lied* by Lynda Obst, or *Hollywood, Interrupted* by Andrew Breitbart and Mark Ebner. (Read all those books if you want a cold dose of Hollywood realities.)

But now, back to our story. Fitzgerald's *The Great Gatsby* became a smash success that defined a time in American history known as the Jazz Age. For a time, Fitzgerald was America's most celebrated author and its most highly paid short story writer. By the early 1930s, though, he was in financial straits. The medical expenses of caring for his schizophrenic wife, Zelda, were overwhelming, and he might have been ruined if Hollywood had not come to his rescue. Fitzgerald had tried screenwriting in 1927, when he worked on *Lipstick* for United Artists, but he had been disappointed when the movie was not produced. In the spring of 1932, once again unable to ignore the vast sums paid by Hollywood, he returned to work on *Red-Headed Woman* (1932) for Metro-Goldwyn-Mayer. Zelda suffered her second nervous breakdown in February, however, and Fitzgerald would not remain in L.A. for long.

In July 1937, deep in debt, Fitzgerald returned to Hollywood for a third time. He signed a six-month contract with MGM at the then princely sum of $1,000 a week, and in December, his contract was renewed for another year at $1,250 a week. In 1938, he finally received what would be his only on-screen credit, for the movie *Three Comrades* (1938). He would work on many other films—*Marie Antoinette* (1938), *Madame Curie* (1943), *Winter Carnival* (1939), even *Gone with the Wind* (1939)—but would never again see his name on screen. If you check under Fitzgerald's name on the Internet Movie Database (www.imdb.com), you will see that all the other films that do not derive from one of his novels or short stories read "uncredited."

That doesn't do much for a writer's ego, but that's Hollywood, and the process is pretty much the same today. You might earn the roughly $100,000 Fitzgerald was paid for writing motion pictures, or even the adjusted-for-inflation equivalent of around $1.3 million, but it is highly unlikely that your on-screen credits will equal the number of scripts you actually write. Nevertheless, if you have something that Hollywood considers valuable enough to become a movie—whether it is an article, a short story, a true story, a non-fiction book, a novel, or an original screenplay—you can do well. In the words of a friend who became an "A-list" screenwriter, you can make "crazy money."

In 1940, F. Scott Fitzgerald was killed by two heart attacks. The first one came at the legendary Schwab's Drugstore on Sunset Boulevard. At the time, Zelda was living in a mental hospital in North Carolina where she would later die, and Fitzgerald was sharing an apartment in Hollywood with his lover, newspaper columnist Sheila Graham. His relationship with Graham would later be memorialized in the movie *Beloved Infidel* (1959), starring Gregory Peck and Deborah Kerr. The second heart attack kept Fitzgerald from finishing his novel, *The Last*

Tycoon, which he had been unable to sell in serial form to *Collier's* magazine.

Fitzgerald passed on thinking he was a failure and feeling defeated by Hollywood. One has to wonder whom in Hollywood, specifically, might have engendered such feelings in Fitzgerald. Well, *The Last Tycoon* was inspired by Irving Thalberg, a legendary film executive and producer who died in 1936. (Fitzgerald also based his short story "Crazy Sunday" on a party he attended at Thalberg's home.) Thalberg was known for his belief in making quality pictures that brought prestige to his industry, and after his death the Motion Picture Academy created the Irving Thalberg Award in his honor. The special Oscar is given to recognize excellence in film production. But Thalberg didn't necessarily believe everyone in "the business" should be recognized for his or her excellence. As one of the thirty-six founders of the Academy of Motion Picture Arts and Sciences, he once said: "The writer is the only absolutely essential element of Hollywood, and he must never find out."

Yes, the rich are different, and even more so in Hollywood.

Things haven't changed much since the 1930s. Substitute "current Hollywood power players" for "the rich," and you'll be prepared for this town. Most people who approach the film business from the outside, hoping to sell a screenplay or some other literary property, don't realize how drastically different a world Hollywood is from their own. Successful people in the film and television business are usually astonishingly rich, and a great many of them simply do not operate by the same logic or rules as normal people. If you don't think that there are extreme neurotics and sociopaths abounding in the film capital of the world, you suffer from an incomplete education. Remember the scene in *Get Shorty* (1995) where Danny DeVito can't simply order something that's on the menu, but must have something specially prepared? That's typical, but it gets worse. As I began this book, a certain studio head had lunch with a certain high level investor at the investor's office. Before they could have the meeting, the studio head's personal chef had to have a lengthy discussion with the investor's caterer, to see that the studio head's culinary necessities were fulfilled to exact specifications. Or so a little bird told me.

Still, you will find a great many fine people in Hollywood, and a lot of them are at the top. For example, in *real* life, Danny DeVito once stopped by to say hello at a dinner my family was having at The Magic Castle in Hollywood. He'd read a script of mine and liked it. DeVito pretended to be the maître d' and my mother, not knowing who he was, thought he was "such a nice man."

Good or bad, some things are true for just about everyone in Hollywood. You can get lost trying to figure out the personalities, but if you understand the motivations you can use that to your advantage. Here's something to remember:

HOLLYWOOD RULE #1—*Just about everyone loves the movies.*

Hollywood's search for the next big thing is never-ending. For your sake, and because I love movies, I hope you have that next big thing, and that it's great. If you also have that rare quality called talent and a persistence that will keep you from being ignored or forgotten, sooner or later you can break through. As F. Scott Fitzgerald's lover Sheila Graham once said: "You can have anything you want if you want it desperately enough. You must want it with an inner exuberance that erupts through the skin and joins the energy that created the world."

Hollywood recognizes passion, exuberance, and creative energy. Like Fitzgerald, you might need three (or more!) sojourns here before you start making crazy money, but dreams really can come true.

Hopefully, you will not end your Hollywood career thinking you are a failure, only to have your best work filmed after your demise. And let's not be too harsh on Hollywood; even though Fitzgerald was famous for saying, "There are no second acts in American lives," his own literary second act was better than the first, thanks to film. Without the recognition of his work that came via motion pictures and television, it is doubtful that Fitzgerald would have been honored in 1998 on one of fifteen

My movies were the kind they show in prisons and airplanes, because nobody can leave.

—**Burt Reynolds**

32¢ U.S. commemorative postage stamps in the "Celebrate the Century" series. Thanks to the movies' recognition of his genius, F. Scott Fitzgerald had a happy ending after all.

So now, let's embark on your Hollywood education with another important maxim:

HOLLYWOOD RULE #2—*It's a people town.*

Information about who they are, where they are, and what they expect may surprise you at first, but by the time we're done, you will have a store of information that took me and a lot of friends decades to discover. Buckle up, turn up the soundtrack, and let's get rolling. We'll start our journey in the place you call home.

Your Reality vs. Hollywood Reality

On a given day in Burbank, the "Media City" where I live, I might drive by NBC where people are waiting in line to get in to see Jay Leno and *The Tonight Show*. I might have lunch with someone who wants to option something of mine at The Smokehouse restaurant across from Warner Bros. (best garlic bread in Los Angeles). I might take my kids to a show at the Falcon Theatre in Toluca Lake, which is owned by producer/director Gary Marshall. Just down the street from the place I get my hair cut is the Bob Hope estate; I had the pleasure of interviewing Hope once and I envy his amazing career. And most days, I'm sitting at home on the couch writing.

Certain aspects of my activities might dazzle you but they don't excite me at all unless I sell something. It doesn't mean a lot to me to take a friend to meet an agent in Beverly Hills unless I can get that friend signed by that agent. I'm interested in results.

That goes for anyone who matters in Hollywood.

So now you know something about me. Unfortunately, I don't

know you or anything about you, your likes, dislikes, hatreds, or passions. I don't know what results you expect, and neither does anyone else in Hollywood. They only know what results they are after, which usually translate into money. They don't really care that you've taken a $100 "master course" in Writing a Great Query Letter over the Internet. Many of them will probably just toss your letter in the trash. Some will not open your envelope or your email. They might even block you from sending them a fax.

If you send them a screenplay, or even pitch your screenplay at a weekend pitch festival in Los Angeles, it will probably be read (if at all) by the lowest-level employee. Believe me, he'll probably be much more interested in seeing that his boss's dry cleaning is picked up on time. And since he might have twenty screenplays to read on the weekend during his "time off," that reader might only read five pages of a script it took you a year to write before tossing it into the trash.

And why not? There are produced writers with established agents who write new screenplays all the time. That doesn't mean they'll be great scripts, but those scripts, along with books slated for publication, get more attention. Those properties have a built-in recommendation because they come from a known person or agency. In the case of books and novels, someone took them seriously enough to publish them. And in case you didn't know, top Hollywood production entities employ people to scout out hot new novels; they read the manuscripts well before they are published. They're looking for the next big thing and they tend, often wrongly, to equate quality with cost. These days a studio movie costs more than $100 million. That means a producer usually needs a script by a top writer (which might cost $1 million) to interest a top director and a star whose starting salary is $25 million. What? You have a script that you swear won't cost over $10 million to shoot? Who wants to read something that isn't even a low-budget $20 million movie? Which means that somehow you have to greatly impress someone; do something to "get yourself on the radar" as I call it. You can't just be a "good writer." You must demonstrate with your property that it has a

Hollywood is a town that will nice you to death.

—Mel Brooks

great possibility of being highly profitable. And brother, do they need profits in Hollywood!

Allow me to elaborate. In his March 2004 annual report to the ShoWest convention on American box office trends, Jack Valenti, head of the Motion Picture Association of America (MPAA), explained that U.S. movie theater admissions shrank by 4 percent in 2003. He called the competition for box office dollars "a lacerating catalog of rivalries and marketplace antagonisms" at a time when the combined cost of producing and marketing a studio film was $102.8 million. That expense was up 15 percent from the year before. The total box office take for 2003 was $9.5 billion, the second best ever, but the "conventional wisdom" in Hollywood often failed. At the time Valenti made his report, Mel Gibson's *The Passion of the Christ* (2004), personally financed by Gibson for $25 million and *not* distributed by a Hollywood studio, was on its way to becoming the greatest R-rated box office success of all time. By the end of March it had grossed more than $300 million, after only a month in release. Not a single Hollywood studio had wanted to make the movie. As soon as *Passion* started topping the box office, though, the copycats came out in force. TV networks ran miniseries and other programs about Jesus, and suddenly religious-themed movies were buzzing in *Variety* and *The Hollywood Reporter.* In Tinseltown, profits are everything.

The runaway success of *Passion* was reminiscent of the PG-rated breakout hit of 2002, *My Big Fat Greek Wedding,* which made almost $250 million in fifty weeks and became the most successful romantic comedy of all time. With a production budget of only $5 million, *Wedding,* like *Passion,* was non-studio financed and distributed, and featured relatively unknown stars.

This is the good news for you. Regardless of what most studios believe about the relationship between cost and quality, in recent years, some of the biggest movie successes have *not* been generated in Hollywood. Major Hollywood players have been involved, but they didn't depend on conventional studio financing to make their hits.

Let's take a look at why that is by examining what *Wedding* and *Passion* might have cost with major Hollywood stars who have been referred to as members of "The $25 Million Club" (their price for starring in a movie). What if Tom Hanks had been the male lead in *My Big Fat Greek Wedding*? After all, his wife, Rita Wilson (who has Greek heritage), produced the movie. Hanks may be a great actor, but he was forty-five years old when the movie was made. OK, how about Tom Cruise? At forty, too old. Could Cameron Diaz have played a dowdy Greek girl? The age was right, but I don't see it.

How about Jim Carrey as Christ? In *Bruce Almighty* (2003) maybe, but Jesus? No way. Mike Myers? He's forty, bay-bee. Mel Gibson's in the $25 million club, but he wasn't vain enough to try to play the King of Kings, and besides, he's almost fifty.

Adam Sandler, Will Smith, Bruce Willis, Harrison Ford, Julia Roberts, Chris Tucker (he reportedly made $25 million for *Rush Hour 2*, 2001)—none of them seem right for either film. And then, bumping down to the $20 Million Club, we have Nicolas Cage, George Clooney, Russell Crowe, Leonardo DiCaprio, Vin Diesel, Eddie Murphy, and Denzel Washington. Could you see them starring in either movie?

Which brings us back to your backyard. If you're reading this book, you probably have a personal vision that you want to share with the world via film or TV. So why don't you try to make your own movie? The films discussed above and other, much smaller budgeted, career-making movie phenomena of recent years like *El Mariachi* (1992), *The Blair Witch Project* (1999), and even *Clerks* (1994) reached the public because the people behind them had vision and persistence. They also had something else that *Passion* and *Wedding* shared—a great story. Which brings us to something you can offer Hollywood that is usually in short supply here:

HOLLYWOOD RULE #3—*Everyone loves a great story.*

All those movies I just mentioned had entertaining stories. *Blair Witch* had the least interesting narrative, but it was cleverly marketed via the

Internet. I saw newsgroup posts designed to make you think real footage of real deaths were in the film. And the movie's backstory reminded people of similar legends in places where they grew up, of local mysteries, old witches, and hauntings.

Do you have a great story, real or imagined? That's what Hollywood wants from you. What makes a great story? Well, think about it. How many times have you commented on a movie with a friend, or had someone tell you about a "great book" they've read? Although Hollywood executives are often portrayed as cold, calculating machines, remember, they love movies. If you don't believe it, just attend a screening of an old celebrated film at an Academy of Motion Pictures Arts and Sciences put on in Los Angeles or New York. I fondly remember one of *Damn Yankees* (1958) where many of the cast members and the director commented on making the movie. (See www.oscars.org for details about the screenings.) This 1958 film adaptation of a hit Broadway musical was about a Washington Senators baseball fan who makes a deal with the devil to help his team win the pennant. It was remade for television in 1967 and is being remade as a feature film.

> *I'd hire the devil himself as a writer if he gave me a good story.*
>
> **—Samuel Goldwyn**

That's one example of a great story. I'm sure you know many more, and I hope you have one to sell, because they're hard to find.

Learning acceptable screenplay structure and clever marketing is secondary to great storytelling. In fact, just about everything is secondary to a great story. The question is, in what form is it presented? That could make a difference in how easy it will be to sell your property to people in Hollywood. Let's take a look at some specifics.

Are You Selling with an Audience Attached?

As long as I've been writing about Hollywood, I've consistently told people that this is a copycat town. There is a great deal of fear here, which is understandable. That's why Hollywood executives, like all good businesspeople, consider the market before they write checks. If they don't make profitable movies, they lose their jobs, or maybe even their studios. If you make a film that costs $10 million, and it only brings in $600,000 at the box office, it's difficult to get someone interested in making another movie with you. Ask Madonna if she's still *Swept Away* (her 2002 movie that bombed). Contrast that flop with *Harry Potter & The Sorcerer's Stone* (2001). Budgeted at $130,000,000, it was released in a record 3,672 theaters and went on to gross around $1 *billion* world-wide. Madonna's movie came from an obscure 1974 Italian film, while the *Potter* books dominated the bestseller lists before being acquired by Warner Bros. While Madonna had never done well at the box office as the singular star of a movie, her director husband, Guy Ritchie, was hot in Hollywood because of the popularity of his excellent film *Lock, Stock and Two Smoking Barrels* (1998). No doubt the distributors of *Swept Away* thought that Ritchie (who also wrote the movie) would ensure success. If so, that was a very costly miscalculation. So, when you're thinking about that property you're trying to sell to Hollywood, remember this:

HOLLYWOOD RULE #4—*Your property will probably sell to Hollywood only if there is a substantial perceived audience.*

Now let's go over the usual sources of movie stories. If you have a kids' toy that you think is unique enough to inspire a great film, good for you, but I'm not going to cover how to sell "the next Barbie" to Hollywood. I'm only discussing "the usual suspects."

TRUE STORY—A great many films have been made from real-life events. In recent times, due to the immediacy of television and the Internet, a true story is more likely to end up on television as a news item or television movie than as a feature film. If one becomes a feature, it usually revolves around a major social issue and numerous victims, such as *Erin Brockovich* (2000) (toxic poisoning) or *The Insider* (1999) (tobacco companies). Most likely, that true story must come to the attention of Hollywood via major media before anyone gets excited. For example, *The Insider* was based on a CBS "60 Minutes" episode that aired in 1994. Though it wasn't national in scope, *Erin Brockovich* was a well-publicized story in California. If you have a true story that you think would make a great movie, you would probably be wise to try to get it written up in a major newspaper or magazine (read: U.S. national) first. Although the true story that became the film *The Straight Story* (1999) took place in the Midwest, it came to the attention of Mary Sweeney, the producer, via an article in *The New York Times*. Richard Farnsworth, who came out of retirement to play the lead role, got an Oscar nomination for his work. It appealed to a lot of people because it was a great human-interest story that anyone could understand. The movie told the story of a seventy-three-year-old man in Laurens, Iowa, who wanted to mend his relationship with his ailing, estranged older brother in Mt. Zion, Wisconsin. Denied a driver's license, Alvin Straight embarked on his journey riding a lawn mower!

Later in this book, I'll discuss a company that makes its living off finding great true stories and matching them with both national reporters and movie and television executives for potential movies. But remember this:

HOLLYWOOD RULE #5—*If you want to sell a true story to Hollywood, it better be about something that people deeply care about.*

A great true story from any time period can make a great movie. *In the Mood* (1987), produced by Robert Kosberg, was based on scandalous tales of fifteen-year-old Ellsworth "Sonny" Wisecarver, who made national headlines in 1944 after he had sexual affairs with two adult women. Naturally, the scandal of 1944 became a 1987 comedy. Since producer Kosberg is convinced that any good idea can make a movie, he set up a Web site at www.moviepitch.com to field people's pitches.

Book—If a story is "big" enough for a feature film, it's probably worthy of a nonfiction book contract. If you publish a book, you can make money: (a) on the advance, (b) on the sale of the rights of the book to a producer, and (c) (if you're lucky) the chance to write the screenplay. If you want your book made into a movie, don't hold your breath unless you've garnered substantial publicity. Here's an example of a big story and a movie you've probably never seen. In March of 1991, Alliance Atlantis Motion Pictures bought Gary Ross's nonfiction book *Stung*, which described how Brian Molony, a mild-mannered Toronto bank manager with a gambling problem, gambled away $12 million in the largest one-man bank fraud in Canadian history. The $10 million movie *Owning Mahowny* (2003) starring Philip Seymour Hoffman and Minnie Driver, took in barely more than $1 million at the box office.

A much more successful book-to-movie was *A Beautiful Mind* (2001), the story of mathematician John Nash that garnered numerous Academy Awards. Problematically, as Pulitzer Prize–winner Ellen Goodman explained in a column in the *Boston Globe*, the movie distorted the truth horribly. Even though the movie came from the popular book by Sylvia Nasar, Goodman said it "left out Nash's first son and the boy's mother, who were, in his biographer's phrase, plunged into 'Dickensian realities' of poverty and neglect. It left out Nash's arrest in the men's room in Palisades Park in California that cost him his job and maybe greased the downward spiral into paranoia. It left out divorce from the marital love story. It left out his second son's schizophrenia. That's just the beginning." Of course, that would make Nash look less like a genius saved by an understanding wife as depicted in the film. And who knows whether Russell Crowe would have wanted to play the real Nash.

Unfortunately, such fact skewing is typical in Hollywood. When advance word on the miniseries "The Reagans" (based on the book *First Ladies Volume II* by Carl Sferrazza Anthony) was leaked in 2003, the public outcry against perceived factual distortions prompted CBS to abandon the project. It aired on Showtime (sister cable channel under corporate parent Viacom) instead. I could share many similar stories, but let me instead offer another maxim:

HOLLYWOOD RULE #6—*If you sell your story to Hollywood, don't expect it to be faithfully reproduced on screen.*

NOVEL—It might surprise you to learn that the *Harry Potter* movies were not initially an easy sale at Warner Bros. even though they were topping the bestseller lists. At the time, they were seen as "kids' movies" with little crossover potential to an adult audience. However, with the success of those films and the incredible *Lord of the Rings* (2001–2003) trilogy by Peter Jackson and company, production companies and movie studios will be enamored of novels for years to come. The catch is that you probably need to write a bestseller to interest Hollywood if you envision a feature film. You can sell self-published novels, electronic novels, and comic books to Hollywood, but it's such a complex subject I devote a chapter to it later in this book.

STAGE PLAYS—In the days of the "studio system" when the top actors were contract players and writers were on staff at a studio, there was a natural conduit from the legitimate stage and Broadway to Hollywood. That simply doesn't exist anymore. A massive stage hit such as *Angels in America,* when dramatized on film, appears on HBO or some other cable channel. Hollywood is more likely to travel a reverse path these days, with Disney musicals of their hit animated films, or the adaptation of a great comic movie like Mel Brooks's *The Producers* (1968). If you are a playwright and want to succeed in Hollywood, you'd better learn to adapt your plays into screenplays and direct, like David Mamet. Which brings us to:

HOLLYWOOD RULE #7—*Hollywood usually doesn't work the way you've seen it dramatized in the movies.*

While Hollywood people love seeing great stage plays, and you can get very well-known actors to work in Equity waiver productions (theaters with ninety-nine seats or under) for nothing to showcase some aspect of their acting, don't hold your breath on having your brilliant play discovered by "the movies." Although the Westwood Playhouse across the street from UCLA became the Geffen Playhouse due to the investment of one of the Dreamworks founders, they probably won't put on your play. TV and film producer/director Garry Marshall owns the Falcon Theatre in Burbank, but productions there are mostly generated by people already working in Hollywood. If you somehow get your play or musical performed on Broadway or even the Mark Taper Forum in Los Angeles, you might be on the way to a movie deal, but it could take a few years to materialize. So if you can't wait, turn your play into a screenplay.

Now, before we discuss the next possible source for a movie, let me provide another thing to keep in mind:

HOLLYWOOD RULE #8—*Don't try to sell Hollywood on something right under its nose.*

AN OLD TV SHOW OR MOVIE REWORKED—Mel Gibson's *The Passion of the Christ* was knocked out of the #1 spot at the box office by a remake of a 1978 horror movie, *The Dawn of the Dead.* That in turn was dethroned by *Scooby-Doo 2: Monsters Unleashed* (2004). The same weekend, the feature film reworking of the old TV series *Starsky & Hutch* (2004) was in the top ten, and a remake of a British comedy classic called *The Ladykillers* (2004) was at #2 after *Scooby-Doo.* I've constantly heard from readers over the years that they had an idea to make an old favorite TV show or film into a new version. Well, so what? Usually, those properties are owned by a major film or television entity that, if they don't produce a remake themselves, want a lot of money for the rights. And if they decide to do a remake, it's either based on an established public appetite or the involvement of major players who decide (for whatever reason) that they would like to make a feature. Unless you have the wherewithal to actually produce a movie based on some old property you're in love with, or unless you own such a property due to inheritance or some other stroke of luck, you'd probably best forget trying to sell Hollywood on your "great idea" that they own.

SHORT STORY (or any other property in need of substantial development)—Filmmaker Aaron Schneider won an Academy Award in 2004 for "Two Soldiers," a forty-two-minute film he wrote and directed, based on a short story by William Faulkner. Schneider made the film with the help of the North Carolina School of the Arts, a ten-year-old film school in Winston-Salem. When he thanked people at the school in his acceptance speech, it was perhaps the first time a film school had been thanked at the Oscars. It also prompted an overload of "hits" on the school's Web site. Such is the power of the Oscar telecast. Still, this was not a feature film, and it's very difficult to get anyone interested in developing a short story into a feature film. What short story is that good, or covers enough literary territory to fill one and one-half to two hours on screen? In this day of inexpensive digital filmmaking, if you have a short story that you want to develop into a feature film, you have two choices: (a) make a short film to showcase your abilities; or (b) flesh it out into a full feature-length screenplay. And if you intend to do the latter, why aren't you writing the novel first?

Along that line, one of my favorite films is 1982's *Blade Runner*, which came from the novel *Do Androids Dream of Electric Sheep?* by Philip K. Dick. Short stories by Dick have also been made into major feature films and TV series with major stars. *Minority Report* (2002) came from a Dick short story while *Total Recall* (1990) (inspired by the short story "We Can Remember It for You Wholesale") was also a TV series in 1999. While Hollywood might pay a cool $1 million for the rights to a Dick short story today, he unfortunately died in 1982 before realizing the extent of his lasting influence.

Yes, just like F. Scott Fitzgerald. Which prompts the following observation:

HOLLYWOOD RULE #9—*If you dream of fame and fortune in Hollywood, be prepared for a very long haul, maybe even an eternal one.*

Legendary Hollywood actors Clint Eastwood and Burt Reynolds, who ruled the box office in earlier decades, were both released from their contracts at Universal Studios the same day. In interviews discussing their movie *City Heat* (1984), both actors agreed that it took each of them approximately fifteen years to "make it" in Hollywood. That is, to achieve the pinnacle.

For your sake, I hope you sell your first screenplay and move immediately into a long and distinguished career. Honestly, though, I've rarely seen it happen that way, in almost two decades in Hollywood as a journalist, editor, author, producer, playwright, director, and screenwriter. Although I have never solely concentrated on writing scripts, it took a decade after I had my first property optioned to the time I actually sold a feature screenplay. And then, after selling another feature within a couple of months, I quit the business and turned to writing books and novels for ten years. That's because the production budget was in the bank to make both movies, yet neither got made due to financial shenanigans of the producers involved. I was a new father and wanted a stable life for my family.

And that, dear reader, brings us to my last bit of advice about the way things are in the film capital of the world:

HOLLYWOOD RULE #10—*The rules in Hollywood change all the time.*

In this book, I will bring you an overview of how Hollywood works based on my own experience and that of many others who know the business. This doesn't mean that what we share with you is written in stone. It just means you're along for a nice ride with people who know their way around. I can only be your chauffeur and point out the attractions along the way. I'll deliver you to certain destinations, but I can't accompany

> *Shoot a few scenes out of focus. I want to win the foreign film award.*
>
> **—Billy Wilder**

you to the meetings. I can offer alternative routes, but you'll have to figure out your arrival. Ultimately, I'll step out of the vehicle and turn the driving over to you. And that's the only way it should be. The people whom I've seen make it in Hollywood won't give up the race, and have the talent and eye necessary to get across the finish line even after everyone they know had thought they were finished.

So now let's move on, to a discussion of how to sell that ultimate Hollywood road map, the one that all the great productions have in hand before a single day of shooting begins. Let's talk about what it takes to sell the greatest of Hollywood literary properties, the screenplay.

CHAPTER

2

The Goods:
What It Takes to Impress
Hollywood Buyers

*Television and film demand that people at all levels have brass balls or
brass ovaries. Unfortunately, we live in the reign of the eunuch.*

**—Rita Mae Brown, Starting from Scratch:
A Different Kind of Writers' Manual**

I n 2003, one segment of the Hollywood entertainment business made
$27 billion worldwide. I'm talking about video games, not movies,
and that figure includes hardware and software. These days, executives thinking about a high budget studio feature think of a high action
video game at the same time. They might even release the game prior
to the film, to build "buzz." If you don't play games, you probably have
a younger person in your house who does, or you know someone who is
devoted to gaming. When you approach Hollywood with a property that

could logically be both a video game and a studio feature, you're likely to get a better reception. You might even find that someone will urge you to create the game first, and that forty people and $10 million will go into making your game happen. Of course, a $10 million budget is high-end for video games, but a studio movie budget averages almost $100 million more. So you might have trouble breaking in at the top in either arena. Still, the idea that a hot commercial property could be a game or a movie, or both, is shared by just about every high-level studio executive. People who do not live and work in Hollywood often don't realize that considerations like this take place, just as they don't keep up with the latest developments in "the business." The old saw that "writers should just write" isn't quite right anymore. In Hollywood these days, writers should just write something they can sell.

Even if you are not exposed to Hollywood on a daily basis, there are a number of things that can get you in Hollywood's door and change your career from "hopeful" to "sold." Selling to Hollywood is a game, and you need to know how it's played. If you don't, it could play you.

One of the great things about show business is that it is constantly being reinvented. New forms of entertainment are always coming along to fascinate the public and generate billions in income. Each time, even though pundits will predict how this latest hot thing will take over everything, the new medium generally blends in with the established media. It's always been that way. The only entertainment medium that ever receded into oblivion was vaudeville, but even that one rebounds on occasion in the form of a television variety show or in some "period" movie.

New entertainment platforms blossom and thrive, threaten the establishment, then happily assimilate.

When motion pictures arrived in the U.S., people thought they might replace theater and vaudeville. Instead, we have scenarios today like Mel Brooks's film *The Producers* (1968) (a vaudeville tale if ever there was one) morphing into the all-time Tony Award–winning success on Broadway.

Here's another example: When television first began, all the programming was freely broadcast via sponsors who put their company name in the title of the show such as 1947's "The Admiral Broadway Revue." Radio stations thought they might be driven out of business. Instead, over time, the two media learned to complement each other. Then, in the 1960s, the boom of FM radio made it seem like AM radio would die. Flash forward to today, and television channels do simulcasts with both AM and FM stations, while AM talk radio hosts like Rush Limbaugh fuel the popularity of all-news cable channels such as Fox News. Meanwhile, Internet radio shows have proliferated and for-pay satellite radio offers a commercial-free equivalent of cable television.

As a recent illustration of how a new entertainment platform threatens the establishment, consider how hip-hop and rap has changed the music industry. But what has happened with rap superstars? They go mainstream in established media, particularly movies. Multi-millionaire rapper Eminem made a hit movie with *8 Mile* in 2002. Many people in Hollywood were surprised, but many Hollywood executives ignored the legions of Elvis Presley fans in the 1950s when he began to make movies, too.

As you can see, there is a long history of fat cats of the reigning champion medium sneering at newcomers. For years after the advent of television, movie studios and movie stars would have nothing to do with it. Eventually, lucky accidents happen. A copyright lapse allowed *It's a Wonderful Life* (1946) to be broadcast across the U.S. Christmas after Christmas, and moviemakers realized the power of television to make hits. (Frank Capra's masterpiece was a dud in theaters, deemed too sentimental by people who had suffered through World War II—they called it "Capra-corn.")

By sheer numbers of viewers, TV became a breeding ground for future film stars. Once, it was big news if a movie studio like Warner Bros. got into television production with a Western like *Cheyenne*. Now most studios have their own television network. The line between movie star and television star has also become unimportant, and many top actors work easily in each medium without their career being impacted adversely in either medium. The changes continue: As I wrote this book, NBC bought and merged with Universal Studios.

Since it's hard to predict what will happen year to year, one thing an entrepreneurial writer can do is pay attention to any group that doesn't have a "voice" represented at the movies. The latest Hollywood hot movie genre is the "urban" film, which translates into a mostly all-black cast making their own movies for a mostly black audience. Credit Spike Lee for beginning that trend with his hit *She's Gotta Have It* (1986), but despite his success and that of others like him, Hollywood executives were still surprised by the success of the comedy *Barbershop* (2002). Hollywood is a big ship, and it takes a long time to make it turn.

Here's an example of how a "new thing" can grow from nothing and crack the Hollywood sidewalks. The last time I wrote a book about selling to Hollywood, the big buzz was Web shows. Mini-TV in the workplace, if you will. At the time, I had just sold a show called "Office Monkey" to a company called WireBreak.com. That company was founded on the idea that young people with broadband connections at the office would take five-minute breaks to watch entertaining original programming, and that advertisers would line up to reach them. We had visions of generating buzz about the show on the Web then getting picked up by a TV network. And why not? New media always piggybacks established media for publicity.

Unfortunately, "Office Monkey" never made it past the pilot stage, but another Web show called "Undercover Brother" did. This animated show from UrbanEntertainment.com was the first online series to get a film deal. Imagine Entertainment picked it up in 2000 for a cool $1 million. Two years later, the film, made for around $25 million, had a respectable box office take of more than $38 million. Not bad for something that started as a cartoon on a computer screen.

A good film is when the price of the admission, the dinner, and the babysitter was well worth it.

—**Alfred Hitchcock**

The "Undercover Brother" deal was brokered by the then up-and-coming Endeavor talent agency. Endeavor is now considered one of the big agencies in Hollywood, and their attention to signing creators of "the next big thing" helped get them there.

Think you have the next hot item? Find an agency or management company with the same brash enthusiasm Endeavor showed then, and you might get a hit.

Sadly, there were few success stories like "Undercover Brother," and Web shows have faded into being just that, despite the fact that broadband connections are now more widespread than ever. One can still hope. With President Bush calling for total broadband connectivity in the U.S. by the year 2007, who knows what might arise by the time most of the United States gets high-speed Internet connections.

All this is meant to show you, the person with something to sell to Hollywood, that you should never discount the possibility of anything taking off. You just have to find a way to sell it that will get you on the show biz radar, and "it" could be anything. If you have the rights to an old radio show your grandfather wrote in the 1920s, you might get a deal if you generate enough listeners by revamping it on your own Internet radio site. Got a script you rewrote from an out-of-copyright silent film? That might work, too. Do you admire animated cartoons from the 1930s and want to do something in that style? That's what Kerry Conran did with *Sky Captain and the World of Tomorrow* (2004), and he ended up with major stars in his first feature film.

Of course, you might also create an original Macromedia Flash show for the Web and end up with a television and movie franchise, like Trey Parker and Matt Stone, the creators of *South Park*.

Becoming a "player" *to* Hollywood (not just *in* Hollywood) is possible from many directions, and doesn't have to depend on creating a great screenplay from scratch.

That said, let's now cover what Hollywood buys, week to week, month to month, year to year—including screenplays.

Television and the Movies

To understand the different types of motion pictures that are filmed by Hollywood, all you have to do is watch television. More on that in a moment. All too often, I receive scripts to read that fit no general classification. That makes it very difficult for me to even describe them to an agent or producer, so how can I help the writer? Each time, I'm reminded of an exercise that I used to teach in a writing class at UCLA. Most of those students there wanted to write a novel. I would ask what genre of novel, and many of them couldn't easily answer. So I had them, outside of class, visit a large chain bookstore and report to me about the classification signs on display: Romance, Crime, Western, and so forth. When they came back to class, many expressed shock. Suddenly they realized that bookstores had to classify the wares they sold, so it wasn't too much to expect a writer to write within a genre. Never again did one of those students start describing their work with, "Well it's kinda hard to describe . . . "

If you are a screenwriter looking for an agent and you cannot accurately depict what type of screenplay you have to sell, if you can't show that you have at least a rudimentary knowledge of the classification of products created by Hollywood, you will probably not get an agent.

I'm not talking about *genre* with regard to your screenplay. Your script could be action, adventure, crime, comedy, family, horror, or any mix. That isn't my main concern. More important things to keep in mind are: (a) the audience (the primary viewers of your proposed movie); and (b) the budget necessary to make that movie.

Which takes us back to television and types of movies, and please note that I'm only discussing here the North American television (and movie) audience.

"A major network event" on one of the major free networks (ABC, CBS, NBC, and Fox) usually means a movie was a theatrical box-office hit. It could have been a big-budget movie like *Spider-Man* (2002) with major stars, or a low-budget surprise hit like *My Big Fat Greek Wedding* that featured actors who were not major stars before that movie came out.

Could you see your screenplay/movie being advertised that way?

"The network premiere of . . . " almost always means a studio feature with major stars, whether it was a hit or not, that had a theatrical release. It could also mean a movie that first aired on a premium cable channel like HBO.

Would that more likely describe your project?

Neophyte screenwriters occasionally tell me that they've written a script they think would make a good "movie of the week." Don't ever say that to a potential Hollywood buyer. "Movie of the week" does not exist. Movies made directly for television were named that when they began, but no network makes and exhibits movies on a weekly basis any more.

"Miniseries" is something you should almost never try to write as an original creation. Major miniseries suppliers like Hallmark derive miniseries from public domain stories like ancient legends or major novels in the way *Roots* came to television (and began the major miniseries tradition).

So what kind of script do you have for Hollywood?

1. A screenplay that would interest major stars and possibly be worthy of getting made for more than $108 million at a studio level (the average cost of a studio feature these days)? Advice: This type of script is almost never sold by beginners.

2. A screenplay that would interest major stars because of its subject matter or content that might not cost much to make ($10 million or even one-tenth of that)? Advice: A much more likely sale for a beginner because it will probably be made by an independent producer, who will take a beginner's phone call.

3. A story so sweeping in scope and broad in story that it really should

be a novel first? Advice: Write the novel, sell it, sell the rights to Hollywood, and see if they'll let you write the screenplay.

I know; you have something different. Your work is artistic, hard to explain. Then you should make it yourself, and let the film explain itself. Meanwhile, let's continue our journey through the Hollywood "bookstore."

What do you know about movies that actually are made for television? More specifically, cable television? It's a big market these days, and the categories are easily broken down for you by cable channel. For example, if you've made an independent film that was shown at the Sundance Film Festival, it will probably air on the Sundance Channel. If you want your movie to air on Turner Network Television (TNT), it needs to be based on a book because they do classy movies like *Gettysburg* (1993) that can also cross over into theatrical distribution. Robert Katz, the producer of *Gettysburg* and several other movies with TNT, is a friend of mine; he told me about TNT's unspoken book "rule."

If you grew up dreaming of aliens and wrote a science fiction script that could be filmed for about the same amount as an independent film ($3 million or under), it might get made for the Sci-Fi Channel.

Movies for Lifetime are not as obviously based on women in peril as they used to be, but if you have a "woman in jeopardy" script, a producer who works with Lifetime might try to "set it up" at that network. Who works with Lifetime? Watch the channel and see! Then figure out how to find those producers. Successful writers in Hollywood are aggressive about finding contacts. Tell you what. I'll help you out a little. Read about their movies at their Web site, http://lifetimetv.com. Then look up information about the movies at the Internet Movie Database (www.imdb.com). After that, use an online database like ShowBiz-Data (www.showbizdata.com) and find out how to locate the production company.

Wasn't that easy?

To get a movie made on a cable channel, you usually need to submit your script to producers who have already worked with that cable channel. The influence of these producers can mean everything; at one time it was almost impossible to get a movie made at USA Network without the involvement of Wilshire Court Productions.

Here's another tip. Pay close attention to how well a cable channel is doing in the ratings. If viewership booms, the channel will want to expand its horizons. For example, Nickelodeon has done very well with theatrical movies based on its hit TV shows. Once, when a writer approached me with a World War II script, I told him that it might have little chance of getting made as a feature, but that History Channel was doing well and he should submit it to them.

"But they don't do their own movies!" he said.

"They will," I responded. And they did, but not his.

If you write a family-friendly movie, you might get it made by a major network, but you'll need to find a producer the network approves. If it's a "topical" movie, or one "ripped from the headlines," forget about writing the script. Even before the story is buzzing across the news channels, some producer with news connections will be pitching it to a network. On the other hand, channels with specialized audiences offer you a chance to break in. If you write a script with a teenage girl in the lead, most agents' and producers' first thought would be Disney Channel.

You need to know the players, the plans, and the nuances.

If you have a script that could be a major feature budgeted at $100 million or more, great. It's easy to figure out where to send that, but chances are Steven Spielberg won't take your phone call. If you have written anything different, however, you should pay attention to television for a clue on where something might find a market. You should be able to quickly tell someone who asks where your script fits in. That makes it much more likely that you can get someone to read your work.

Screenplays are not works of art. They are invitations to other to collaborate on a work of art.

—*Paul Schrader*

Getting on the Radar

If you don't have a screenplay to sell but rather something else entirely such as a true story, "life rights" (the authority to sell someone's life story or a part of his or her life story), or a nonfiction book, Hollywood buyers might be interested. They know that the public loves to see "Based on a True Story" as a film begins. It adds a little extra buzz of anticipation, and often there will be a built-in audience for a particular story. I don't always recognize how important a built-in fan base can be. For example, when I first heard about *Titanic* (1997) and *Pearl Harbor* (2001), I thought, "Who cares?" even though they were being made by major producers (James Cameron and Jerry Bruckheimer, respectively). After all, didn't we already know those stories? Hadn't movies already been made about them?

Then I realized lots of people were highly interested in each of those subjects. I reminded myself that Civil War reenactment aficionados had fueled the box office for *Gettysburg* and even helped it get made by supplying costumes and weapons and being extras on the set.

So both *Titanic* and *Pearl Harbor* were instantly on the radar of large numbers of the movie-going public.

That's the kind of thing you need to think about when trying to sell to Hollywood. No matter what it is you're trying to market, it helps if people know something about you before you approach them. Barring that, it's a benefit that they know something about the subject of your property. Whether you've lived it, written it, or not, some type of advance publicity usually helps get you in the door.

That's all an agent or manager does; provide generally reliable publicity. Like a trusted radar operator in the Navy, he or she will tell a "higher officer" (someone who can get a check written or write one) the Hollywood equivalent of, "Sir, you'd better take a look at this."

Even if you have a true story, life rights, or a nonfiction book that didn't get enough national notice, it could be difficult getting Hollywood to pay attention. There are only so many hours in the day. On the other hand, if you wrote a movie-friendly article for a periodical that Hollywood buyers read, like *L.A. Weekly* or a New York magazine like *Vanity Fair,* you probably won't have to worry about getting on the radar. So what do you do if you or your story aren't already famous?

And what if you're not even a writer, but just know of a great story that Hollywood should know about? The next *Erin Brockovich* (2000), perhaps. Well, you could go to your local newspaper and tell a reporter about it, and that reporter's editor would try to sell it (once published) to an international news service. It might get picked up by a reporter for *The New York Times* and then get noticed by a writer/producer such as Mary Sweeney, who discovered a story in Iowa that eventually became the David Lynch movie *The Straight Story* (1999).

Naturally, that process could take some time. What if you're convinced it's a timely story worthy of national attention that someone needs to know about *now*?

A pause here for the uninformed—if you are interested in securing someone's life rights to turn into a movie, you'll need a lawyer to make sure you're covered under the laws where you live. *Don't ever try to sell anything to Hollywood that you do not legally control.*

If you're simply trying to get a true story noticed, I have a connection that can help you with both the news media and Hollywood. Industry R & D, Inc. (IRD) is the nation's only "middleman" service for people involved in breaking news stories. They are an independent story provider for all major national media, and act as a no-cost go-between for victims, story participants, witnesses, or relatives involved in compelling events. The company can assist in setting your story up with writers and editors of your choice. Since the company's creation in 1992, they have delivered more than 10,000 personal stories to TV programs such as ABC's *20/20* and CBS's *48 Hours.* They've placed print stories in publications such as *Reader's Digest, Newsweek, People,* and *Redbook.* Two dozen IRD stories have become TV movies or feature films (for example, *Fly Away Home,* 1996).

While the service is free to you, the only catch is the type of story. IRD founder Tom Colbert says: "My specialty is stories that tug heartstrings. They're in my blood. They're my high. I fell in love with the idea of story."

As a former journalist for CBS, Colbert knows that many of the best stories dug up by media hounds in L.A., New York, and Washington were first sniffed out in small towns. "For years, TV and print have done nothing but rip off local journalists," Colbert says. "Big media outlets employ people to read regional papers, scan the Web, or monitor local TV news from around the country, then send items to national producers and writers to rework for their own venues."

Now you can beat the system with IRD. As mentioned, there is no charge for getting your story on the national media radar via IRD. I've known Tom Colbert for many years and have never known him to treat anyone unfairly. If you have a story for them, let them know. Their toll-free national number is (800) 995-6808 or you may send a fax to (800) 995-7978.

Ideas That Sell

If you have any doubts about whether Hollywood would care about a story you control, consider this. On March 31, 2004, New Line Cinema bought "The Zenith Man" from writer Mark Bailey. *The Hollywood Reporter* said the true-life murder story was the first acquisition for New Line's Chief Operating Officer Mark Ordesky since he oversaw and executive produced *The Lord of the Rings: The Return of the King* (2003), which won the Oscar for Best Picture. The story centered on a lawyer in the small town of Ringgold, Georgia.

Ah, but Bailey somehow gained access to New Line and COO Ordesky. You usually only get that kind of Hollywood access if you are a known quantity with film or TV credits that executives recognize or respect. You can move to L.A. and work your way up in the business to acquire those credits, or you can find people who have the ear of others in the business. That might be a producer they are already doing business with or someone they'll consider doing business with.

One producer with connections who actively entertains projects from outside sources is Robert Kosberg. He has long advertised that he will take anything, even an idea. If he likes what you bring him, he will make a deal with you and pitch it to people at major studios. Kosberg has sold many pitches and is very clever at them. One he sold about a mad dog was described as "Jaws on paws." The fact is, however, many producers who like the kind of material you have to sell will generally listen to your idea, if it is presented to them properly. If you are certain you have an idea that will sell, use a Kosberg trick that he explains in the seminars he presents around the country. Hollywood readers, he explains, frustrated over not finding anything suitable despite reading all weekend, might take story pitches on Monday mornings, before the boss arrives in late morning.

"Read anything good this weekend?" the producer asks.

Gulp. If the reader says "no" too many times, the producer might offer that reader a permanent weekend.

"No," replies the reader. "But Bob Kosberg came in with a great pitch . . . "

> *Just because a film is made under the commercial umbrella does not mean it is not valid as art.*
>
> *—Alan Parker*

If Your Ideas Don't Sell

The truth is, I've never known a successful Hollywood writer who wasn't brimming with ideas. If your creative well has run dry, however, or if you want to be involved with Hollywood, but haven't come up with an idea that people like, you just need to stir up your imagination. Media resource PRNewswire.com is one place to start. Their ProfNet Wire (connections to university professors) provides journalists with experts willing to speak on a plethora of topics while their "Public Pulse" from Roper Reports, updated every Friday, "provides intelligence from over 30 countries to help journalists understand public trends around the globe." The catch is, you have to prove you're a working journalist to gain access. If you think you might qualify, email them at mediasite@prnewswire.com or call (800) 387-8448. You could also write PR Newswire at: 810 Seventh Avenue, New York, NY 10019, but something tells me they wouldn't believe you're a working journalist if you didn't email or call.

I've repeatedly heard from readers who want advice on why their ideas, stories, books, novels, or screenplays weren't selling to Hollywood. Sometimes, they simply need to stir their imagination. In other cases, they only need to keep writing until they come up with better screenplays. A lot of Hollywood success is merely hanging in there long enough. I often refer people to www.wordplayer.com, where very successful screenwriter Terry Rossio explains how, at an early, frustrated part of his career he realized that people in many professions take a decade before they have a career breakthrough. After that, Rossio relaxed about his career curve. Since then, it's gone straight up, with movies like *Aladdin* (1992), *The Mask of Zorro* (1998), and *Pirates of the Caribbean* (2003).

If you are determined to have a career in Hollywood, but your ideas don't sell at first, be patient. Keep digging and keep thinking. While talent is important, 98 percent of Hollywood success is built upon persistence.

A Career by Stages

In the early days of talking pictures, playwrights did well, and were often hired as studio writers. A great many classic movies were made from hit stage plays.

That doesn't happen so much any more, but that doesn't mean a stage play you've written can't become a film. To get there, though, you'll probably have to learn to be a screenwriter, and maybe even a director like David Mamet who first got the notice of Hollywood with his play *A Life in the Theater* in 1979. There simply isn't a large market these days for original stage plays on television or in film.

I love the stage, and some of the first attention I got in Los Angeles came when I staged a couple of my own one-acts that got a nice write-up in the *L.A. Times*. One of the things I learned from that production was that well-known actors will perform in an Equity waiver setting for free. Their exchange is that they can invite fellow professionals and casting directors to see their work. This kind of thing happens all the time in Hollywood, with famous actors appearing onstage to do readings of new plays for playwrights they admire, or appearing in plays to show another aspect of their acting. For example, a soap opera actress might want to show how she could also do comedy.

You often don't really know just how good an actor is until you see him onstage. I watched David Schwimmer of *Friends* fame participate in a reading of a Jeffrey Sweet play at the Coronet Theatre in West Hollywood. Schwimmer had amazing presence onstage, and suddenly he was a lot more to me than simply "Ross" on a hit sitcom. If you want an idea of the type of play that will attract actors of the caliber of Schwimmer to an L.A. reading, see www.jeffreysweet.com. Sweet is the author of *The Dramatist's Toolkit* and also has some Hollywood credits.

If you check David Mamet's credits on the Internet Movie Database, you'll see that he wrote an episode of the gritty TV police drama *Hill Street Blues* in 1981, the same year he made a screenwriting breakthrough with the remake of *The Postman Always Rings Twice* (1981). Good playwrights are generally great with dialogue, which makes them natural candidates to succeed in television. If they also offer a unique flavor, like the clever plot twists and raw human emotions that Mamet is so good at, screenwriting and directing success can't be far away.

One playwright I know, Jim Henry, thought he was doing well when his play *Angels of Lemnos* won some awards on a Los Angeles stage. To his chagrin, however, no Hollywood studio called Jim at his Chicago area home. When he first contacted me, it was because he couldn't get the screenplay version sold. I consulted on the script and made suggestions about marketing that included a title I thought might be more easily understood by movie people. The script, centering on a mentally disturbed homeless person, still didn't sell, but Jim's talent told me he would eventually make headway in Hollywood. The next time I heard from Jim he had written an original screenplay called *Moon-shadows*. It was excellent, and I introduced him to a producer friend who read the script and immediately tried to set it up with a cable network. That deal didn't happen, but another producer optioned *Moon-shadows* later. When Jim told me he was moving his family to southern California, I knew it was inevitable that he would sell his screenplays while continuing to do well with his plays. He simply had that admirable combination of talent, desire, and willingness that every successful screenwriter I know possesses.

Then there's playwright Jon Dorf, who took a studious route to making it in Hollywood. Jon's plays have been produced in more than twenty states and on three continents, and he has been a resident playwright in several places. When I first met him, he was living in Philadelphia. Despite a B.A. Magna Cum Laude in dramatic writing and literature from Harvard, he wasn't having much success breaking into Hollywood. So he moved to L.A. and acquired his MFA in playwriting from UCLA, where he won the Hal Kanter Comedy Writing Award and the Marty Klein Comedy Writing Award. In addition to writing original screenplays, he made his first short film. I was impressed by Jon's talent and energy, so I introduced him to the people who own the Writers Store (see www.writersstore.com), who were looking for someone to write about the stage on a Web site in the way I had written for them about screenwriting (see www.screenwriting.info for tips from myself and others). Next thing I knew, Jon had created the information presented at www.playwriting101.com, which is a valuable resource for anyone writing for the stage.

If you can somehow gain notice as a playwright and turn that into a Hollywood career without venturing to southern California, I salute you, but that transition is rarely accomplished without a good amount of time spent here.

One thing is certain about theater and Hollywood. If you have a good stage play and stage it in Los Angeles, you might be surprised at the familiar faces that will show up to audition. You might even discover that highly successful actors will help you with a staged reading of an original screenplay, if they think you have talent. I speak from experience here; I wrote an entire chapter about how to go about a staged reading in my *Complete Idiot's Guide to Screenwriting.* It's a common practice among the pros.

From Page to Screen: Why Published Works Wow Hollywood

I realize that writing a screenplay is a current grand dream of hopeful writers in America, the way writing the "Great American Novel" was once the rage. I don't care what people write—if it fascinates enough people it might make a good movie someday. There is a simple reason why I have always advised new writers to attempt a novel instead of a screenplay, though.

They'll potentially make a lot more money.

Consider the following. If you sell a novel, you can make money in the following ways:

1. An advance against royalties. Depending on the novel, you could get lucky and get a six-figure advance. Don't hold your breath for the big bucks if it's your first novel, but such things happen.
2. If a producer, production company, studio, or network wants to make your novel into a movie or even a video game, they have to buy the rights to do so. And they often read the manuscripts or bound galleys of novels before the public ever sees the finished product.
3. Often enough, some producers will give a novelist a chance to write at least the first draft of the screenplay. That's particularly true if the novel is published in hardcover. (More expensive books have more clout because the publishing world took them more seriously.)

4. If the novel is published in hardcover, the author might also make money with a paperback version, and if a movie is made, even more paperbacks will be sold.

5. If the movie is highly successful, a television network might want to make a TV series. You might end up with a long-running franchise.

6. If your novel or nonfiction book eventually morphs into a TV series, you might become one of the producers or writers. If the show runs for three seasons or more, you'll probably become a multi-millionaire from producing alone.

7. If your book inspires a movie or TV franchise of some kind, but you're tired of your creation, novelizations of the movies or shows can make you a lot more money.

Now contrast that to simply selling a screenplay. How many times can you get paid from a script?

a. You get paid for the script, but you might not get a chance to do the rewrite (there's almost always a rewrite). Why not? Because producers figure that the script you sold is the best you can do with that story.

b. If the screenplay is made into a movie, there might be a paperback novelization, but you might not get the chance to write that type of Hollywoodized novel. They're written by people the studios trust to deliver, who have experience writing novelizations.

c. If your movie is successful, you might not even get a chance to write the sequel, although you'll probably get some money and credit.

Know this. Hollywood respects published authors because a printed book shows that someone took you seriously. It also means you might have a following. Why do you think Stephen King has had so many movies and miniseries made?

When you write a novel, you have room to engage in deeper story development than a screenplay. That means someone adapting a script from your novel has plenty of stuff to throw away that doesn't fit with the visual story flow. That's good—there's nothing so bad as padding a script.

Needless to say, a lot more novels are published than screenplays filmed, so you have a better chance of success. And when you're published, people in Hollywood get impressed. I first noticed this when I was pitching a show to the TV exec at Steven Spielberg's Amblin Productions. All the novels and books were stacked on her desk or arranged neatly on shelves. The screenplays, even those sent over by major literary agencies, were stacked on the floor. And when I came back to Hollywood after half a decade's absence, during which I wrote and sold books and novels, I found that old friends were extremely impressed that I had had so many titles published. Suddenly, I was solidly on the radar.

Hollywood is often impressed by published works, no matter what form in which they are printed. As I was putting together this book, one of the students in my screenwriting course who had self-published five novels had garnered the attention of one of the hottest young actresses in Hollywood.

I've long believed that Hollywood considers itself a secondary, less important cultural medium to books and novels. That may or may not be justified, but it seems so, particularly in recent years when studios are more and more cautious about how they spend their hundreds of millions.

While Hollywood studios buy a lot of properties that never see the screen, television networks generally air most of the properties they buy, particularly bestselling books and novels. With viewer levels decreasing every year, major networks don't have a lot of money to spare for projects they'll abandon.

Even if you have a nonfiction book, if circumstances are right, and you appeal to a family audience, you might end up with a TV show. That happened with W. Bruce Cameron, who wrote the book *8 Simple Rules for Dating My Teenage Daughter: And Other Tips from a Beleaguered Father (Not That Any of Them Work)*. The book hit #14 on the *New York*

If my books had been any worse I should not have been invited to Hollywood, and if they had been any better I should not have come.

—Raymond Chandler

Times bestseller list and became the hit sitcom *8 Simple Rules* on ABC. For details on how it came about, see www.wbrucecameron.com.

Then there's that great American invention, the comic book. It ain't what it used to be, movie-wise. After the disappointing box office showings of *The Hulk* (2003) and *Daredevil* (2003), which executives hoped would turn into movie franchises like *Batman* (1989), *X-Men* (2000) and *Spider-Man* (2002) had done, studios got a little skittish about that big budget comic blockbuster. Not that they'll quit making comic book movies—if you've created a comic book, show it around. It can easily serve as a convenient, elaborate "storyboard" that shows a busy reader or exec exactly what you have to sell. Even a comic book might get you more respect than a screenplay, but it might not bring the money it once would have. If you've created a comic book that does well, chances are some producer will find you, or maybe even a video game designer. As a matter of fact, I wouldn't be surprised if the comic book artist you work with (if you're not the artist) is a game designer, too.

Whatever print product you present to Hollywood, if it's been published it shows something simple and valuable. Someone took you seriously enough to invest some money in you. In copycat Hollywood, that's a valuable thing indeed.

Lightning in a Bottle

In my third *Writer's Guide to Hollywood,* I described how an old friend, David Ayer (see chapter 7, "The Independent Route") sold a project called *Squids,* based on his real-life experiences in the U.S. Submarine Service, for $1.5 million to producer Art Linson. *Squids* was the first major buy of Art Linson and David Fincher's Indelible Pictures. As of this writing the movie has still not been made, but it doesn't matter. With credits behind him like *Training Day* (2001) and *S.W.A.T.* (2003), Dave is an A-list Hollywood screenwriter, and he has more work than he can handle. He makes "crazy money," he told me after he became popular.

The script that put him on that A-list was *Training Day*. Based on interviews Dave did with locals and police in the rough-and-tumble Ramparts division of Los Angeles, where Dave was living at the time, *Training Day* provided a role that Denzel Washington used to win an Academy Award. It was Dave's first script, however, that got him his first rewrite job to be filmed, Jonathan Mostow's *U-571* (2000).

Here's how that script came about. Dave began to take himself seriously when encouraged by another successful writer, Wesley Strick (*Cape Fear,* 1991, and many others). While at Strick's house doing electrical work, Dave shared some true-life sea stories from his time in the Submarine Service in the U.S. Navy. Strick told Dave he liked his ear for dialogue and strong sense of character. So Dave wrote a script, read some screenwriting books, and Strick was impressed enough to give Dave's first script to a development person on the lot at Disney. That script was the original draft of *Squids.*

It took a while to become successful, though. Dave wrote several scripts before finally growing frustrated with getting close but not selling. When he realized he wasn't writing what he cared about, but instead trying to second-guess producers, he decided to write something he cared about, whether other people liked it or not. As he wrote it, he didn't think anyone would pick it up. That script was *Training Day*, written far in advance of the real-life L.A. police corruption scandals. When *Training Day* began circulating around town, he found that people either loved it or hated it. Then, when the subject matter became front-page news in the *L.A. Times*—same guys, same division in his script—suddenly he had a hot project. His script wasn't just on the radar; it was filling the screen.

Before long, he signed with International Creative Management (ICM) and the offers began to flow. These days, he'll finish a job on a Friday and start a new one on Monday.

When I asked him if there was any key thing that everyone in Hollywood was looking for, he had a quick reply.

"Lightning in a bottle," he told me.

No form of art goes beyond ordinary consciousness as film does, straight to our emotions, deep into the twilight of the soul.

—Ingrid Bergman

What does that mean? I knew instantly. Impossible magic from the truly creative mind. The good screenwriters I've known seem to have it from the start. And the great ones know how to keep the sparks alive.

"Hollywood wants a fresh voice to bring into the fold," he told me. "After you go through the development process a few times and get some cuts and bruises it can take the fight out of you and you can start internalizing all the rules of the road, which is kowtowing to the lowest common denominator of acceptability. Success is a difficult process. It's almost like death in the sense that your old life dies and you have this new life and things are different and you're not sure how. The message you grew up with is that money is the solution to all problems. I don't have to worry about rent and theoretically I should have some freedom, but the reality is that I work all the time. I really haven't had a chance to go out and enjoy the money. You can get to the point where it becomes abstract. You stare at your bank statement and feel great about it. That's natural. Then you get to the point where you know that you are still you, still the same person. I didn't grow up saying I wanted to be a writer. I failed high school. Writing found me. I didn't pursue it. It's a blessing because I had a set of skills I didn't know I had. Talent, that's what they're paying for. You can have all the studious dedication you want, learn the craft, and write a zillion scripts, but unless there's some intangible core talent there it's not going to get anybody's attention. I really can't explain what it is I do. I think a lot of it is being able to write good characters. And it's ideas. Not necessarily the big commercial script idea, but little nuts and bolts about how things work in the real world that'll link up Rube Goldberg devices in your imagination. You're nothing without imagination."

David was adamant about the hard work of an A-list screenwriter. He called it the loneliest job in the world. Why? "A screenplay is one of the most difficult forms to write," he told me. "It takes a long time to learn how to get it right."

If you do get it right, though, you might become a million-dollar screenwriter like David Ayer. You might be demonstrating that you, too, are lightning in a bottle. Remember that old saw about watching what you wish for, though. Once they capture your lightning, Hollywood executives want to keep it in the bottle. To paraphrase Mark Twain's comments about eggs in a basket, they want to put all their lightning in one bottle and keep an eye on that bottle.

Lightning Buyers & Lesser Sparks

There are several ways to keep track of who buys what in Hollywood. After all, in any business it helps to know the market. You can forego the trouble and simply find a literary manager or agent, or figure out which producers are most likely to buy what you have to sell. Or you could subscribe to either *The Hollywood Reporter* or *Daily Variety*, in print or online. You might also look into an online contact and information service like www.ShowBizData.com. There are many Web sites with Hollywood information, some reliable, some not. We'll go into those later in this book.

Meanwhile, thankfully, one man offers a one-stop-shop of information about recent literary sales in Hollywood. If you want to know what any given producer, company, or studio purchased and who sold it to them, surf www.hollywoodlitsales.com. Before Howard Meibach created this comprehensive and helpful site, he wrote several editions of the *Spec Screenplay Sales Directory*. The original book covered more than three hundred "spec" (written under the speculation that it would sell) script sales. A decade later, the site's searchable information is updated daily, offers an address/phone list database of agencies, production companies, guilds, law firms, and organizations, as well as a free email newsletter. There's even a "Scripts Wanted" section. You can also order the latest edition of the book via the site or you can order it via The Writers Store by calling (866) 229-7483 (toll free in the U.S. and Canada). The *Los Angeles Times* saw fit to rave about Howard's book, and so do I.

On the other side of the entertainment business, another way to keep track of who is buying what in the publishing business, and who in Hollywood is buying *from* the publishing business, take a look at www.PublishersMarketplace.com. For little more than your email address, you get a daily email called "Publishers Lunch" that updates you on business dealings and gossip in the publishing world, as well as a weekly email that lists who sold what to whom. For a few dollars a month, you can also find editors, publishers, and agents, create a Web page about literary properties you have for sale, and generally navigate publishing sales as easily as Howard Meibach helps you navigate Hollywood sales.

And by the way, I'm a customer of both sites.

Selling Onward

One last caveat about delivering "the goods" to Hollywood. Show them the lightning your first time out. First impressions really do mean a lot. I've had people remember scripts I wrote fifteen years after they'd first read them. Unfortunately, too many of those people with long memories had short bank accounts.

But that's not the point. What's important to remember is that you need to make a bigger impression when you hit the "Hollywood radar" than you will once you are already established. But guess what? It's that way in any business. If you keep at it and don't give up, if you keep continually improving your wares, sooner or later you'll be invited into the insiders' club and you might feel like you always belonged there. When your properties begin to sell, people who wouldn't let you in the door will invite you into their homes, your phone calls will be returned, and you'll think there's no business like show business.

Whatever it is you have to sell to Hollywood, I hope you impress everyone immediately, and show us all some lightning.

CHAPTER

3

Hollywood:
It's a People Town

I'm astounded by people who take eighteen years to write something. That's how long it took that guy to write Madame Bovary, and was that ever on the bestseller list?

—Sylvester Stallone

I f a Hollywood star commenting on great literature seems laughable, just think of how many people Sylvester Stallone influenced with his "Rocky" movies alone. Now contrast that to the fans of Gustave Flaubert, the author of *Madame Bovary*. Stallone has won many awards, been nominated for an Oscar, and has a star on the Hollywood Walk of Fame. He gets things done. When Stallone was starring in *Nighthawks* (1981), the original director, Gary Nelson, left the project in the middle of the shoot. When Nelson's replacement, Bruce Malmuth, was unable to take over in time to direct a scheduled train chase, Stallone directed it himself. There is a typical "can do now" attitude in Hollywood, particularly among those like Stallone who possess great talent. Talent keeps careers alive. For actors, it persists when physical beauty fades. For writers, it lasts as long as one can put entertaining words in print.

In all fairness to Flaubert, his great novel has been made into a Hollywood film eleven times. Just as he got no respect from Stallone, though, screenwriters don't often gain the public recognition enjoyed by others in the business.

Then again, why should they? Moviegoers don't often look at screenwriters' names on movie posters. They pay attention to actors. Living vicariously through characters on screen, they expect a good story told with physical beauty, charm, humor, and a brilliant interpretation of written scenes by the director and actors.

Therein lies the difference between what the moviegoing public and the Hollywood community care about. People who make movies know how very important good writing is, so the name of the writer is often the first thing they consider. In turn, when the script is good enough, a director comes on board who can attract the talent. In this instance talent means A-list actors who might sign onto a project because they have always wanted to work with a certain director. Nevertheless, A-list actors who have the freedom to pick their projects will more often than not make their final decision based on the screenplay.

However, an actor might only agree to do a project if a certain writer does the screenplay. I knew a producer once who had the life rights to the Bob Wills story. Wills was, in his heyday, an enormously popular musician whose most famous hit song was "San Antonio Rose." He made several Hollywood movies during the 1940s and at one time sold more recordings than Bing Crosby, who had been the #1 musical act in the nation for a long time. Waylon Jennings, who was rock 'n' roll superstar Buddy Holly's bass player before becoming a country music legend himself, once wrote in a song: "I don't care who's in Austin, Bob Wills is still the king." And so he was; when Wills died, the story goes that hundreds of despondent women showed up at his funeral, to the chagrin of Wills's wife.

Back to the movies. Not only did my producer friend have the rights to Wills's story and a great potential soundtrack, he also had the agreement of Jack Nicholson to play Wills. Instant greenlight on the project, wouldn't you think?

Not really. Nicholson wouldn't go forward unless one writer and one writer only wrote the script. That man was Thomas McGuane, who wrote a number of decent films and a rather forgettable one starring Nicholson and Marlon Brando called *The Missouri Breaks* (1976). At the time my friend had the rights and no studio would finance a McGuane picture because *Breaks* had done so badly at the box office.

So there my friend was, lacking the $250,000 "start writing" price then demanded by McGuane. "Well, heck," I told him, "let me write the script for free. I'm from Texas and I'm a musician, too. I know Wills's music. If Nicholson likes the script then I'll get paid."

"Jack only wants McGuane," I was told.

And so the project never got made.

That story is all too typical in Hollywood. It usually takes great writing, good timing, persistence, some luck, and the right connections to make a success. Hollywood is a people town. For the writer, that means that if the people don't know you or your writing, you're at a distinct disadvantage. No matter how excellent the material you are selling, it's often hard to get it read by someone who can help you, and even then you might only get one chance with him or her. Whether you are selling a true story, life rights, an article, a comic book, a novel, an original screenplay, or anything else, once your project is ready for sale you have one task and one task only. You need to find that special person or team of persons who will champion the project through to a sale.

Specifically, you need to find someone to love it.

"You can seduce a man's wife [in Hollywood], attack his daughter, and wipe your hands on his canary. But if you don't like his movie, you're dead."

—**Josef von Sternberg,
director**

Someone's Gotta Love It

There is a very simple reason why someone has to love a project to get it made in Hollywood. You've heard the phrase before, though perhaps not in a Hollywood context.

Life's too short.

These days, producers often have to spend years getting a project made. In the days of the studio system, when feature film writers were paid a weekly salary and actors were on contract, movies were made in assembly-line fashion. Television production today is the only equivalent. Perhaps the greatest American director, John Ford, helmed almost one hundred fifty feature films, mostly under the studio system. These days he would be lucky to make fifty films in a career. The producers I know count on spending three years or more of their lives getting a project "in the can" (finished). They have to acquire the property, find a director, secure financing, help line up the actors, make a deal with a distributor, and much, much more. Thus they rarely go forward on a project simply because they like it. They want to *love* it.

Producers who make movie after movie are passionate about the business and are willing to do whatever it takes to get each project made. Directors and stars choose carefully, too. They also want to love it, because in Hollywood "you're only as good as your last picture." If they miscalculate and are part of a box office dud, their asking price could plummet by millions of dollars. So they want to at least be able to say that they loved making that particular movie.

It's a very high-stakes game in which top-end feature film budgets now are in the $200 million neighborhood. That's more than the Gross National Product of some small countries. When a studio is picking where to invest each of their $100 million to $200 million "pies" each year, they're understandably cautious. While they want to guarantee return on investment and profit, they are dealing with filmmakers who might be more passionate about a project than financially realistic.

Thus the "lovers" must be persistent.

I've often reminded people that it took director Sir Richard Attenborough twenty years to get *Gandhi* (1982), a biography of one of the great world leaders of the twentieth century, onto the screen. I tell them how producer Wendy Finerman spent ten years of dogged persistence before getting what was arguably Tom Hanks's greatest role, *Forrest Gump* (1994), filmed. I describe how producer Mace Neufeld put a film into production after twenty-two years of trying.

The amount of passion people can have for any one project never stops astounding me. When Fox released the Regency Enterprises movie *Man on Fire* in 2004, it was a hit for Denzel Washington. What most moviegoers didn't know was that the unique story of revenge came about due to the more than twenty-year determination of producer Arnon Milchan, the head of Regency. While producing the Sergio Leone *Once Upon a Time in America* (1984), Milchan interested Robert DeNiro in *Man on Fire,* a novel by A.J. Quinnell. Ultimately, DeNiro didn't work out, so Milchan made the movie in Italy with Scott Glenn in the starring role. The movie didn't do well at the box office, but Milchan was convinced it should be remade. Two decades later, he finally saw the vision he originally conceived brought to the screen with *Man on Fire.*

Because of the unswerving persistence that some filmmakers will exhibit, smart screenwriters learn to never give up. An unsold screenplay can impress people for years before someone finally finds a way to get it made. *Unforgiven* (1992), which won a number of Oscars and garnered a Best Screenplay nomination for David Webb Peoples, was well known in Hollywood for almost *twenty years* before Clint Eastwood decided to make it. The movie was only the third Western to win the Best Picture Oscar.

To use a favorite Hollywood phrase, "Who knew?"

Do you have that kind of persistence? If you cannot maintain personal passion about your project, how can you expect it of someone else? You have to love it yourself. You need to feel that yours is a story that someone *must* champion, that *deserves* to get made. You are asking a producer to spend at least the next two years of his or her life on your property, so you'd better be willing to spend as long as it takes to find the right producer to champion that project you care so much about. You even have to be willing to make the movie yourself.

You gotta love it, or it won't get made. No matter how small the production, or how large, that's almost always the way it is.

But, but, but . . . how do so many bad movies get made? Well, that's simple. Different people have different loves.

Finding Someone to Love It

Though the studio system is long gone, most successful producers that I've known come up through the ranks. They learn how to read scripts for commercial quality, learn how to analyze them, break them down for production costs, and learn how to physically produce them. People who have learned the craft of filmmaking while maintaining their love for the art form are easy to spot in Hollywood. They're self-confident and are not threatened by new arrivals. In fact, they believe in "giving back," a Hollywood term meaning helping newcomers because you were helped when you began.

As one successful friend told me: "It's very important in this business to find a mentor."

That's true, but too many people I've known who are new to Hollywood look for just anyone to guide them in the business. They take any agent they can get, even when their intuition is telling them to put on the brakes.

I ask them if they would marry just anyone at all.

"Of course not!" they exclaim.

"Well then," I reply, "Maybe you shouldn't do business with just anyone, either."

Every book of advice on selling to Hollywood that I have written has one constant theme running through it—*contact people who are most likely to resonate with what you have to sell, and you'll have far less disappointment.*

The last time you visited a shopping mall, did you notice that the businesses had certain specialties? You wouldn't try to buy lingerie in a bookstore, would you? Similarly, it is folly to approach certain producers, directors, or even agencies with certain types of projects. A producer who has been making teenage movies for the Disney Channel is unlikely to produce your epic tale of the Battle of Xerxes. An agent or manager whose top clients are in their twenties and writing gross-out comedies probably won't care about your thoughtful romance set in Regency England.

You need to know Hollywood to sell to Hollywood. That means knowing what your prospective buyers have liked traditionally and any other information you can find on them that will give you some idea of what they might like. But first, you need to know the language. Here are some basic terms that might help.

How to Speak Hollywoodese

If you understand the following terms, you might fool your friends into thinking you're a Hollywood player. Some of these terms appear on a Web site put up by the Writers Store that I contributed to, www.screenwriting.info. I have not included terms that are technical screenwriting definitions like those covered in my *Complete Idiot's Guide to Screenwriting.* Rather, the purpose here is to provide a list of terms in daily use in the business.

A-list: A person who, by being involved in a project, can help it into production much more quickly. This person can be an actor, director, producer, or writer.

Above the line: The cost of hiring actors, a director, and other creative talent for a film. So named because of the way a production budget sheet is laid out.

Above the title: An A-list actor's name usually appears on screen before the title of the movie appears. Others' names may appear above the title as well.

The Academy: The Academy of Motion Picture Arts and Sciences, the group that puts on the Oscars each year

AFM: The annual American Film Market in Santa Monica, California, at which foreign buyers buy product for exhibition in their home territories. Hollywood aspirants without a pass to the upper floors of the hotel hang around the lobby bar hoping to meet people. "Are you going to AFM?"

Against: A term describing the ultimate potential payday for a writer in a film deal. $400,000 against $800,000 means the writer is paid $400,000 when the script is finished (through rewrite and polish); when and if the movie goes into production, the writer gets an additional $400,000.

Alan Smithee: A fictional name taken by a writer or director who doesn't want his or her real name credited on a film

Approved writer: A writer whom a television network trusts to deliver a good script once hired

Arbitration: Binding judgment by members of a Writers Guild of America committee regarding proper on-screen writer credit of a movie; arbitration is available only to WGA members or potential WGA members.

Attached: Agreement by name actors and/or a director to be a part of the making of a movie. (It usually takes money to secure attachment.)

A/V: A dual column audio/visual screenplay with video description on the left and audio and dialogue on the right, used in advertising, corporate videos, documentaries, training films, and reality TV. In contrast, movie and TV scripts have direction and dialogue interspersed.

Back-door pilot: A two-hour TV movie that is a setup for a TV series if ratings warrant further production. The logic behind them was that at least they would have a movie to sell if the series didn't go. These are rare today; if a network wants to test a project, it often only finances the one-hour drama or the 30-minute sitcom pilot and nothing else.

Back end: Deferred payment on a movie project to be seen when profits are realized

Backstory: Experiences of a main character taking place prior to the main action, which contribute to character motivations and reactions. A writer will rarely be asked to explain the backstory of any project, but doing so briefly in a pitch may help sell the project.

Bankable: A person who can get a project financed solely by having his or her name attached. This usually means an A-list star.

Beat: A high point of a scene in a script. A development executive might ask about a story or script: "So tell me the beats." In the second meaning, a beat is for actors, a parenthetically noted pause interrupting dialogue, denoted by (beat) or ellipses (. . .).

Beat sheet: An abbreviated description of the main events in a screenplay or story

Below the line: All the costs of actually making a movie excluding creative talent such as actors, the director, and others. On a production budget sheet these costs take up many more entries than the "above the line" costs.

Brads: Brass fasteners used to bind a screenplay printed on three-hole paper. The preferred type is the Acco #5 solid brass brad, generally accepted as having the highest quality.

Bump: A troublesome element in a script that negatively deflects the reader's attention away from the story

The Business: The Hollywood production of movies, television shows, videos, DVDs, and video games

Button: A TV writing term referring to a witty line that "tops off" a scene, usually in sitcoms

Buzz: Gossip about the worth or non-worth of a person or project in Hollywood

Cannes: Pronounced "con." A major film festival held each year in the south of France. "Are you going to Cannes?"

CGI: Computer Generated Image; a term denoting that computers are used to generate the full imagery

Character: Any personified entity appearing in a film. An actor on a set may lose his or her own personality altogether and become their part, thus being "in character."

Character arc: The emotional progress of a main character during the story, usually revolving around a specific thing, such as resolving a crisis of confidence

Cheat a script: Fudging the margins and spacing of a screenplay on a page with a software program in an attempt to fool the reader into thinking the script is shorter than it really is. (They don't like it when they find out.)

Colored pages: Changes made to script pages after the initial circulation of the production script, which are different in color and incorporated into the script without displacing or rearranging the original, unrevised pages

Commercial: The type of property, such as a screenplay, that garners the attention of an A-list actor who would love to play the lead, appeals to general audiences who easily understand the film's concept, and that easily fits into an established genre

Conflict: The heart of drama; someone wants something and people and things keep getting in the way. You could be asked while pitching: "So what's the conflict?"

Consider: A reader notation that an evaluated screenplay should be read by the boss for possible production. Usually, the best a writer can hope for is a "consider."

Courier 12: The main font in use in the U.S. by the Hollywood film industry. Other forms of Courier such as 12 pitch Courier New are also acceptable.

Coverage: A reader's report about a property for sale. Usually one to two pages, it rates the project on things like character and story.

Development: The process of readying a script for production after it is acquired

Development hell: The dreaded "hurry up and wait" malaise that occurs when the development process lasts too long

Dialogue: The conversations between characters in a film

Direct-to-video: A movie that might have been intended for release in theaters, but for whatever reason was instead sold only as a video or DVD. Some lower budget films, or sequels to studio hits such as Disney animated films are also made for direct sale to the public.

Feature: A movie made for distribution in theaters

Gaming: The conception, writing, and creation of video games, a $10 billion industry that has become as influential as Hollywood moviemaking

Genre: A French term describing the type of story. If you are asked for a "genre film" that usually means a horror, thriller, or some other easily categorized project.

Greenlight: To OK a project for production. Only a small number of people in Hollywood, fewer than ten at this writing, can greenlight a picture at a major studio level.

Gross: Percentage point participation in project profits recouped from the beginning of box office revenue. Usually reserved for A-list talent and the producers of the project only. (See "net" below.)

Heat: Positive gossip about a project in Hollywood. "It's getting a lot of heat around town."

High concept: A brief statement of a movie's basic idea that is felt to have tremendous widespread public appeal. Different from a logline (see below) in that high-concept movies are more likely to be high-budget feature films.

Hip pocket: A casual relationship with an established agent in lieu of a signed, formal agreement of representation. If you find an agent to hip-pocket you, that means you'll do the legwork in selling and if someone asks who your agent is, you can refer them to that agent.

Hook: A term borrowed from songwriting that describes that thing that catches the public's attention and keeps them interested in the flow of a story

Housekeeping deal: A producer or director who has an office on a studio lot with utilities, a secretary, and other basics paid for, but does not receive a salary from the studio. In exchange, the studio usually gets a first look at any project the producer or director develops.

Improv: Improvised dialogue in which actors make up what they say in real time on the movie set. For older actors the phrase ad lib (from the Latin *ad libitum,* "in accordance with desire") may be preferable.

Indie: A production company that operates independent of major film studio financing and/or a housekeeping deal

"Let's do lunch": A term that might mean what it says, or could be a sarcastic person's way of telling you to get lost

Logline: A "twenty-five words or less" description of a screenplay

Master scene script: A script formatted without scene numbering. This is the only kind a potential buyer expects to see from you.

MIFED: Pronounced "me-fed." The Mercato Internazionale del Cinema e del Multimediale is an annual international event in Milan, Italy, eagerly anticipated in Hollywood. "Are you going to Mifed?"

Miniseries: A long-form movie of three or more hours shown on successive nights or weeks on U.S. television networks

Montage: A cinematic device used to show a series of scenes, all related and building to an emotional conclusion. It's probably not a good idea to describe a montage during a pitch because amateurs use them, but rarely well.

M.O.S.: Without sound, so described because a German-born director wanting a silent scene told the crew to shoot "mit out sound." If you describe a scene as "M.O.S.," a filmmaker will understand you. A non-filmmaker might not. (Which is why using technical terms might not always be smart.)

Multimedia: Writing and filmmaking encompassing more than one medium at a time which, script-wise, usually refers to CD-ROM games or Internet-based programming

Net: Percentage point participation in project profits that are recouped after all expenses have been paid back. Due to the great creativity of Hollywood accountants, the chance of actually collecting net monies owed is so unlikely that actor Eddie Murphy called them "monkey points" because you'd have to be a monkey to believe you'd get paid.

Notes: Ideas about a screenplay shared with a screenwriter by someone responsible for moving the script forward into production, which the screenwriter is generally expected to use to revise the screenplay

One-hour episodic: A screenplay for a television show whose episodes fill a one-hour time slot, week to week

One-sheet: Originally a studio term for a movie poster. These days, used by development people and others to describe a single-spaced description of a screenplay.

Opening credits: On-screen text describing the most important people involved in the making of a movie. Never describe the opening credits of any movie; to do so says "amateur."

Option: The securing of the rights to a screenplay for a given length of time, whether paid or not

Package: The assembly of the basic elements (i.e. main actors, director, producer) necessary to secure financing for a film. Agencies "package" projects because they get an additional 10 percent fee for doing so.

Pass: A rejection of a property by a potential buyer; the notation made most by script readers

Pitch: To verbally describe a property to a potential buyer in the hope it will be bought

Points: Percentage participation in the profits of a film, whether gross or net. A point is one part of 100 percent.

Polish: In theory, rewriting a few scenes in a script to improve them. In practice, a writer is often expected to do a complete rewrite of a script for the price of a polish.

Production script: A script in which no more major changes or rewrites are anticipated, which is used day by day for filming on a movie set

Property: Any intellectual property in any form (including a screenplay) that might form the basis of a movie, television show, or any other show-business product

Reader: A person who reads screenplays for a production company and writes a report about them, sometimes on a salary, sometimes paid per screenplay report

Reality show: A series such as "Survivor" in which real people are put in created situations to see how they react. Reality TV changed the face of television in the early 2000s.

Recommend: The notation about an evaluated screenplay that almost never comes from a reader because his or her job could be on the line if the project is made and fails

Release: A legal document given to unrepresented writers for signing by agents, producers, or production companies, absolving said entities of legal liability

Scene: Action taking place in one location that (hopefully) moves the story to the next element of the story

Screening: The showing of a film for test audiences and/or people involved in the making of the movie

Screenwriter: The most important and simultaneously most abused person in Hollywood

Screenwriting: The art of writing scripts for any visual medium

Script: A blueprint of a movie story that provides visual descriptions, actions of characters, and their dialogue

Shooting script: A script that is ready to be put into production; the one the director works from daily

Showrunner: A writer/producer ultimately responsible for the production of a TV series, week to week

Sitcom: A situation comedy; a normally 30-minute (in the United States) television show revolving around funny situations the main characters repeatedly fall into

Soaps: Daytime "soap operas" so named because these dramas were originally sponsored by the makers of laundry detergent in the early days of television

Spec: A script written without being commissioned on the *speculative* hope that it will be sold

Stock shot: A sequence of film previously shot and available for purchase and use from a film library

Sundance: The Sundance Film Festival begun by Robert Redford that is the Mecca of independent filmmaking. Also refers to the Sundance Institute, where the careers of writers and filmmakers who fit Redford's philosophy are nurtured.

Synopsis: A two- to three-page, double-spaced description of a screenplay

Tentpole: A top-end budget film like *Spider-Man* that is a major summer or holiday season release; so named because it is like the main ring attraction at a circus where a huge pole holds up the main tent.

Thriller: A fast-paced, high-stakes story in which the protagonist is generally in danger at every turn, with the most danger coming in the final confrontation

Treatment: A scene-by-scene description of a screenplay, minus all or most of the dialogue. Originally meant (during the studio system days) a document of forty to eighty pages; these days a treatment might mean only a double-spaced page and a half synopsis. In the gaming world, however, a treatment might run upward of two hundred pages.

Tweak: A minor change made in a scene or portion of a screenplay. Illegally by Writers Guild rules yet too often, writers may be asked to tweak something for no extra pay.

WGA: The Writers Guild of America, the main union for screenwriters in the United States, with chapters in Los Angeles and New York. The New York guild was originally formed for people in theater and radio, the LA guild for screenwriters. Now both guilds handle film and TV and attempt to gain influences in other media over which they have little voice, such as animation and gaming.

WGA Signatory: An agent, producer, or production company that has signed an agreement to abide by established agreements with the Writers Guild of America

You might also want to read through the excellent "Slanguage Dictionary" glossary developed by *Daily Variety* and available for free on their Web site at www.variety.com. You may have to use the search function to find it. Slanguage isn't normal Hollywood speak—many of the terms like "ayem" (a morning hours TV show) were coined by *Variety* journalists to be catchy to the ear and look good in print.

Inside the Producer's Head

No matter how much you know about normal everyday language in Hollywood, things change here all the time. Trust your intuition about any encounter and remember that any person you're dealing with when trying to sell a property is probably as interested in finding a great property as you are in selling one. Toward that end, let's examine a typical independent producer, which is the kind you're most likely to sell to first. Here are some things he or she considers when contemplating working with anyone or any project.

1. *Do I Know You?* A great number of producers will not accept projects sent in by writers they don't know. Unless they have spoken to a writer or the writer's representative about a project, they won't look at it unless a release has been signed, and not even then unless they like the high concept or logline pitched over the phone or via email. Thus, most busy producers prefer to have projects referred to them via agents, managers, and other producers whose opinion they trust.

2. *Do You Know Who I Am?* Successful people in the business expect you to do your homework before you approach them. If someone tells you about a producer, but not much about their history, do whatever you can to find out about them before contacting them.

3. *How Did You Find Us?* If you merely go through a reference book and send them a script with a cover letter, that could be considered bad etiquette. Call first if you can, email if that's your only option, or send a short letter. A fax is acceptable to some, but completely unacceptable to others due to legal worries. If a producer doesn't know anything about a writer or a project sent unannounced, the project will probably be immediately returned unread (or more likely, thrown away) because it's unsolicited.

4. *Hmmm, That's Interesting.* If you pitch your idea over the phone or via a short email and the idea sounds interesting, the producer or production company might offer you several options. First, you can send it in through an agent, manager, or lawyer. You might be asked to sign a release form they'll send you. If they really like what they hear, they might ask you to messenger it over. In the rare occasion you hear the last option, that producer would consider you someone who knows

this business and is already working in it. In any of these options, there has to be a "paper trail," because people have to protect themselves from possible litigation. So you'll have to include a cover letter however you get the project to them.

5. *It's Not for Me/Us.* Just because a producer rejects a project, that doesn't mean it is without value. Some producers just don't "get" gross-out comedy. Others might not have a clue how to make a thriller. More often, though, "it's not for us" is a nice way of saying a project has been rejected due to amateur writing and/or low grades by a reader or character, dialogue, story, or other screenplay elements. Too many checks in the Poor or Weak boxes mean your script gets rejected. Unfortunately, you won't be shown the coverage due to potential legal problems.

6. *How Much Work Does It Need?* The ratio of projects submitted to what gets bought or optioned for development is very small. A producer needs to be willing to fight for a project or even spend his or her own money on it. Just about every project "needs work," because filmmaking is a constantly evolving, collaborative process, even in production. Every major project requires a screenplay, so the closer a script is to being ready for production, the better it is for any producer.

7. *Is This a Writer I Want to Know?* Even if a producer passes on a screenplay, if they find your writing interesting they might take a general meeting with you, to see if you could develop a harmonious working relationship. That can often lead to a rewrite job or a recommendation to someone else. They might also tell you: "Send us anything you write."

8. *Will Someone Else Make Money off This?* If you ever wonder how three baseball movies could be made by three different studios in one

year, or why a spate of Christian-themed projects appeared on television and in film after the surprise success of Mel Gibson's *The Passion of the Christ*, just know that fear is a big reality in Hollywood. Even if someone isn't in love with your project, if it's similar to something else that's making money, or if it's so good they're afraid someone else will make millions off it, the producer might get in business with you.

When you "click" on a project with a producer, it's a great thing. The producer might become your friend, invite you to his or her house, to parties, and introduce you to friends. Suddenly you'll realize what I mean by saying that Hollywood is a people town. I often refer to it as being admitted into "the club." Once you are seen as someone with marketable commercial talent, the barriers of the past seem like ghosts that never should have hindered you.

So where do you find those people who will fall in love with your project or with you and get you into "the club"? There are a number of ways, and it depends not only on where you're coming from, but where you actually live.

Where to Find the People: In Hollywood

I've found there are two types of people who come to Hollywood: those who mix well, and those who don't. Unless you are represented so well you don't need to physically be here at least briefly, you will need to be someone who likes to mix with people and can "work" a party. How do you do that? Well, it's as simple as introducing yourself and being genuinely interested in all types of people, because there are all types of people in Hollywood. One night I watched my then twelve-year-old son Haley do that at a pool party at the Hollywood Roosevelt Hotel. He spent a couple of hours entertaining Nia "Big Fat Greek Wedding" Vardalos and her husband Ian. "Your son was the life of the party!" Nia

> *Studio executives are intelligent, brutally over-worked men and women who . . . wake up every morning . . . with the knowledge that sooner or later they're going to get fired.*
>
> —**William Goldman**

told me as we were leaving, and I promised to see her movie. (I had no idea how big a film it would be, so shoot me.)

If you don't naturally mix well, there's another thing you can do, which is simply be friendly. When I wrote the first edition of my *Writer's Guide to Hollywood*, one agent told me that her first advice to new writers was to make friends. That might be the best advice I could give any "newbie." Although you've no doubt seen movies like *Swimming with Sharks* (1994) that paint Hollywood as a cutthroat town, the truth is that successful people here have great and lasting friendships. For example, it warmed my heart one day when I learned that the greatest screenwriter I've ever had the pleasure of meeting, Ernest Lehman, counted producer David Brown as his best friend since elementary school.

It would be folly on my part to try to list every single place in Hollywood where you could meet people, because hot spots change all the time. A bit of simple logic should tell you where to find people who can change your career, namely, where they can be found.

Here's what I mean by that. I once lived in West Hollywood and regularly ate breakfast at the Beverly Hills delicatessen Nate 'n Al. One day Aaron Spelling and his wife were in the next booth. Another morning, Fred Astaire came around the corner and said "Good morning!" Not far away, in the parking lot of a grocery store I met director Richard Donner. Another time at the same grocery store, I returned Steve Martin's wallet to him after it slipped out of his pocket. (No tip from Steve—I think he thought I lifted it.) I met Michael York in a photocopy shop. And all because I lived in the same general area.

So what if you move to Los Angeles but can't afford a certain neighborhood? Well, they have to eat, don't they? I ran into producer Brian Grazer at The Grill in Beverly Hills one day. I can't count how many times I've seen similarly dressed agents from major agencies at Beverly Hills eateries. Of course, I happen to know what these people look like, but you could accomplish that by reading certain publications and/or *Daily Variety* online (where pictures accompanying the articles can be downloaded).

And then there are the nighttime activities. Director Gary Marshall once claimed he could accomplish a year's worth of business by attending three parties, including one at the Playboy Mansion. Such options might not be available to you, but certain activities that are open to the public will allow you to mix with Hollywood movers and shakers for very little money. Ever heard of The Academy?

The main organization that just about everyone in Hollywood wants to belong to is the Academy of Motion Pictures Arts and Sciences. By simply surfing to www.oscars.org and clicking on Events you'll find a place to sign up to be automatically notified via email of current events, public programs, and events of the Academy Foundation that include "film-related exhibitions, screenings, lectures and seminars, and the Student Academy Awards, among many other activities." Who could you meet at such events? Just about anyone. Remember, most movie stars, directors, and producers are film fans, too.

Similarly, by surfing to www.emmys.org and clicking on Events, you can sign up for email updates on activities at the Academy of Television Arts & Sciences in North Hollywood. These events include "behind-the-scenes evenings with the most popular and acclaimed shows currently on the air, as well as workshops and seminars on employment, career and social issues, and conferences on emerging technologies and information systems." And by the way, if no one told you this, most of the work in Hollywood for writers is in television.

Speaking of writers in Hollywood, the organization most screenwriters aspire to join is the Writers Guild of America, west. The Writers Guild Foundation is a 501(c)3 nonprofit organization that works in concert with the Writers Guild of America, west. This educational entity was formed to encourage excellence in writing, to educate the public concerning the role of the writer in film, television, and radio, and to promote further education and communication within the writing community. They put on events like the "Writers on Writing" seminar series held at the Writers Guild of America, west headquarters at 7000 West Third Street, Los Angeles. The series showcases an outstanding motion picture or television writer each month discussing how their careers have developed, their approach to their craft, and so forth, with each interview followed by an audience question-and-answer period. Most of these events are open to the public, with a substantial discount for students who present valid student identification. For more information see the Web site at www.wga.org or call (323) 782-4692.

There are public venues unique to Hollywood that support and celebrate the business and offer people an opportunity to meet like-minded people, successful or pre-successful. For example, ArcLight Cinema (www.ArcLightCinemas.com) offers events like this one:

> Hollywood's Master Storytellers Presents:
> *Superman: The Movie* (Expanded Edition) and
> Q&A with director Richard Donner. Expanded
> edition of this 1978 film that made a star of
> Christopher Reeve incorporates more than twenty
> minutes of unseen footage and some reworked
> special effects.

Chances are, at an event like that, even if you didn't get an opportunity to pitch your project to Richard Donner, you might meet someone else who could help your career or who at least might become a friend.

In general, the main "bible" of happenings in Los Angeles is published every week in the free newspaper *L.A. Weekly* (see www.laweekly.com). Favorite restaurants, neighborhood movies, best clubs—it's all in the *Weekly.*

Lastly, since any club is only as successful as its ability to attract and keep patrons, it hires event producers to get the public to their venues. One whose events I generally like is:

MacAfrica

Event Producer

P.O. Box 18784

Encino, CA 91416

Phone: (818) 342-2171

Fax: (818) 342-2789

Email: macafrica1@earthlink.net

Signing up for email notices about Mac's events (Mac is a lady) might get you an invitation to a place like Barfly, "The most SPECTAC-ULAR BAR in L.A., Where they serve the BEST DRINKS!" or a similar establishment. You might also learn about a performance by one of the many actors who are also musicians, like Dennis Quaid or Jeff Goldblum.

There are a great number of hangouts, parties, clubs, and net-workers in Los Angeles, and I could probably write an entire book about that alone. Just know this: You can find like-minded people rather easily, and if you approach established professionals on a friendly, open basis and *not* as a fawning fan, in most cases you can strike up a conversation that could (but might not) lead to something mutually beneficial.

Where to Find the People: From Out of Town

Since the late 1990s, there has been an explosion of events in Los Angeles for aspiring screenwriters. Usually held on a weekend, these events attract people from all over the world, some of whom will dress like the main character in their script. The atmosphere can be competitive: Many people will ignore the other attendees, taking three times longer than their allocated pitch time, as though their project was the most important in the universe. In case you've never been to such an event, you usually only get a maximum of five minutes to describe your project to the person listening. That's about the amount of time you might get in a phone call, which is usually less expensive than a plane ticket.

Let me break down, roughly, how a pitch event usually goes:

a. more people will sign up than will get seen;

b. the majority of the attendees will forget to read the rules and fail to sign up for the company they want to see;

c. inevitably, some production companies will simply fail to show with no explanation, thus causing the event promoter to shift around the hopefuls to other company reps who might not be right for them;

d. you'll be allotted five minutes to share the idea you could have spent years perfecting in screenplay form; and

e. if the chemistry isn't right or if you've picked a company that simply doesn't do the kind of material you own, you're dead in the water before you even start talking.

I've helped put on such events, taken pitches at such events, refereed, and more. After years of being involved, I now feel that, generally, most of these events are not worth your time. Here's why, other than cost of attendance: Unless you are dealing with a small production company, one which will likely offer you only a small paid option if not asking for a free one, the people who will show up to hear about your project are almost always the lowest-ranking people at a company. That doesn't mean they're not great people, or future producers. It just means you probably won't get any further with them than you would if you called them.

Once you sign up for an event, you'll get all sorts of offers in the mail and via email, so I'll leave it to you to sort out which ones sound worthwhile. Meanwhile, there are three ongoing institutions in Los Angeles that I feel have proven their worth to writers year after year.

Every couple of years or so (there is no specific schedule) the aforementioned Writers Guild Foundation holds an event known as "Words into Pictures." This generally three-day event is not simply famous screenwriters telling tales. It also features panel after panel of top film and TV executives discussing the current state of Hollywood,

A film is never really any good unless the camera is an eye in the head of a poet.

—Orson Welles

how some projects made it while others failed, as well as other items of interest to Hollywood hopefuls. For more information see the event Web site at www.wordsintopictures.org or call (323) 782-4692.

If you can only attend one event per year in Los Angeles, here's what I recommend. In its third year in 2004, the Screenwriting Expo put on by Erik Bauer and the creative team behind *Creative Screenwriting* magazine is the world's largest screenwriting conference. It offers almost three hundred seminars, workshops, and panel discussions on every aspect of writing and selling to Hollywood. One of those seminars, I'm happy to say, will be given by yours truly. Jeff Arch, who wrote *Sleepless in Seattle* (1993) and other top scripts, said: "The Expo is exactly the kind of thing they didn't have when I was coming up. I wish to hell that they had." Priced to be affordable to just about anyone, this three-day event offers the opportunity to pitch projects to dozens of producers, development executives, managers, and agents. It features a $50,000 Screenplay Contest, a three-day screenwriting tournament held during the Expo, and the chance to make thousands of friends in attendance. For more information call (800) 727-6978 or visit www.screenwriting-expo.com.

If you find that neither of these events fit with your schedule, one organization with ongoing events might be exactly to your liking. It's the only organization of its kind that I recommend without question. Sherwood Oaks Experimental College has no fixed classroom. Its students meet at hotels and movie studios and often share breakfast or lunch around a table with someone who can buy their work or sell it for them as soon as that very day. Sherwood Oaks events offer attendees a chance to meet numerous development executives, producers, and other working professionals. Would you like to sit inside a boardroom at Sony or Disney and tell an executive from a company with an on-the-lot deal about your project? That's the kind of opportunity you get via Sherwood Oaks.

Former schoolteacher Gary Shusett started Sherwood Oaks in the late 1970s and has alumni like James *"Titanic"* Cameron. Gary's brother Ron is a very successful screenwriter with numerous credits, and just about everyone in the business knows Gary or his reputation. If you can't afford one of the weeklong or weekend programs, Gary might work with you on a work/study basis. For more information contact: Gary Shusett, Sherwood Oaks Experimental College, 7095 Hollywood Blvd. #876, Los Angeles, CA 90028; phone (323) 851-1769, fax (323) 850-5302, or see the Web site at www.sherwoodoakscollege.com.

I'm sure I'll get email along the lines of: "But Skip, I went to Joe Blow's Weekend Pitch Powerhouse and got an agent immediately!" I hope people do have such successes. It's just that I've been around this town a long time, have seen a lot of things come and go, and I know what I trust.

Where to Find the People: Online

In the last edition of my *Writer's Guide to Hollywood* I touted the potential of a few "script trackers" and "coverage services" accessible via the Web. I've since seen the error of my ways. There have been too many people promising too much and delivering too little, so no longer will I offer them the opportunity to reach my readers. I'll only tout those I've personally found to be worthwhile. The novelty of the Internet and email has worn off in Hollywood. Some people are very protective about being contacted in any fashion unless they have some idea who you are. That means they might not be eager to Instant Messenger you about that project you're so enthusiastic about.

The facts are simple. You can locate email addresses and contact information at Web sites such as www.showbizdata.com or www.hcdonline.com. You can try bulk email promotion services like www.scriptblaster.com and look up contact information for actors at www.whorepresents.com. Sooner or later, though, you'll need to deal with people personally. That means you'll have to pick up the phone or (much better) go meet people in person. If you can find a better way, good for you. I only know what has worked for me and just about every other successful writer I know. In this people town, people want people before they want email.

One online resource I will recommend unequivocally, however: "Skip's Hollywood Hangout" discussion group at Yahoo! You'll find a link to it on my personal site at www.skippress.com. You can also take a look at the group at http://movies.groups.yahoo.com/group/hollywood-writers.

Getting Inside the Club

My first film will be a very simple one. I'll need only $10 million. The film will be about a boy, his dog, and his budget.

—Robin Williams

Please remember this about Hollywood "gatekeepers." That includes the person who is paid a low wage to answer the phone, make coffee, and read enough scripts to make his or her eyes permanently bloodshot. They are needed for this reason: *Most scripts received are not commercial by Hollywood standards.*

I'm nice to gatekeepers because I've seen them move up, usually after finding a hot property that their boss produced. My thought is: "The one I'm selling is their ticket up." I always believe that. So call me an optimist.

Any club has its rules of entry, and Hollywood is no different. When you get on someone's radar you'll find that person to be someone with whom you or your material will resonate, usually from the very beginning. Once you can write a good screenplay, the good ones will sense it. I can't prove that to you—you'll just have to find out for yourself.

When you've done your research about any one particular person or company, you might be surprised what you can accomplish with a simple query, whether by phone, email, or letter. A pitch over the phone that is effective will also work in person. It's confident, to the point, and exciting. When it's exciting enough, it gets buzz going. People will tell the person in the next office, pick up the phone and chat about it, type out a description in an email. That's called "word of mouth" and it works with finished movies, but you don't have a studio publicity machine, only yourself. So you have to take off your "writer as artist" hat and put on your "writer as sold professional" hat.

One caution here: Don't buy into the conventional wisdom about the type of person who can sell to Hollywood or the circumstances under which you have to sell here. For example, you might have been told that you can't sell anything if you're over forty. Baloney. I knew a man who sold his first script at fifty-eight. I knew a woman living in Maine who sold a screenplay to the Disney Channel via an agent I told her about. I knew a fifty-three-year-old author living in New Mexico who sold a screenplay to a German company after seeing a post on a newsgroup and got a job on an animated Hollywood TV show. One of my readers sold his first screenplay at age twenty-eight, though English is his second language.

Of course, one highly successful author friend who wanted to sell screenplays had to come to Los Angeles for a week before I could find her an agent, but that's not the point. The fact is, if you show any kind of screenwriting talent at all, you can get noticed. As long as you know your own strengths and write commercially interesting screenplays (the kind people will pay to see), you're in the running.

The catch is making that initial connection. If you send a query letter to an agent or producer, it's a toss-up whether they'll read the letter at all. That's why I advise calling instead and emailing only if you know they're open to hearing from you that way. Whether you write a query letter or an email, keep the following elements in mind:

a. Never send a "To Whom It May Concern" query or anything that looks like it's going out to several people at the same time. Find out who receives scripts and *spell his or her name correctly* (very important).

b. Don't bother trying to tell them how wonderful they are. Get right to the point and describe what you're selling.

c. Explain why you chose to write to him or her, indicating that you've done some research (and you'd better have really done it or you could be found out, then your credibility will be shot).

d. Briefly introduce yourself. Tell them whether you have any credits at all, any particular qualifications for writing your script (like being an emergency-room doctor for twenty years if it's a medical thriller), or any prizes for your writing.

e. State when you are available to talk about the project. If you work during the day and can give out your work number, do so. If you have a cell phone, give that one first. People in Hollywood pick up the phone more often than they email. Try to be as "reachable" as you can without sounding desperate.

f. If you'll be in their city soon, let them know that you're coming to meet with some other people (you don't have to say who) and use that to stoke their interest in meeting "busy" you.

Any letter should be a page or less, emails much shorter. I doubt there is one person in ten who will read a query letter longer than a page. The average agency, particularly any agency listed in a well-known contact book, gets *thousands* of query letters every year.

Forget tricks, chocolates, dancing delivery people, Amazon.com gift certificates, or the like. They've seen it all. Do not waste your money sending a query letter to anyone overnight or by special delivery, or use any kind of special envelope to make it get noticed. It won't help. In Hollywood, scripts are messengered from place to place. How letters arrive doesn't matter; they just go in the pile.

If they will read an emailed script, they'll tell you. Otherwise you'll need to send a printed script. I've never met anyone who would download a script from a Web site and read it—there are simply too many computer viruses around.

You can get just about anyone's attention briefly. That's why you need to know the logline of your property cold. From there, you probably don't have more than a minute to get your point across. Let's go over an imaginary conversation that might take place over the phone.

If you call and don't know whom to ask for, you would request the Director of Development or the Creative Executive. Since you want to appear to have done your homework, it would probably help to know who this person is prior to calling. It might go like this . . .

"Mega Pictures."

"Hi. I wondered if you could help me. Is Blair Branson still your Director of Development?"

You could be some person updating a Rolodex for another Hollywood executive, couldn't you?

"Yeah, this is Blair."

And there's an example of why you should call. With a name like Blair, how do you know if this is a man or woman? A phone call would probably reveal that.

"Hi. Mr. Branson, this is Jane Screenwriter. I have a script I think you'll be glad you read."

"We don't accept unsolicited submissions."

"I understand. I can send it in with a release."

Hmmm, Branson thinks. She's got her own release form. She's serious about this. "Well, all right. What've you got?"

"It's a story of how an MI-6 friend of mine personally stopped the Russians from winning World War III."

Now, you may be thinking that sounds far-fetched, but I'll bet it would get your attention. It also happens to be true and that's pretty much the exact phrase I used to get a pitch meeting with the woman who ran Sean Connery's former production company. Of course, a fellow I knew happened to be the Director of Development there, but it's my educated guess that if I used that same pitch to a production company that did big-budget action thrillers I would have had a warm reception.

Here's how I would've approached a company with an email query on the same project.

Let's start with the subject line, which can be all-important. How many emails do you read if you don't know the sender or at least are intrigued by the description?

> *This film cost $31 million. With that kind of money I could have invaded some country.*
>
> **—Clint Eastwood**

My subject line would be something like: "Why the Russians never won World War III."

From there, I would introduce myself, explain in twenty-five words or less what I had to offer, and ask if I could call and speak to someone. Maybe this:

"I'm a screenwriter with a number of sales, and I have the rights to the story of how an MI-6 agent personally stopped the Russians from winning World War III. I would love the opportunity to pitch it to you."

If the only way I could approach a company was a written letter or even a fax, it might read as follows:

"I'm a screenwriter with a number of sales, and I have the rights to the story of how an MI-6 agent with the help of a beautiful Russian spy stopped the former USSR from starting and winning World War III. While this might sound far-fetched, I could produce this person for a meeting and explain in detail how the world reached the brink of nuclear war and staggered backward into peace. The story would make a great action thriller and I would love the opportunity to pitch it to you.

"If we brought along a Russian-made eavesdropping device that would allow you to listen to someone speak through six feet of solid concrete, would that convince you we might be telling the truth?"

So tell me, would you be intrigued by that letter? Unfortunately, because of a terrorist element to the story and the fact that September 11, 2001, happened not long after we made that pitch, the project in question fell by the wayside. Sean Connery dissolving his production company was another reason.

Lastly, writers often ask me:

"How long should I wait after contacting someone before I follow up?"

My standard response is "at least six weeks." Chances are good that if you don't hear from them by then, you're not going to hear from them. I'll usually just cross that name off the list and move on to the next. If you're convinced they're simply the perfect agency or production company for you, and it's been six weeks or more, you might call or post a very short, polite follow-up.

There's another thing to remember about Hollywood. Personnel at production companies change all the time. Companies move from one studio to another, depending on projects. They might switch area codes. Normally, a production company will have an answering machine to provide its new numbers (including fax) to callers, and it probably will *not* record messages.

You don't have to live in Hollywood to make it here, but living here isn't bad. Show me some other place where you can ski in the morning, surf in the afternoon, and have lunch in a restaurant where you can see the star of the latest blockbuster. (Or more likely, shop at a grocery store where they're also trying to find fresh produce.)

So far, we've looked at the nature of Hollywood, and what it takes to break into the business. I've simply taken for granted that you might have something up to Hollywood standards, ready to sell. If you find, however, that despite your best efforts you're not having the success you imagined, you might need more education. We'll cover people and places for that in the next chapter.

CHAPTER

4

A Hollywood Education

Everything has its limit—iron ore cannot be educated into gold.

—Mark Twain, What is Man?

If you display natural storytelling talent, Hollywood will probably become interested in you. I say this from observing many successful screenwriters and from my own experience. At its core, Hollywood is about story, because that's what people love.

From the time I first started writing, I got noticed. I wrote a twelve-page poem in high school about the fatal charge of Confederate troops at the Battle of Gettysburg; the teacher wouldn't let me turn it in because, she said, "It might embarrass the other students." I still shake my head at that one.

When I first ventured into Hollywood it was courtesy of winning a lot of money on a game show called "Knockout." Having the luxury of not working for a while, I took my time trying to perfect my first screenplay. I didn't sell that script, but it got me an agent. The story had impact, apparently. Fifteen years later, a producer remembered the script and urged me to rewrite it. I was about to do that when the movie *Elf* (2003) came out; mine was so similar I abandoned the rewrite.

The second screenplay I wrote got me another agent, who remembered it over a decade after he read it. I was again amazed that someone would remember it and said so. "It was a great story," he insisted.

The first screenplay treatment I wrote impressed in this order: director Richard Donner, actor/director Robert Redford, and actor/producer Michael Douglas. Donner said I should make a novel of it before a screenplay. Redford had a project he thought was too similar. Douglas offered to option it and pay me to write the screenplay. Unfortunately, the producer who took it to him botched the deal.

That treatment and the second one I wrote landed me one of the top agents at International Creative Management. The second one was optioned by someone from ICM who left to become a producer, and the agent who negotiated that deal is now President of the Writers Guild of America, west.

If there's a pattern here it's a simple one. I've been writing interesting stories from the beginning. If you can do that *and* learn how to network and persist through the natural disappointments of Hollywood, you have a chance of making a success here.

Breaking Through

In recent years, while writing books and teaching courses, I have had little time to write screenplays. Nevertheless, I had one of my old scripts optioned for a decent amount of money. Another that I managed to rewrite was optioned about a month after I completed it.

The recounting of my successes above was only intended to illustrate that some people are natural storytellers and can break in almost immediately. Take my friend Mirko Betz. After arriving in Los Angeles from Germany, he took a screenwriting class from Linda Palmer at UCLA, wrote his first script, and quickly sold it to director/producer Roland Emmerich. Mirko's cycle from zero to sold took all of eleven months. His next script landed him a literary manager and an agent, and I expect him to sell many more screenplays.

Mirko and I had some things in common. We both started in our twenties and each of us found good teachers. He attended UCLA; I took classes at Sherwood Oaks Experimental College and read the only book I could find at the time: *Magic Methods of Screenwriting: A Practical Handbook of TV and Movie Scriptwriting* by Donna Lee.

And guess what? The principles I learned still apply. Donna Lee founded the Hollywood Scriptwriting Institute in 1976 and has been teaching writers to create stories they truly believe in while being "crassly commercial" for almost thirty years. She has been particularly helpful to first-time writers, if the alumni success stories on her Web page at www.moviewriting.com are any indication:

- Cindy Rosmus sold her script "Jury of Wives" to Fox Studios for $150,000.
- Edward Case sold his script "Alexander the Great" to LLP Productions for $30,000 plus $150,000 upon the film's release.

If you'd like to find out more about what Donna Lee has to offer, you can call (800) 727-4787 (1-800-SCRIPTS), email info@moviewriting.com, or visit the Web site.

Meanwhile, there are a lot of screenwriting teachers and programs out there, so let's try to sort through them.

I always tell the younger filmmakers and students: Do it like the painters used to . . . Study the old masters. Enrich your palette. Expand the canvas.

—**Martin Scorsese**

A Hollywood Education Is Like . . . Family

These days, I would not advise anyone to try to make a career solely as a screenwriter.

That shouldn't shock you. I'm merely being realistic. In this day of inexpensive digital moviemaking and an explosion of "reality television," the message is clear—*If you believe in it that much, do it yourself.*

Many of the people who make a big splash in Hollywood these days are "hyphenates." Starting with a fine basic knowledge of screenwriting, some writer/directors, such as Quentin Tarantino, Robert Rodriguez, and James Cameron (who attended Sherwood Oaks Experiment College classes at about the same time I did) produce their own films.

Other hyphenates grow up in the business, which is an education itself. For example, teenage actress/writer Nikki Reed's cowritten, somewhat autobiographical *Thirteen* (2003) earned several awards and nominations. Reed is the daughter of Seth Reed, a very successful Hollywood art director.

The point is that it doesn't matter *how* Hollywood noticed these people, it's that they weren't content merely being screenwriters. The script was where they started, but they did whatever it took to get their vision onto the screen.

And even though Nikki Reed grew up around Hollywood, she still had to deliver the goods. That's always the case. Sofia Coppola did not become the third woman ever nominated for a Best Director Oscar only because Francis Ford Coppola is her father. The Academy simply thought her *Lost in Translation* (2003) was that good. Similarly, HBO did not buy the documentary *My Uncle Berns* (2004) from Lindsay Crystal because her dad Billy Crystal and mother Janice executive produced it. Steven Spielberg might have discovered Gwyneth Paltrow in a movie theater near his summer home on Long Island, but her wistful looks and obvious talent got her working and kept her working. So what if her mother is noted actress Blythe Danner? She can't do Gwyneth's lines for her.

All the people mentioned above, whether they had relatives in Hollywood or took classes here, had something major going for themselves, other than talent.

Simply put, they had proximity. You can get proximity, too. All you have to do is physically connect.

Hollywood is a cornucopia of schools and teachers, and if you can pay the tuition (sometimes reasonable, sometimes exorbitant) you can have access to them all. If you click with a teacher, you'll find that person might even become like family to you. They'll be curious about your progress after you leave them. They'll introduce you to people who can help you, and become a friend in the business. Hollywood professionals take pride in helping others build careers. When I met legendary director and producer Robert Wise (who edited *Citizen Kane* [1941] early in his career), I mentioned director Martha Coolidge for some reason I now forget. Mr. Wise smiled and told me how Coolidge started out with him as an intern.

I've been giving back for years myself. The covers of my *Writer's Guide to Hollywood* books have advertised me as "Your friend in Hollywood," but truth be told, I don't know you. I don't know what you like to write, what type of film you want to make, or even if I'd want to be your friend. Without knowing these things, it would be impossible for me to tell you exactly which teacher might be best for you, so I can only discuss institutions and individuals who have stood the test of time and whose students have prospered.

I am atypical of writing teachers in Hollywood. I've sold feature films, yet never have had one made. Had I solely concentrated on writing features, maybe that would be different. Instead I've been a staff writer for a TV series, had both novels and nonfiction books published, edited magazines, made how-to videos, produced international events, and been a successful playwright and director. So I know a little about a lot of things. Other teachers in Hollywood have a more singular focus.

They've worked in television and they teach television. They've worked in features and they teach features. Or they worked a long time ago, aren't currently working, and so they teach. Not that there's anything wrong with that, but I try to find teachers who are actively working in their field of advice.

Whatever teachers you decide are right for you, I would suggest some simple criteria in evaluating them:

1. Have they personally achieved what they are telling you how to do?
2. If not, have their students gone on to substantial success?

I'm not sure a Ph.D. helps when it comes to telling people how to write screenplays. Unless, that is, you've also written and sold screenplays, or even won awards like Lew Hunter, former co-chairman of screenwriting at UCLA. Anyone can sit down with a stopwatch and notepad and make note of recurring patterns. Certainly, you should know such things, but where's the art? All too many screenwriting gurus make a living commenting only on what others have done. To me, that tends to make their advice a bit like "paint by numbers."

This prompts complaints from people like Frank Pierson, President of the Academy of Motion Pictures Arts and Sciences and the writer of great films like *Cool Hand Luke* (1967). Pierson has been vocally agitated about the cookie-cutter approach of many modern films. This might have a connection with some of the current crowd of screenwriting teachers who are not themselves screenwriters, or maybe not. Some great writers can't teach, and some great teachers are not the best of writers. You'll have to do your own investigation.

Before I get into schools, let's go over the texts that I have found to be most helpful in learning screenwriting. Many of the current gurus learned from some of them, one of which is more than two thousand years old. It wouldn't take long to read all of the following books—you might even learn enough to write and sell your first script.

My Top Ten Hollywood Reads

Despite the library of screenwriting how-to information that has proliferated in recent years, the basics remain the same. Picasso learned to do perfect figure studies before he painted his masterpieces, so I hope you will give these books a thorough study before you attempt to write your first script or attend your first class. You'll be ahead of most of your peers if you do.

1. *Poetics.* Writing about successful Greek playwriting techniques, Aristotle set down basic dramatic principles that are merely rephrased today by some screenwriting gurus. For example, if anyone ever tells you about the importance of plot reversals, where progress made is lost, that was known as "perepetia" more than two thousand years ago. Lew Hunter told me he rereads this book once a year.

2. *The Art of Dramat!c Wr!t!ng: Its Basis in the Creative Interpretation of Human Motives,* by Lajos Egri. (The exclamation points you see are actually in the title.) Egri's theories are used in major universities with good reason..He was an influential teacher in Hollywood. When some of his students put together some software called *Collaborator,* it was the best script development program of its kind. To understand character and motivation, read Egri's book.

3. *Screenwriting Tricks of the Trade* by William Froug is still one of the best screenwriting books I've ever read. Lew Hunter called Bill Froug "*The* premier screenwriting teacher in the history of motion pictures." The late great screenwriter Jeffrey Boam called Froug (in the Foreword) "the screenwriter's best friend and advocate." I insist you read this book, and here's one reason why: Froug tells you to learn about writing movies by *watching movies,* whenever possible. In his book you'll know what to look for, while watching. William Froug brought Lew Hunter into teaching. With that kind of lineage, it's no wonder that Julius Epstein, one of the screenwriters of *Casablanca* (1942), said this of *Lew Hunter's Screenwriting 434:* "If it is not possible for you to enroll in Professor Hunter's class at UCLA, then immerse yourself in his book. It can be the quickest, surest path to a screenwriting

career." Lew retired from UCLA and now does seminars and workshops, and his advice is still in high demand. In addition to teaching, Lew won several top awards; not many screenwriting teachers can make similar claims.

4. Although the title *So You Want to be a Scriptwriter and Make a Million Dollars* is a little odd, Irving Elman scriptwriting knowledge came from experience that included more than two thousand television shows. He wrote his book after he found that he couldn't recommend any to his students at Santa Monica College.

5. *The Writer's Journey: Mythic Structures for Writers* by Christopher Vogler began as a memorandum that changed Hollywood. Vogler was working at Disney when he finally convinced Jeffrey Katzenberg of the wisdom of plots based on the "myth structure" of Joseph Campbell. Hit movies ensued. Of course, it helped that George Lucas credited Campbell's work with helping him finish *Star Wars* (1977) and that George Miller used Campbell's writings to frame his *Mad Max* (1979, 1981, 1985, 2005) series. Campbell was an academic and philosopher, so read this book first to understand him in a Hollywood context.

6. Once you've studied Vogler, you should read *The Hero of a Thousand Faces* and every other work by Joseph Campbell that you can find. Campbell's distillation of the great stories of world religion and myth will enliven and embolden your storytelling.

7. *The Secrets of Action Screenwriting* pulls no punches. It's all proven methods used by William C. Martell to sell dozens of feature screenplays, seventeen of which have been made, *all without an agent*. If your focus is on action or thriller (easier genres to sell) this book is for you.

8. *Secrets of Film Writing* by Tom Lazarus. Lazarus is the award-winning screenwriter of *Stigmata* (1999) and other films and TV series. He teaches for UCLA Extension Writers Program and knows what working screenwriters face because he is one.

9. *Television Writing from the Inside Out: Your Channel to Success* by Larry Brody. The proprietor of the excellent TVWriter.com covers just about everything in television in this book. He offers tips on every genre, including animation, as well as sample teleplays and tons of business advice, all based on years of TV writing successes.

10. After I had written the first two editions of the *Writer's Guide to Hollywood*, I was given the opportunity to write the first edition of the *Complete Idiot's Guide to Screenwriting*. I hesitated until, like Irving Elman above, I found that no book covered everything I thought beginning screenwriters needed to know. So I told them about the history of storytelling, Shakespeare, the history of Hollywood, the influence of psychology on the industry, and a lot about the screenwriting craft. So, at the risk of making a shameless plug, it must have been pretty good, because a Russian publisher translated it, and I was asked to write a second English language edition, which covers such things as "the Shaping Force," which is a person, item, or idea that arrives in the middle of the first act, with usually a hint or two of it before its arrival. It revisits at various points of the film, helping keep the "spine" of the story aligned.

The process of shaping successful screenplays is continually evolving. As video games and Hollywood movies grow increasingly hard to distinguish from each other, expect even more changes. With regard to books about the craft of screenwriting, I urge writers to read everything they can, if they think it might help improve their writing.

If a Guru Falls in Your Woods on the Path Not Taken

In the past, I've tried to be all things to all people with screenwriting and marketing advice. With this book, I simply don't have the room. I no longer have the patience with some people I see as more interested in their own bank account than they are of their clients' success. Most people who write screenplays hoping for a Hollywood career don't have a lot of money. Therefore, wanting them to get their money's worth is a major concern for me. It's one reason my own six-week screenwriting course is inexpensive. I'm just not so sure that several hundred dollars for a weekend seminar is always a good idea. Aspiring screenwriters might be better off renting great movies and studying them closely, then writing and rewriting their own scripts.

I'm convinced that paying $5,000 to have a screenplay analyzed is way too much when the Writers Guild minimum (the price paid for the majority of screenplays) is in the low $30,000s. I suppose the money is worth it if it helps you improve your script so that it's purchased for $50,000 or more. I knew one retired executive who hired *every* top consultant (including myself) to comment on his screenplay. Maybe you have that kind of money to spare. But guess what? He didn't sell that screenplay. What you pay is a matter of judgment, and I don't know your budget. I only know that all too many hopeful writers I've known don't have much of a budget at all. So I try to watch out for them.

Since not everyone can move to Los Angeles or another major media center and attend classes, they learn from the gushing gurus, people profuse with information and frequent flyer miles. If you can't attend the annual Screenwriting Expo, you might discover that a guru will be traveling to your city, or offering information via an online class or via audio, video, or DVD.

One way I judge potential teachers is by their attitude. If they spend too much time touting how great they are, that's trouble. I know one who does that, and I know how his background in a cult encourages him to be that way. What he doesn't know, probably, is how many people have told me how turned off they are by both his pushiness and what they perceive as disguised recruiting for his quasi-religion.

Another criterion I use is openness. If I inquire about a program and find the proprietors reluctant to give me information (which has happened in the past more than once), I feel they're hiding something or are too arrogant to bother with little old me. I inevitably hear bad reports about them.

> *I always thought the actors were hired to ruin the writers' lines.*
>
> **—Robert Benton,**
> **screenwriter**
> **and director**

Next, I try to determine *what student success came directly from what they learned from a guru.* When instructors make statements that can be misinterpreted in their favor, what does that say about their core honesty? One of my former students won the first Sundance Online Film Festival, but he didn't learn filmmaking from me; he was in a college English class I taught. One of my readers wrote an Academy Award–winning animated film, but I doubt anything he read in any of my books contributed to the script. I've been teaching screenwriting and consulting on screenplays for only a short time, and I want to make a living writing, not teaching and touring. So while I'm glad that my students, clients, and readers win contests and awards, I'm much more interested that they make a living at writing or at least make sales. Thus I'm only interested in telling them about gurus I feel will help them do that, not people who will thank them for sharing and pat them on the back while cashing a check.

Lastly, I prefer that someone teaching me how to do something has actually had success in the real world doing what he or she is telling me about. So here's what I suggest to you. If you are looking for a teacher or seminarist to learn from, look up their writing credits on the Internet Movie Database (www.imdb.com). If they don't have a *writer* credit, how much do they really know about screenwriting? Despite all the feel-good advice you might have heard in the past, in my experience, the marketplace tends to sort out the worth of people's scripts fairly well.

All that said, here are people listed alphabetically that you'll find on the seminar and workshop circuit who also have writer credits on the IMDb.

Gurus with Actual Writing Credits

Syd Field—Credited as Sydney Field, this prolific screenwriting teacher wrote *Spree . . . aka Las Vegas by Night* (1967), the last film that Jayne Mansfield completed before she was killed in an automobile accident. As Syd Field, he has a more recent story credit with *Mnemosyne* (2002), which was based on the ancient poem "Thunder, Perfect Mind," a visual journey of the human race, "an homage to power, strength, and individualism" according to IMDb. While that might sound terribly esoteric, Syd has been teaching the basic Hollywood three-act structure for as long as anyone and with his book *Screenplay* is the one who got the cottage industry of Hollywood screenwriting advice started. Though it was originally published in 1979, it remains one of the most popular and bestselling screenwriting books. No stranger to production, he came up with the structure chronicled in his books when, as a film executive, he saw the same pattern repeated over and over in scripts that got made. To read about his many products, classes, and speaking engagements see www.SydField.com.

Michael Hauge and Christopher Vogler—The author of *Writing Screenplays That Sell* teamed up with Hollywood's expert on Joseph Campbell to do an event that became a CD/DVD worth watching. You can read about "The Hero's Two Journeys" at Hauge's site, www.screenplaymastery.com. I was skeptical of Hauge when I first heard about him because he would emphasize things like the "fifteen most effective principles of plot structure" and the "seven steps to screenwriting success." His numbers game sounded too cut-and-paste to me. Plus, Hauge had no writing credits I could find, only a development, story editor, and producer background that seemed nebulous. Then I heard him speak at a "Selling to Hollywood" conference where I was also speaking and liked his ideas. One that was appealing was that major characters have a "wound" that they need to heal during the process of the story. Other teachers might call this a "ghost"—I call it the "inner need." While Vogler's site at www.writersjourney.com has been up and down over the years, Hauge's is updated regularly and offers a newsletter. He gets around a lot so don't be surprised if he'll show up in your city soon. Their recorded dual lecture, which is available as an audiobook, is certainly worthwhile.

Lew Hunter—Although he retired as chair emeritus of the

screenwriting department at UCLA, Lew Hunter has remained very active since moving back home to Nebraska with speaking engagements and workshops around the world on an ongoing basis. Most intriguing is a two-week screenwriting colony held in his Victorian mansion in Superior, Nebraska each summer starting in late June. Similar to the Sundance Workshop, it offers "twenty beginning and advanced screenwriters an opportunity to immerse themselves in focused daily workshops that are modeled after the UCLA MFA screenwriting program's story development process, which has launched more successful careers than any other screenwriting program in the world." The former UCLA prof is pleased to point out, "In 1998 alone, writers who came from the UCLA program wrote nine of the top ten box-office grossing films." If this sounds interesting, visit www.lewhunter.com and see if it's right for you.

Bill Martell—When I first met Bill he had just published *The Secrets of Action Screenwriting*. When I suggested how eager people would be to read his book and hear him speak, I offered to help him find a bigger publisher, but he told me he "wasn't in the book business." As for public speaking, he said he wasn't very good at that. Nevertheless, this always-busy screenwriter has been very busy in recent years with appearances in London and other venues. Upcoming action writers love Martell statements like: "The bigger the villain's plan, the bigger the movie." He offers a great deal of free advice at www.scriptsecrets.net. Go see if he'll be speaking near you, and learn why Roger Avary of *Pulp Fiction* (1994) fame said: "This book is dangerous. I feel threatened by it."

Robert McKee—Probably the most animated and engaging of all the speaking gurus, McKee has a Ph.D. in philosophy from the University of Michigan, where his creative writing teacher, Kenneth Rowe, had other students such as playwright Arthur Miller and writer/director Lawrence Kasdan. Immortalized in the film *Adaptation* (2002), McKee did not, as many people believe, play himself. That part went to character actor Brian Cox, despite the fact that as a child actor McKee appeared on Broadway with the legendary Helen Hayes. McKee has been a story analyst, written for top TV shows, been on the faculty at USC, and hosted the series *Reel Secrets* for British television. Although many people love his 1998 book *Story,* I didn't learn anything new. Nevertheless, his weekend seminar is a unique experience. As you might notice, the Endorsements page of his site at www.mckeestory.com lists a number of very successful writers who have attended his lectures, and an equal number of executive and magazine accolades. McKee is so famous in Hollywood circles it's not unusual to hear people say they took his seminar just so they could "speak McKee" (know his terms) more effectively.

John Truby—I like John Truby because he attempts to be all things to all writers. I don't think you actually *can* pull that off, but Truby certainly tries, with a plethora of audiotapes and lessons available via www.truby.com. In recent years, Truby has found an audience in Europe and has spent a good bit of time consulting there. Larry Wilson, screenwriter of *Beetlejuice* (1988) and *The Addams Family* (1991), describes him as "the best of all the teachers" but that's just the type of hyperbole you expect to see on any teacher's site. I do know that Truby's multi-level story organization and instructional software, "Write a Blockbuster," is pretty darn good, although some might find it a bit expensive. Truby's main writing credit was story editor on the TV series *21 Jump Street.* One of his students produced it, but he proved his own worth when he wrote and directed the feature film *All-American Boy* (2004), which won Best Dramatic Feature at the Houston International Film Festival.

To L.A. or Not to L.A.?

I've long advised that anyone serious about a Hollywood career should spend at least a year in Los Angeles. A summer retreat, a weekend workshop, or even a week-long program can be good, but it's nothing like living in a place and learning how it works to give you that legendary "lucky break." Although there are now worthwhile screenwriting programs available all over the world, the most skilled and produced screenwriters live in southern California—and you're likely to find them teaching at least part-time in the greater Los Angeles area. Listed alphabetically, here are brief descriptions of what you might find at schools that have traditionally helped launch Hollywood careers.

American Film Institute—With campuses in both northern and southern California and in Maryland and Washington, D.C., AFI is more geared to a full filmmaking curriculum than specialization for screenwriters. The AFI Conservatory's graduate screenwriting program is headed by *Kiss of the Spider Woman* (1985) writer Leonard Schrader, whose designation is senior filmmaker-in-residence. The AFI also offers unique programs like the Catalyst Workshop, an intensive two-day focus on the screenwriting craft for scientists. While AFI Conservatory screenwriting graduates include top screenwriters such as Scott Frank (*Get Shorty*) and Susanna Grant (*Erin Brockovich*), AFI is a great overall resource for screenwriters because of all the educational events and special programs available. See www.afi.com for details.

> *I don't take the movies seriously, and anyone who does is in for a headache.*
>
> **—Bette Davis**

The Learning Annex—While people might have laughed at me in previous years for including The Learning Annex on the same pages as major schools like AFI, UCLA, and USC, Steven Schragis has helped change that. This former marketing executive at Cahners (the parent company of *Variety*) has brought in top Hollywood talent for nighttime and weekend classes, such as a screenwriting class by Alec Sokolow, who was nominated for an Academy Award for writing *Toy Story* (1995). With more than forty screenplays to his credit including *Cheaper by the Dozen* (2003), Sokolow just might know something about scripts. See www.learningannex.com for myriad seminars offered on many subjects in a number of cities.

The University of California at Los Angeles (UCLA)—There are several ways to learn screenwriting at UCLA, the public university of the "big two" in L.A. (the other being USC below). The primary UCLA possibility is the four-year Master of Fine Arts in screenwriting, which prompted *The London Times* to dub UCLA "the Harvard of film-writing schools." Of course, that was in 1992 when Lew Hunter was running the program; a lot can change in a decade. Now the school offers a similar online program in three segments: (a) Professional Program in Screenwriting Online; (b) Advanced Program Online (second-year students); and (c) Summer Program Online. Many faculty for the online courses teach in the Professional Program on campus and in the MFA Program. Unfortunately, I've often found the Web site hard to navigate. Therefore, if you have trouble locating the site at www.tft.ucla.edu/filmtv/ftvframe-home.htm, call (310) 825-6827 or email UCLA Professional Programs at: professionalprograms@tft.ucla.edu.

UCLA Extension Writers Program—Although it shares the same campus, UCLA Extension has always been self-supporting. It is the largest school of its kind in the world and features a huge list of industry-related courses taught by working professionals. I taught for a year at the Writers Program and enjoyed it thoroughly. See the much more easily navigated site at www.uclaextension.edu for information about the certificate programs in feature film writing and television writing or call (310) 825-9415. They also offer online courses that address several levels of advancement. Given what I know about instructors like Linda Palmer and Corey Mandell, I would advise anyone serious about learning screenwriting from people in the know to choose Extension first and the larger UCLA program second. I would also highly suggest an on-campus in-person course over an online curriculum because of Extension's emphasis on classes taught by working professionals.

University of Southern California (USC)—Like publicly funded UCLA, Los Angeles' premier private university also offers a Master of Fine

Arts with a track in screenwriting, from its School of Cinema-Television. For information try www.usc.edu/dept/publications/cat95/cntv/cntv10.html, but if you have a problem simply use the search feature at www.usc.edu. You can also call (213) 740-3339 or email admission@cntv.usc.edu. A great number of USC teachers such as Richard Krevolin have written books on screenwriting. The key difference (other than tuition cost) that I find between the UCLA and USC programs is the stronger emphasis on overall filmmaking at USC. Consider this class from Norman Hollyn, author of *The Film Editing Room Handbook: How to Manage the Near Chaos of the Cutting Room.* Hollyn's "Editing for Scriptwriters" is designed to show how movies change drastically from the page to the screen; you usually only get that kind of information from actual production. Want to make digital features? The USC School of Cinema-Television's 3500 square foot Robert Zemeckis Center for Digital Arts, funded by a $5 million gift from the USC alumnus and Academy Award–winning director, was the country's first and only fully digital training center when it opened its doors. And let's not forget the MFA offered in USC's two-year Peter Stark Producing Program. Graduates seem guaranteed for a career as a film or television producer or film or TV executive.

When choosing a screenwriting program, it may not be as simple as figuring out which degree would give you the best alumni network. That's because Hollywood is about business, and commerciality of projects. This sentiment was reinforced when I spoke with Samantha Plotkin, who has been working professionally as a screenwriter for hire, a script doctor, treatment writer, and script analyst since 2001. She also writes for magazines like *Creative Screenwriting.* With several programs to choose from, she settled on USC's Master of Professional Writing. "It's not as connected to Hollywood as the film school," she told me, "but it's a better program for literally mastering writing because you are forced to study the different writing disciplines (short stories, narrative, TV writing, screenwriting, playwriting). You have to master all of the disciplines (to the best of your ability) before you can graduate. The best thing about the program was interacting with other people with the same dream, focusing on writing full-time. The only flaw is that it's not focused on the business of writing or how to sell your script once you graduate. They told me that my thesis script would be a great 'calling card script,' but when I got out into the real world, I was told over and over again that good writing is not enough to make you a salable writer—you need to be a good, commercial writer."

Ah, commerciality. The path to your dream home in the Hollywood Hills is paved with commerciality. Can you get that from a structured program? Maybe, maybe not. You might discover that the person who will teach you commerciality is not someone working in a structured program, but operating independently. It could be a working writer, or it might be someone who makes a living nurturing budding screenwriters.

Someone to Watch Over You

If you can't find a way to spend time in Los Angeles, and you're simply not getting ahead as fast as you'd like, you might consider hiring a script consultant. That can be tricky; I've found that the majority of script consultants got their start in the business not in writing but in working in production offices as a reader. Not that there's anything wrong with that—a number of successful producers I know started that way. Syd Field developed his structure matrix based on what he saw from reading and working with scripts. Therefore, I'm only listing below (in alphabetical order) consultants whose work I know personally. You'll find, oh, about five hundred others out there.

Robert Flaxman—Selected as best consultant in Los Angeles by *Creative Screenwriting* magazine, Robert pursues the writer's true meaning. "I'm always trying to get something from their subconscious," he once told me. "That's why I like to work with clients over the phone.

When we discuss the script that way, it's more a meeting of minds. We don't have distractions and can simply focus on the script. I want to know a writer's background because the process has to be personal. If my asking about things puts them off, they might not be honest about their script. I want writers to know I'm on their side in order to make the consultation as vital as possible." His advice isn't cheap. He spends a lot of time on any screenplay he takes on, with a method that includes multiple reads. A phone consultation might run eight hours or more. His main rule about a screenplay is that the reader cannot know more about what's going on than a member of the audience. While this might sound simple, it's a principle often overlooked by writers who have never participated in a production. Flaxman has a filmmaking background and, like anyone who has participated in the script-to-screen process, knows how and why things can change in getting a story in front of a paying audience. "No script is easy," he believes. "There are no shortcuts." You can reach him via his Web site, www.deepfeedback.com.

The cinema is not a slice of life but a piece of cake.

—*Alfred Hitchcock*

Colleen Hunt—Raised in the theater in both Los Angeles and New York, Colleen brought "a passionate love of the printed word and those brave souls who write them" to the fourteen years she spent as a story analyst at Columbia Pictures and Twentieth Century Fox. Her development job was at Fox on the Oscar-nominated Sidney Lumet/David Mamet film *The Verdict* (1982). She then became story editor at John Davis's first production company, worked at The Walt Disney Company, and worked as an analyst with Roy Disney at the Television Division Creative Group developing the now defunct Movies of the Week. Her mentors have included studio heads Sherry Lansing and Jeffrey Katzenberg; her favorite development project was *What's Love Got to Do With It* (1993), Tina Turner's biopic. Also a director and producer, she has taught at the UCLA Extension Writers' Program, and is expert in the area of dialogue and acting/character choices. She feels that most beginners don't understand Hollywood, and the proliferation of screenplay analysis services offered on the Internet hasn't helped. "I believe almost every writer can get work seen or read," she told me, "providing it goes through the proper submission channels. The truth is, no matter how a script manages to get in the door, it is given to a reader to analyze; if the script is shot down or passed on by the reader or an executive, that's it. You may only get one shot. Having championed so many writers and seen so many be rejected for problems that could have been worked through, I want my clients to have the *best* shot possible the first time out." You can reach Colleen at Storyconsultant@aol.com.

Donie Nelson—The lady I call the Fairy Godmother of Hollywood is known for her ability to personalize advice to fit the goals and needs of each client. She began in Hollywood as a development executive for MGM Films and has worked at developing feature films, movies for television, drama series, sitcoms, and even a documentary. All of her studio jobs focused on working with writers and scripts, whether she was in development or supervising production. Within a year of going to work at MGM, she became executive supervisor of MGM's unionized story analysts (readers). A consultant for more than a decade, Donie likes to experience each script on its own merits. "I never read coverage, summaries, or even loglines before opening the script," she related. "I only read the script once because this mirrors how an agent or producer will read it. I see everything that's obvious, both the positive and the negative. If the script is well written, I may have no notes to share. If there are problems, my comments give the client an overview, not a blueprint for a rewrite." Feeling that the biggest mistake most novice screenwriters make is marketing their scripts before they are ready, she works with writers to develop their craftsmanship and also instructs them on networking. Contact Donie Nelson at wrtrconsult@earthlink.net.

Natalie Lemberg Rothenberg—With her Insiders System for Writers, Natalie Rothenberg has advised almost two thousand clients over the last twelve years. She doesn't advise anyone to seek quick success. "You need to structure a life that includes enjoying the process of writing and networking," she emphasizes. "Writers who are ready for it should consider working in L.A. as an assistant or P.A. (production assistant) to learn the business, but the spec script market is such that anyone anywhere can create a product that—if they're good enough and lucky enough—can sell." Rothenberg's emphasis is taking each writer to his or her own next level. When she started the Insiders System, her goal was to tell writers constructively what buyers and representatives say behind their backs. And she would know. She's worked for companies such as Fries Entertainment and James Cameron's Lightstorm and in personal management as well. Check out her "Doorway Between Undiscovered Writers and Top Industry Decision Makers" at www.InsidersSystem.com.

Linda Seger—As the author of *Making a Good Script Great,* Linda Seger has built a worldwide reputation as a consultant. Although she has apparently never written a screenplay of her own, she's written several other books including *Making a Good Writer Great.* Some writers swear by what they've learned about fixing scripts from Linda. Visit www.lindaseger.com for more information.

Marc and Elaine Zicree—These successful writer/producers are not so much script consultants as career advisors. Via their "Supermentors" six-week class, they work from your end career goal backward. Then, week by week, they refine your game plan for marketing your work to Hollywood. Guest speakers include people such as screenwriter Paul Guay, who wrote the Jim Carrey hit *Liar, Liar* (1997). For those not able to attend in person, the Zicrees offers audio and video versions, as well as one-on-one phone coaching sessions. At regular weekly get-togethers for graduates, pros, and friends, they network to pursue a goal of creating "an oasis for professionals and hopefuls longing to live in the Hollywood that *ought* to be . . . a Hollywood where everyone's dreams are treated with respect." For more information, surf www.zicree.com.

Finding Friends in Tinseltown

After the year 2000, I quit counting all the online groups, pitch events, and various hope-to-be screenwriter possibilities around the world. There were just too many to investigate and still make a living. Instead, I listened to my readers and researched on my own when I had the chance.

It's different if I only want to keep up with Los Angeles. I know this town pretty well, and the screenwriter support groups that have lasted over the years are the ones I know will continue to be helpful associations. As of this writing, there are three that I feel I can fully recommend.

If my films make one more person miserable, I'll feel I have done my job.

—Woody Allen

Hampton's Round Table—In 1999, the aforementioned Zicrees founded a group "to coach writers, actors, directors, and others in the Industry and aid them in accomplishing their creative and career goals." When the group grew to more than three hundred members, they called for a moratorium on new members. Meeting in Burbank every Thursday night, they've accomplished quite a lot through networking, so if you can get invited you'll be in good company among a number of working professionals.

Scriptwriters Network—Meeting at venues such as Universal Studios on a monthly basis, this group has proven to be the most professional and reliable of all for up-and-coming writers. Their Producers Outreach Program can get your script read by any of more than one hundred producers, and the producer who reads it will be someone who likes the type of material *you* write. Each script submitted must get a "Recommend" by two group members, plus a third "Recommend" by a committee reader before notification is sent to the appropriate producer. See www.scriptwritersnetwork.com to get an idea why Oscar-winner Marc Norman said, "I found the Scriptwriters Network to be the best group I ever spoke to, as far as the intelligence and energy of the people who came. I was very impressed with the organization."

StoryBoard Development Group—One of the best things about this more intimate group of writers is their monthly guest moderator, which is always someone with great knowledge of the industry and perhaps even some influence (I've spoken there more than once, but maybe they couldn't find anyone else). There may be several dozen participants, and each discussion revolves around a currently playing or about-to-be-released feature film. I've known writers who drove hours to reach a meeting, which usually takes place at a movie studio on the West side of L.A. such as Sony. Sound interesting? You can contact StoryBoard Chairman Scott Burnell at (323) 936-0672 or email sburnell@earthlink.net.

Meeting Other Masterminds

Whatever route you take to your Hollywood education, travel with patience. While it's easy to get excited after reading about an "overnight success" who sold a script for a million dollars, much more often such an "overnight" can take a decade or longer. You'll need talent to make it in Hollywood, then knowledge to shape that talent. After you learn how to write a good, commercial screenplay, you'll probably put as much work into selling your script as you did in writing it. And you'll probably sell it only when you find someone who shares your vision and does whatever it takes to help you bring that vision to the screen.

CHAPTER

5

Just the FAQS, Ma'am

Just the facts, ma'am.

**—Attributed to "Sergeant Joe Friday"
in the 1950s TV series Dragnet**

Many people who have seen the original *Dragnet* TV series from the 1950s believe that writer/producer/director Jack Webb, in the lead role of Sergeant Joe Friday, often said: "Just the facts, ma'am." In reality, throughout the 275 episodes of the show's eight-year run (1951–1959), Webb would either say "All we want are the facts, ma'am" or "All we know are the facts, ma'am." But that's how people often are; they want something simple, and that's what the show delivered. The story structure of *Dragnet* was as steady as the deadpan dialogue of Joe Friday, and the show became a Hollywood franchise. Even

Conditions in
the [movie]
industry
somehow
propose the
paradox:
"We brought
you here for
your individuality
but while you're
here we insist
that you do
everything to
conceal it."

—F. Scott Fitzgerald

the episode titles were predictable. Except for the inaugural "The Human Bomb," every show was titled "The Big" something or other: "The Big Actor," "The Big Death," "The Big Mother," or "The Big Counterfeit" (the last episode of the original show).

Hollywood buyers don't like to have to invent a classification for a new project. They prefer easily labeled projects like *Dragnet,* and at any given time in Tinseltown, some genre is hot. You know a genre is cooling when spoofs appear, but I advise writers to not try to predict trends. Instead, I tell them they'd better know where their property fits in, genre-wise. In a decade of giving advice to writers I've repeatedly had to tell them to put their work in a category if they want a quicker sale.

To illustrate, let's look at the history of *Dragnet.* Derived from the 1949 radio series created by and starring Jack Webb, *Dragnet* has had many incarnations. It reappeared as a TV series in 1969, again starring Webb and Harry Morgan (who later starred in *M.A.S.H.* on TV) as Joe Friday's partner "Officer Frank Smith." The show resurfaced once more in 1989, this time as a comedy/drama called *The New Dragnet.* Its most recent television appearance was in 2003 as a serious drama starring Ed O'Neill of *Married . . . with Children* sitcom fame.

Popular from the beginning, this crime show was a groundbreaker. At the beginning of its run on television, *Dragnet* ran concurrently as both a TV series and radio program. It was the first American TV show to give birth to a feature film—called *Dragnet,* naturally—in 1954. A 1953 episode called "The Big Little Jesus" was network TV's first half-hour color program (and the only color show of the original series). The second *Dragnet* feature film, a 1987 comic spoof starring Dan Aykroyd and Tom Hanks, inspired the 1989 comedy-drama series.

And now we get to some information that can help you sell your own projects. The way the 1987 movie was sold reveals how the right idea, properly presented, can be used to secure a greenlight deal with amazing speed.

I first met producer David Permut when he was producing the 1987 *Dragnet* movie. Ten years later, while writing the first edition of

The Writer's Guide to Hollywood, I learned how he sold it. His story brought home to me the importance of writing and selling projects that are not only exciting but also easily remembered. Why easily remembered? Because any idea that generates great word of mouth around a production office or studio will usually do the same with the public.

Here's what Permut did to sell his *Dragnet:*

The 1987 comedy was made at Universal Studios, where Permut knew top executives. While "channel surfing" one night, he saw a rerun of an episode of the 1950s show. Click, next channel. The man on the screen was Dan Aykroyd in a rerun of *Saturday Night Live.* Click, back to *Dragnet.* Jack Webb: "All we know are the facts, ma'am." Click, Dan Aykroyd: "Jane, you ignorant slut." Permut sat up in his chair, his mind buzzing.

The next morning, Permut called Bernie Brillstein, who was Dan Aykroyd's manager. He explained his concept: he wanted Aykroyd to star in a feature film spoof of the old TV show. "Dan's in!" Brillstein declared. Permut immediately called Frank Price, who was running Universal Studios, and set up a meeting.

Permut didn't prepare a treatment or write anything at all. He simply walked in and sang "Dum, da, dum, dum!" He knew that anyone who knew the 1950s show knew the opening notes of the theme music by heart.

"Dragnet!?" Price said incredulously.

Permut explained that Dan Aykroyd wanted to do it.

"You got a deal," Price said.

It was perhaps the quickest sale ever made from the pitch of a "high concept" (an A-list movie star in a spoof of a well-known TV show). *Dragnet* was one of the first popular TV shows to be adapted for the big screen. But Permut had a problem. He'd sold the project before having a writer. Since he had a deal, though, writers were easy to find, and he ended up with three very good ones: former *Saturday Night Live* writer Alan Zweibel, Dan Aykroyd, and Tom Mankiewicz (who also directed).

That's how a deal can work when the right elements are in place, and it was important to the project's success that David Permut was a Hollywood insider. If you're not a Hollywood insider, you'll have to find one to fall in love with your project, but guess what? The insiders are constantly searching for instant bonanzas like David Permut found with *Dragnet.* When he first told me how the *Dragnet* deal went down, he explained his philosophy: "I'm always looking for good stories, an idea, an original idea I'll have once in awhile, a newspaper article, a true story where we have to track down the rights. It all starts there. The basis of any movie is a good story. If you start off with a story that isn't good or really doesn't have any merit theatrically, or a script that doesn't have any merit theatrically, it's hard to build a house without the foundation. The script is the blueprint and the foundation of any movie, and you see what happens."

Note the word *blueprint.* By clicking between TV channels one night, a producer came up with the basis for a hit movie and the right person to star in it. Once an architect draws up a blueprint, what's next? Someone to build the project, right? In David Permut's case, that "builder" was Dan Aykroyd. Since Permut had many Hollywood connections and a track record of making movies, Aykroyd's manager took his phone call, easily visualized the "blueprint" in his own mind, and agreed that his client would build it. Then came the financing, which Permut arranged the next morning.

I've seen far too many people approach Hollywood with blueprints (usually scripts) that say, in essence, "this house is built on sand" or something much less substantial to a producer in the know. I make that comparison because their project is not easily classifiable or castable with major movie stars. These writers don't comprehend the geography of the industry and don't realize that when people are shopping they like simple and easy directions.

Here's what I mean. Think of a large shopping mall that features, at entrances and other places, large directories that reveal the layout of the facility. The various merchants are grouped by category. If you want women's shoes, you can quickly find a shop that sells them.

The businesses in the mall might change, as things go in and out of fashion, but when a business departs, the people running the mall must find a new one to replace it. And that business needs an attractive sign and the right advertising to attract customers. If it sells a quality product, it will get more customers by word of mouth, with a "buzz" much like the one David Permut created with "Dum, da, dum, dum!"

That's how Hollywood works. Now let's focus in on one of the merchants. Let's say it's a bookstore. When you walk in, you'll find signs above the book aisles that tell you the categories of the books. If you have a question, someone will direct you to the right book or even look it up in an electronic database. When you're satisfied with what you find, you'll probably make a purchase. (Buying this book, I hope!)

That is, again, how Hollywood also works.

Let me break it down further:

a. Think of the mall as Hollywood, except instead of buying you're selling, and you need to find the right buyer in the vast "mall." So you need to study the layout (who's who in Hollywood).

b. The various stores represent people with specialties, like most producers, although there are some "department stores" (large production companies) that do many different types of projects. Those "merchants" buy in quantity and usually from established firms (known writers). So you might need an agent to sell to them, whereas a smaller "merchant" will deal with you personally.

c. Within a major "store" in the Hollywood mall, you'll find different categories, as in the bookstore. If a large production company had defining signs like a bookstore, they might read "Development," "Finance," and "Production." (You won't see signs like that in a production company, but we're working with metaphors here.)

It's really about that simple. Hollywood buys a lot of stuff, so you need to be able to quickly state what it is you're selling. You need to have something they want and also know how to tell them about it in an appealing way.

Dragnet has always been easily understood. The original radio show, and the TV show that followed, were crime dramas about detectives solving crimes in greater Los Angeles. After exposure to one episode, people knew what they were getting, and they either liked it or not. No one involved with *Dragnet* was trying to change society or fight censorship. Jack Webb and his friends were simply presenting a dramatized look at crime from the point of view of the police.

If you walked into our metaphorical mall above and looked under "crime drama," you might find *Dragnet*.

If you wrote a crime drama and walked into a mall named Hollywood Buyers, where would you look on the directory to find someone to purchase your property?

Romantic comedy? Family comedy? Animated feature? Thriller? Horror? Reality series?

Where would you find your own project(s)?

If you can't find a name on the Hollywood Mall Directory that fits your project, your only hope is to go to the Office of the Mall and get a permit to set up a booth or kiosk in the walkways between stores. I'm sure you've seen those, particularly during the holiday season. If you have something that doesn't quite fit within the established "stores," you'll need to build up visibility and work a little harder to convince people that what you are selling has merit.

And the most likely label of a hard-to-classify project would be "independent," which usually means it was shot on a very low budget, but studio standards.

Here's a personal example that happened to me while I was writing this book. I emailed a producer I've done business with about a low-budget digital comedy that I wanted to direct.

"Not what I expected," he replied. "Was hoping for a genre pic . . . but if you show me how you can make it for $50K, I will help you all I can."

Give the people what they want is my philosophy. (As long as it's something I want to deliver, that is.) I emailed my friend back immediately.

"Hey, I got genre," I said. "A *Scream*-like one with a killer title that no one's used." I told him my idea.

"Sounds great!" came the reply. "Really like it, can be funny, too! Can we talk more when I get back from Mexico?"

I'd known this producer for years, and he'd optioned a screenplay of mine the year before. This response was the most enthusiastic I'd ever gotten from him. What had I done right? I'd found the right place to sell that idea because:

- This producer traditionally loves murder mysteries and thrillers.
- He's made a great number of movies for a certain price, usually in the two- to three-million range.
- Because of the nature of my story, he knew it could indeed be made cheaply.
- He loved the title and how the story proceeded naturally and easily from the basic concept.
- Like *Dragnet,* my project fit easily into a genre classification, making it easy to market and much easier to get financed. No one would have to think too hard, from studio marketing to the movie audience, to realize what the movie is about.

So now let's take a look at how you can navigate the vastness of the "Hollywood mall" to find the right place for your property. I can only assume that you will have problems similar to the tens of thousands of others who have contacted me over the years.

See if your situation is in the Frequently Asked Questions (FAQs) below. If you have a different question, send me a brief email. Just the FAQs, ma'am.

Every great film should seem new every time you see it.

—Roger Ebert

Skip's FAQs

I went through almost a thousand computer files to figure out what questions I had been repeatedly asked over the years, both from book readers and students. I consider these people more important than someone who just emails me from out of the blue because I know that with my readers and students I've conveyed at least part of what I know about writing and selling screenplays and other works.

I've arranged the questions and answers in the manner I recalled them most frequently being asked.

Will they steal my idea?

Not unless your work is commercial and you have submitted it to unscrupulous people. Hopefully, what you read in this book will help you avoid such types. You must realize, however, that millions of ideas have circulated through Hollywood, and your idea may not be as unique as you think. A 2003 article in *Variety* revealed that one Hollywood warehouse contained more than a quarter-million unpurchased scripts. Registrations with the Writers Guild of America, west (WGAw) average around fifty thousand per year, and the number keeps increasing because of the online registration option offered by both the WGA, west and East (WGAE registers around 15,000 scripts annually).

How can I protect myself?

Although you'll find some misinformed people who will insist that you must have your work registered with the Writers Guild of America, the facts are as follows:

a. should you ever need to prove registration with the WGA in a legal setting, once you pull the proof from their archives, your protection evaporates;

b. The WGA registration only lasts five years.

Do some reading at www.loc.gov/copyright under the Frequently Asked Questions. A copyright can last a lifetime and is the proof of ownership that a lawyer wants when establishing a "chain of title" when someone buys your property.

Any time you submit a work for consideration, keep a paper trail, meaning a copy of a query or transmittal letter or fax. If you send your work via the U.S. Post Office Priority Mail or Media Mail, you can pay an additional minimal fee for proof of delivery that can be tracked on the Internet. If you submit via email, keep copies of all email with full "headers" (the electronic paths of the messages) and print them out as well as save them electronically. The necessity of maintaining "proof of access" is important and is why it is legally smart to have an agent, manager, or lawyer submit your work for you.

A production company wants to read my script. I don't have an agent or manager or lawyer, but they will read it if I sign a release form. Should I sign? One clause makes me swear I own my own script. Another clause would make me pay all court costs if I sue them and lose!

When a company buys a property or even options it, the first thing their lawyer (or "business affairs" if it's a large company) does is chase down the chain of title. The same thing happens when people buy a house. Companies have to make sure that what they're buying can legally be sold by the person selling it. What if they spend $100 million to get a movie into production, and suddenly someone's lodged a claim for breach of copyright? The legal cost clause is to ensure no one files a frivolous claim. There are always people looking for easy money, and all the sharks aren't located in Hollywood. Bottom line: If a release form doesn't make sense to you and you can't afford an attorney to look it over, ask the company to amend it. If they won't, find another company.

Which is better: an agent, manager, or lawyer?

Most independent producers, those who do not have an exclusive deal with a studio or network, are easily accessible to all writers. If you can't find a producer who will read your work via direct submission, you may not be trying hard enough. That said, managers are generally more accessible; they are not regulated by California law like agents, and they can also produce movies (which agents cannot). A manager usually charges 15 percent, however. Agents can only legally charge 10 percent, but they can also make a 10 percent "packaging" fee by putting together various clients (star, producer, director, and writer) in a package to help get the project financed. There are also a number of agents who will read new writers. Some are listed in this book, and the WGA maintains an agent's list that can be accessed via www.wga.org and www.wgae.org.

Should I pay an agent a reading fee? How about mailing fees and other incidentals?

Never pay an agent a reading fee. While some agents starting out might reasonably request reimbursement for office expenses, how good is an agent if he or she can't make enough money to pay the costs of doing business?

How much money can I expect to make for my script?

You can find prices for scripts under the Schedule of Minimums at the Writers Guild sites. Unfortunately, those prices reflect what Writers Guild of America members must be paid by producers who have agreed to abide by WGA rules. A great number of companies that do projects like straight-to-DVD movies hire writers who are not yet members of the WGA. A non-Guild writer could be looking at as little at $5,000 for a script, with no money on the "back end" (no "profit participation" in Hollywood terms). If someone wants to buy your project, get a lawyer or agent to negotiate (by law a manager cannot negotiate). Try to find out what the overall budget for the movie is, and ask for two percent to five percent of the budget. For example, if the film is made under the Screen Actors Guild Limited Low Budget Agreement, which you can find at www.sag.org, five percent of the $250,000 budget would be $12,500. If non-SAG actors are used, the budget might be so low that producers would want to "defer" the writer's salary and pay for the script only if the film makes a profit. In that case, you'll have to determine if a completed film would help your career, because you might never get paid. At the top end, if you write a script that is made at a studio, you might make six figures or over a million dollars.

Can I sell an idea / pitch / synopsis / treatment?

Forget the short cuts. Forget the "wow" deals you read about. I know a fellow who got a $350,000 advance on a book from a synopsis, but he'd published about seventy-five books before that. Joe Ezsterhas got $4.5 million for a movie synopsis, but before that he'd written *Basic Instinct* (1992) and other films. The buyers thought they could rely on Ezsterhas to write a great screenplay from his idea, just as the publishers knew they'd get a completed book from the author I knew. To shoot a film, someone has to write a screenplay. No matter what producers buy, someone has to write the movie. If you think your idea is that good, write the script. Even if you don't sell it, you'll have a great "calling card" that could get you hired to write or rewrite other screenplays.

I found a great book that would make a wonderful movie. Can I write the screenplay and sell it?

Too many beginning screenwriters don't know that they should never adapt anyone's work without dealing with the author first. You can probably track down an author via:

The Authors Guild
31 E. 28th St, 10th Floor
New York, NY 10016-7923
Phone: (212) 563-5904
Fax: (212) 564-5363
Email: staff@authorsguild.org

I generally advise contacting the author instead of the publisher, because writers understand each other. You might also read "Tutorial: How Writers Can Option Published Material" by Lenore Wright, at www.breakingin.net.

Do you have to be under thirty to make it in Hollywood?
You will find little ageism in the feature film side of the business.

I've had numerous development people tell me they didn't care how old a writer was if he or she came up with a *great* screenplay. I've known of people in their seventies who are writing and selling scripts. In case you haven't noticed, most of the folks who win Oscars for screenwriting have at least a "touch of gray." If it's a project geared to a teenage or college-age audience, however, a producer might want someone young to write it. Television generally has younger writing staffs, which is one reason there was an "older writers" lawsuit filed in recent years (see www.writerscase.com for details). With the American and European moviegoing demographics skewing older, though, experienced writers might become a plus factor.

I'm only a teenager, but I write screenplays that people really like. Will Hollywood take me seriously?

There is no minimum age requirement for selling screenplays. In some instances, your youth could be very helpful, particularly when publicizing the project. Some middle schoolers once sold a script to the "Tiny Toon Adventures" animated series, and actress Nikki Reed was a teenager when she cowrote (in only six days) and starred in *Thirteen* (2003), loosely based on her own life. If your work is of sufficient quality, you can probably find someone to take it seriously, no matter what your age.

Have you ever heard of [fill in producer name here]?

When I first started trying to sell to Hollywood, one publication listing independent producer information had around two thousand entries. Multiply that by five in Hollywood today, and add vast numbers of digital filmmakers around the world. How many producers can you name? Do you know who produced the last movie you saw? When people email me about this person or that, I wonder if they're lazy. You can look up companies and people for free at www.imdb.com. By searching www.hollywoodreporter.com and www.variety.com you can see if they've been mentioned in "the trades." Can't afford to pay for the trades? You might be surprised. I used six thousand unused frequent flyer miles to subscribe to *Daily Variety* (250 issues) via www.milepoint.com. You can find contact information at http://inhollywood.com, www.showbizdata.com and www.hcdonline.com (each of these has free or inexpensive trial deals). Good writers do good research. If you can't find out anything about a producer or director, they probably are not worth dealing with. But then, you could always *ask* them for information. I've found that all too many people are reluctant to do so, but it has *never* caused me a problem.

Does it help to have [fill in actor name here] attached to my project?

That depends on the actor. My normal advice is to not try to get an actor involved in a project unless that actor has an *active* production company of his or her own. In that case, the actor often produces projects whether he or she stars in them or not. Examples of this are Tom Hanks' Playtone, Drew Barrymore's Flower Films, and Kelsey Grammer's Grammnet. If you call an actor's agent, they generally don't care about your project unless you can put up the 10 percent "pay or play" money top actors receive. That means this—if they like your project, they will block off some time on their schedule. If you do not come up with the money for the production, they keep the money, you lose the bet. Some A-list actors require larger amounts of money placed in an escrow account before they will even read a script. On the flip side, movie distributors prefer to have some kind of name to publicize sales, so if you can get a suitable actor committed to your project, it can help. What is "suitable"? That depends on your budget, where the project will be sold, and many other things. Which is why you should try to get your project to a producer first.

How do I know who's hot in Hollywood? For example, I wrote a script that I want to be a TV movie and was told I need an actor with a high enough "Q." What does that mean?

The first time I ever pitched a TV movie someone told me about the "Q" list. I was flummoxed, as I'd never heard of it. "Oh, they use the list but they aren't supposed to," said the producer. "They" being the

> *Cinema is the most beautiful fraud in the world.*
>
> **—Jean-Luc Godard**

American TV networks. If you look at the trade sites, you know that *The Hollywood Reporter* and *Variety* put out various "Who's Hot" lists (it costs you money to get them). But the place they all go to for demographic data and audience preferences is www.qscores.com/performer.asp. Performer Q measures the familiarity and appeal of personalities in a variety of categories to determine targeted audience attraction. This information is expensive, which is why only studios and big companies can afford it. I believe (don't quote me on this) the term originates with the idea of who will "queue up" to see someone (stand in line to see them).

How do I find a director for my movie?

It is usually left to the producer to hire the director for a film. Directors are important; the overall vision of the movie depends on them, and actors will often sign onto a project because they want to work with a certain director. Many directors also produce and thus have their own production company, while some simply go from one job to the next. I've advised people for a long time to spend $25 for a thick book listing all the members of the Directors Guild of America. See www.dga.org for information about it. If you're looking for a specific director, you can also search the member directory on the site.

How long should I wait to hear back from someone?

Which mail do you deal with first, checks made out to you, or bills with your name on them? Since we both know the answer to that question, we should know that Hollywood people are no different. They're busy with things that mean money in the bank before they deal with things that *might* mean money. Nevertheless, if a person can't get back to people in a timely manner—meaning six weeks or less after receiving a property they asked to see—that can be bad business. Sherry Lansing, the head of Paramount Studios, built her reputation partly on attempting to return every call the same day it was received. Unfortunately, not enough people in Hollywood are like that. On a personal note, I have never made a deal with any producer who took a long time to get back to me. If I submit a project to someone and haven't heard from him or her in a month to six weeks, I'll make a phone call. If the person is still interested, that call could put my project on top of the reading list. If they still don't get back to me, unless there are extenuating circumstances that explain their delay, I don't submit to them again.

Which screenwriting software do you use?

The box of ScriptThing screenplay formatting software once featured a glowing quote from me taken from a review I did of the product. ScriptThing is now known as Movie Magic Screenwriter and can be found at www.write-bros.com. (The simpler Hollywood Screenwriter is also good.) I also use Final Draft (once the industry leader), when someone I'm working with uses that software. If people cannot afford such software even with a student discount, I refer them to Online Communicator, where they can find Word and other software add-ons (see www.online-communicator.com/swsoftin.html). Every PC user that I know who has tried the very reasonably priced SceneWriter (see www.virtualamnesia.com) has been very happy with it, too. What mainly matters is that your script looks how it is expected to look on the page, so it doesn't matter what you use as long as the page looks right.

You're only as good as your last picture.

—Marie Dressler

Does it help if you win a contest?

In recent years, screenplay contests have proliferated like mushrooms in damp weather. Even if there is a substantial prize for winning, your first-place certificate won't matter to most Hollywood buyers unless it's a competition with which they are familiar, such as the annual Nicholl contest run by the Academy of Motion Picture Arts and Sciences. (See Chapter 8 for a thorough discussion of contests, fellowships, and other possibilities.)

Do you have to live in Los Angeles to break in?

No, you don't, but you should definitely spend some time in southern California. Movies are being made everywhere these days. I spoke at a conference in Virginia and was amazed to learn there were enough production personnel to make two feature films a year in Richmond. (The 2004 TV movie *Iron Jawed Angels* was filmed in Richmond and other Virginia locations.) What you can gain by living in Los Angeles for even six months is a certainty about the people and activities in the heart of the film business.

How easy is it to get a job in Los Angeles, particularly in entertainment?

Take a look at the job boards at www.showbizdata.com, www.entertainmentcareers.net, and www.hcdonline.com to get an idea of industry-specific jobs. More generic jobs can be found at newspaper sites such as www.latimes.com, www.dailynews.com, and www.laweekly.com. One large agency in town is famous for a job list that appears sporadically. It was put together to help up-and-coming agents build their sales. Most of the lists reveal something telling, however. Many unpaid intern positions are available, but most of them are filled by people who can afford to work for free for a while. People trying to break into Hollywood by getting a job at a production company or studio often don't realize that their competition will include many "trust fund babies" who are in no rush to make a project into a viable product because they keep getting checks anyway. This is one reason why people can expect to make at least 10 percent less working in "the business" because of the "privilege" of doing so. It basically comes down to "How bad do you want this?"

Would it help me to pay for a "coverage service" so that my work would be recommended on a "tracking board" or to a producer or production company? How about a service that gets my logline to thousands of people?

One reader wrote, "Are paid services such as Scriptshark.com worth it? If so, do you recommend any?" Another reader remarked, "The tracking boards seem like some guarded taboo, so I appreciate any help you can offer in taking the mystery out of it."

I told the first reader that I generally find it questionable when people purport to sell access. They remind me of ticket-scalpers; they might be able to "sell you a ticket," but there are more legitimate ways to gain entry. One company, Storybay.com, actively courted producers to refer unsolicited queries to them, then offered to read and comment if the screenwriters paid a fee. Although they might provide a worthwhile service (since newbie screenwriters often write poorly and make lots of mistakes), I have never heard from a hopeful screenwriter who was happy with StoryBay. I came close to a movie deal with Ryan Williams, the head of Script-Shark, so I trust his taste. Nevertheless, the number of successes reported on ScriptShark seem relatively few compared to the number of people who have paid for the service. I caught the proprietor of another site that touts great success in more than one lie; the majority of the production companies he mentions are people I've never heard of, or people operating on very low budgets who pay very little, if anything, for screenplays.

You cannot pay to be mentioned on a tracking board, which is in essence a chat room for people working in development. If you are mentioned favorably, however, it could greatly boost your career. Thanks to the Internet, production company personnel refer writers to their comrades who are more likely to like a certain type of script. Conversely, if a writer is troublesome, annoying, or just not very good, their career can be hurt by negative comments from a "tracker."

Using a service like ScriptBlaster.com, which offers direct email access to more than one thousand film producers, agents, and managers, could help if you don't have the time to acquire the addresses and tailor emails yourself. I've always found, however, that anything that takes away your own personal touch is not as effective. (More on this in chapter 6.)

In summary, you'll probably do just as well contacting production companies on your own, and being as polite and businesslike as you can with everyone.

What does a coverage form look like?

Writers almost never get to see coverage. The only time I was ever shown any concerning my work was when a reader raved about three of my novels, which were subsequently optioned by a production company; the head of development was so astonished by her favorable comments that he offered to show me what she wrote. (A sample coverage form can be found on the next page.)

What do you think of "peer review" sites? In my discussion group, writers read each other's scripts, offer comments, and support, and generally have a good time. You'll find no annual competition and no promises, although occasionally I'll read a script if the logline sounds promising, and if warranted, I will refer the project to someone who might sell or buy it. I haven't personally participated in sites like Helium Peer Review, Project Greenlight, TriggerStreet, or Zoetrope because I wasn't eligible as a professional with sold credits. Nevertheless, I think they have value. One of my group members summed it up this way:

a. Sometimes you can learn something new.
b. You can gauge your own writing ability by reviewing others' writing.

With Project Greenlight, you might get to make a movie, and I've liked the winners so far. I've been on panels with Pete Jones, the first contest winner, whose movie I loved. Francis Ford Coppola purchased a couple of screenplays from Zoetrope members, including one of my readers.

With any peer review site, the question you should ask is "What could I get out of this?" If you'd be happy with the answer "A few more friends I could learn from," you'll probably do well both on the site and in Hollywood.

Where can I find a sample screenplay contract?
I've long recommended attorney Harris Tulchin's Web site because of the free entertainment business contracts he features. Any writer who has been offered a contract and needs something to compare it against, but isn't ready to pay a lawyer should look at www.medialawyer.com/contract.htm.

PRODUCTION COMPANY NAME

Title: _____   Genre:

Author: _____   Circa:

Analyst: _____   Location:

Date: _____

Submitted By: _____

Submitted To: _____

Type of Material/Pages: _____

Publisher/Date: _____

	EXCELLENT	GOOD	FAIR	POOR
Premise:				
Storyline:				
Structure:				
Characterization:				
Dialogue:				

LOGLINE:

COMMENTS SUMMARY:

RECOMMENDATION: Recommend   /   Consider   /   Pass

SYNOPSIS: (usually 1–3 pages)

COMMENTS: (usually 1 page)

How can I keep track of what kind of projects are bought?

While sites that report on screenplay sales come and go, the most reliable is www.hollywoodlitsales.com, maintained by Howard Meibach, author of the *Spec Script Sales Directory*. The database, which is a veritable travelogue of spec script deals of every genre, is totally free. Once you register, you can search the current database, or search the archive of spec sales from 1997. If you only want a daily list of spec sales, you do not need to register. You can see who bought what, for how much, and who was involved in the deals (studio exec, producer, agent, writer). Want to know who to approach about your script, whether agent or producer? It's all there. You can peruse the loglines to see if your own story has already been done, and you'll even find some on-site producers looking for material.

How do I find updated information on who's who at the production companies?

As mentioned earlier, you can find contact information that is updated weekly at electronic databases like http://inhollywood.com, www.showbizdata.com, and www.hcdonline.com. The Pro version of the Internet Movie Database (www.imdb.com) is also worth a look. All of these databases have free or inexpensive trial deals. (Why do I mention it twice? Because no matter how many times I say it, people keep asking!)

If I write screenplays I'm a screenwriter, right?

Not in my book you're not. I tell people not to call themselves a writer unless they've been paid for it. I have that attitude because I've seen too many people use a New Age attitudinal approach and believe that if they tell themselves something frequently enough it will come to pass. That kind of thinking never turned me into an astronaut. There was a time when I'd get very indignant when a professional writers' organization would reject me because I didn't have the credits they required. After I qualified for and joined a number of those organizations, however, I learned that often enough the main benefits of membership were perquisites like cheaper insurance. (Health benefits top the list of perks for Hollywood professional organizations.) If you find yourself at a Hollywood party sometime and tell someone you're a screenwriter, you'd better be able to back it up. If in actuality you have no credits or sales, that might backfire if you're talking to a producer looking for a pro screenwriter. If you said you were trying to become a pro, however, that producer might ask to read something you've written. Honesty has its benefits.

You may have noticed that I didn't include a question about the luck factor in my Frequently Asked Questions. That's because all I know is the facts, man. In my two decades in Hollywood I've found that people generally make their own luck. Here are a couple of examples:

A few years back, I got a package from an author in England named Patricia Finney. She sent me her popular novel *I, Jack* after reading my *Writer's Guide to Hollywood.* Patricia had written her first original screenplay and wanted advice on selling it to Hollywood. I knew a TV executive who was trying to make low-budget films, and I liked the sound of Patricia's script, so I got him to read Patricia's screenplay. He loved it, and called her at home in England to discuss it. It wasn't until she actually came over for a visit, three years later, however, that I was able to get her a Hollywood agent. (Agents like to work with people here in town who can go to meetings at the drop of a hat.)

Another fellow I know is one of the top CGI (Computer Generated Image) experts in the business, with most of his career spent working for George Lucas in northern California. He cowrote a script based on a book that has now seen five printings. I gave him and his cowriter some advice, and they did a rewrite, but when they contacted a producer listed in my *Writer's Guide* who had done three projects based on books for Turner Network Television, they couldn't get an audience. When my friend came to southern California to work on a high-level studio project, we discussed the project on the phone and he explained what had happened. I called my producer friend and told him

Filmmaking is a chance to live many lifetimes.

—Robert Altman

he should read the script, and he told me to have my CGI friend call him at home to discuss it.

That's generally how it goes in Tinseltown. Even if you know all the protocols, you usually get a much different reception when people know you are "in town" and working at success as hard as they are.

A blurb on my *Writer's Guides* declared I was "Your Friend in Hollywood." That got me in a lot of trouble, but I can't say I minded all that much. People were kind to me when I started out, so I've always tried to return the favor. But then, I know what goes on behind the scenes in Hollywood, and you only learn that by being here. Nevertheless, I'll try to clue you in on Hollywood's inner workings, if you'll be so kind as to read the next chapter. Let's have a look at what goes on in the buying and developing of any given project.

CHAPTER

6

Inside
the Gates

What we want is a story that starts with an earthquake and builds to a climax.

—Samuel Goldwyn to Billy Wilder and I.A.L. Diamond

So you've done your homework. You've taken the classes, read the books, written and rewritten your script, and learned how to approach Hollywood. Maybe you've hired a consultant, maybe not. Now you're sure that you're ready.

Hold on a second.

Are you protected? Do you know how to protect yourself?

Just as there are tried and true ways of finding buyers, there are reliable and not so reliable ways of protecting your work. Let's start with the difference between Writers Guild registration and online registration with other services. And let's get one thing cleared up immediately: The best way to protect yourself is with a copyright, period.

Copyright First

Forget any so-called advice like mailing a copy of something to yourself. Did someone tell you that this form of "protection" would stand up in court because of the date stamp from the post office? What if the dated stamp or mailing label falls off? How could you prove you didn't steam open the envelope and put in something else? If you use iffy methods, a million ifs arise. Here's what works.

Under the 1998 Copyright Term Extension Act (CTEA) sponsored by Congressman Sonny Bono, the term for copyrighted material was increased from seventy-five years to ninety-five years. The specific advice from the U.S. government's copyright site (www.copyright.gov) reads as follows:

> The term of copyright for a particular work depends on several factors, including whether it has been published, and, if so, the date of first publication. As a general rule, for works created after Jan. 1, 1978, copyright protection lasts for the life of the author plus an additional 70 years. For an anonymous work, a pseudonymous work, or a work made for hire, the copyright endures for a term of 95 years from the year of its first publication or a term of 120 years from the year of its creation, whichever expires first. For works first published prior to 1978, the term will vary depending on several factors. To determine the length of copyright protection for a particular work, consult chapter 3 of the Copyright Act (title 17 of the *United States Code*).

Let's contrast that protection to what you get if you register a work with the Writers Guild of America, west (WGAw). The following comes from their site at www.wga.org:

> The registration fee provides five years of legal evidence for your material. It also helps maintain the overhead for the department, including the maintenance of the confidential facility where the material is stored for its five-year term.

What about the Writers Guild of America East (WGAE)? (The dividing line is the Mississippi River.) From their site at www.wgaeast.org:

> The Guild East Script Registration Service protects members and non-members of the Guild by establishing the completion date and the identity of their literary property. For as little as $10, the Guild East registration service will protect your script, your screenplay, or simply a great idea, for 10 years. That's twice the protection of any other script registration service.

Any other script registration service except the U.S. government, that is. I'm sure you see the difference. A U.S. Copyright on material you create protects you for your lifetime plus an additional seventy years. Depending on circumstances, the work may be protected for up to 120 years from the year of its creation.

Before the devastating events in New York City on September 11, 2001, plans were in the works to allow the online registration of creative works with the Copyright Office. Unfortunately, that got put on hold. You can, however, register works online with either Writers Guild of America office. First, you need to know which form to use in registering a screenplay for copyright.

If you're an author or journalist you might assume that you would use Form TX for a screenplay because you've used it with manuscripts (it covers literary works and computer programs). Instead, you need Form PA, which covers works in the performing arts. You can download both the long and short versions of either form at www.copyright.gov. On Short Form PA you'll find a box under "Type of Authorship" entitled "Other text (includes dramas, screenplays, etc.)." I haven't tried sending in a screenplay using Form TX to see if it gets rejected, but I know other writers who have used that form to register a screenplay with no problem. I try to find out and follow the rules, however, so I use Form PA. I have registered double-spaced treatments using Form TX, because treatments are laid out like manuscripts. I only had one treatment rejected, and that was because I included a photocopy of an old English painting. Lesson learned: *If you don't own the copyright on everything within a work, the work will be shipped back to you.*

Any copyright questions you may have are easily answered on the site.

If you don't have Internet access (even through a public library), you can get forms from the Copyright Office in person, by mailing in a request, or by calling the twenty-four-hour forms hotline at (202) 707-9100.

If you need to speak to an "information specialist" about something else, call (800) 688-9889 (Federal Citizen Information Center) or (202) 707-3000 [TTY: (202) 707-6737], Monday through Friday, 8:30 a.m. to 5:00 p.m. EST except federal holidays. Recorded information is available twenty-four hours a day. You can order forms and other publications from:

Library of Congress
Copyright Office
Publications Section, LM-455
101 Independence Avenue, S.E.
Washington, D.C. 20559-6000

Completed forms are mailed, along with the appropriate fee, to:

Register of Copyrights
Library of Congress
Copyright Office
101 Independence Avenue, S.E.
Washington, D.C. 20559-6000

The only problem with copyright is proving when you registered it. According to the WGA: "Registration provides a dated record of the writer's claim to authorship of a particular literary material." So does copyright, but the Copyright Office does not provide a quick confirmation of receipt. The site states: "If your submission is in order, you may generally expect to receive a certificate of registration within approximately four to five months of submission." Who wants to wait that long to be protected!? So when applying for copyright, use a carrier like Federal Express, or even the inexpensive mail delivery confirmation offered by the U.S. Post Office, which allows you to track progress of shipment and delivery via the Internet.

Registration Facts and Fallacies

I've had more than one writer tell me that a producer insisted that a script be "Registered WGAw" with the registration number or the producer wouldn't read it. No doubt that's because the producer thought that Writers Guild of America registration offers some type of protection to the producer. If a producer tells you that, and you want to do business with that producer, you can try to educate him or her on the truth, or you can just register with the WGA as well as with the Copyright Office. A sale is more important than quibbling.

I've also heard from people who feel that writing the copyright symbol © on a screenplay gets you labeled as an amateur in the eyes of readers. Well, who cares? Legal protection matters more. Here's what I read about that on the WGA Web site in late 2003 (which I use herein under the "Fair Use" doctrine):

> Initial legal control of a script rests with the copyright holder. Specifically, copyright law vests the copyright holder with exclusive ownership of five rights: 1) reproduction of copies; 2) distribution of copies; 3) performance rights; 4) public display rights; and, 5) the right to prepare derivative works. A creator owns the copyright in a work simply by virtue of having created it. A work should be published with the © copyright symbol or the word "copyright," the date, and the creator's name to preserve the copyright for the creator. Otherwise, the copyright may pass into the public domain—that is, have no copyright vested with anyone—and be freely copied.
>
> A copyright filing with the U.S. Copyright Office establishes ownership of the copyright more securely for purposes of legal enforcement. Registration of material with the Writers Guild Registration Office establishes your possession of the material on the date of registration, which may be a key fact necessary to defend against plagiarism or copyright infringement (whether or not filed with the U.S. Copyright office, see below).
>
> When you write an original script on spec, you own the copyright by virtue of having created the script. Transfer of your copyright ownership to a production company is a common element of virtually all purchase agreements. When an original story, treatment, or script is sold, the writer usually is required to transfer the copyright to the buyer.

A verbal contract isn't worth the paper it's written on.

—Samuel Goldwyn

So there is the official Writers Guild advice. Put the symbol on the page to protect yourself. You don't have to register a copyright to own a copyright because U.S. law protects you as soon it is "affixed to media," which could even mean typing it on a computer screen and storing the file. If you had to prove when you wrote it in court, though, the judge would need a little more than your sworn word.

That is where the WGA registrations come in handy, particularly over the Internet. Electronic registration is almost instantaneous, compared to downloading, filling out, and mailing a copyright form. Here's what you can register with the WGAw: books, commercials, drawings, interactive media, lyrics, novels, outlines, poems, scripts, short stories, stage plays, synopses, treatments, video cassettes/discs, written ideas (radio, television, and theatrical motion pictures). Naturally, you can't register a solid item over the Internet, so items such as cassettes would have to be mailed in or hand-registered.

Registration with the WGAw is valid for five years and may be renewed for an additional five years. If for some reason you lose your original and don't have any copies of what you registered, the WGAw will provide you with your material but guess what? That ends the registration. So if you have to pull the registration to prove something in court, too bad. If you want to register in person or via mail with the WGAw, contact:

WGAw, Intellectual Property Registry
7000 West Third Street
Los Angeles, CA 90048
(323) 782-4500

According to the WGAE: "The goal of the Guild East Script Registration Service is to protect your claim of priority of ownership. So register your material before showing it to a producer or agent; many of them won't even look at a script unless it has been registered first with the Guild." (The myth of registration "necessity" runs deep.) The WGAE "accepts for registration manuscripts as well as material which is not in full script form, i.e. synopses, outlines, ideas, treatments, scenarios." It also offers a ten-year registration period with the option of renewal. So if you live east of the Mississippi River you can save money. If you don't want to or can't register online, you can do it in person or via mail at:

> Writers Guild of America, East
> 555 West 57th Street, Suite 1230
> New York, NY 10019
> Attn: Registrations
> You can also call (212) 757-4360 for recorded instructions.

Other Registration Possibilities

Since you can register online with the WGA (East or west), and some producers ask for a WGA registration, it might not seem to make much sense to use anything else, but there are a few online options worth investigating.

At www.protectrite.com you'll get "the exact same protection as the Writer's Guild registration service for less money and longer terms." Their $18.95 fee is for a ten-year registration. This site from National Creative Registry provides a numbered electronic registration certificate that you can print out and save immediately. For more information you'll have to read the site; this is a service designed to operate electronically. WriteSafe at www.writesafe.com is similar to ProtectRite in that you can protect anything: an idea, drawing, novel, outline, poetry, script, story, or any other computer file. The site will also create a public Web page so that your Web file will be available to WriteSafe's visitors, including agents, producers, studio and network executives, and publishers. Registration is $10, with a discount price of $15 for every two pieces of material submitted. The site also has no limit on file size as long as it is "any reasonable amount." WriteSafe offers a ten-year registration.

What if you don't live in the U.S. or are doing business with countries outside of North America? Most countries respect a U.S. copyright, but if you are doing business with a producer in the United Kingdom or Europe, you might want some additional assurance. A London company, Writers Copyright Association U.K. Copyright Registration Service at www.wcauk.com, offers a simple process and various registrations: five years, ten years, fifteen years, twenty years (all in the U.K.), or a ten-year worldwide registration. Although their service is all done online, you can also contact them at:

WCAUK
T04, Eailing Film Studios
Ealing Green
Ealing, London W5 5EP
Phone: 08707 442 513

Most writers who contact me think they have a screenplay or other property that someone should spend several millions (if not tens of millions) of dollars to put on screen. So I shake my head when I hear complaints about the cost of registering material and copyrighting a property. I offer those writers this question:

If someone actually did steal your work and made a hit movie and you couldn't prove that you owned the original material, how would that $30 look to you?

Consider this also: If a studio made a movie for $100 million and the writer was paid only 1 percent of the budget for the script, the fee would be a cool million.

So now that you know many different ways of protecting yourself and some of the stakes in this business, let's take a look at *you* from the point of view of the person on the inside. Let's step inside a production company.

The Phone Is the Weapon of Choice

There's really no secret about making a cold call to a production company. If someone answers the phone they will probably only offer you two options:

a. They will look at unsolicited material;

b. They will not look at unsolicited material.

Since Hollywood is a "people town," whether or not you can get them to bend their rules (or even talk to you) depends on your people skills. It also depends on how well you've done your research and finding out whether this production company is likely to be interested in your project.

It doesn't matter what kind of project you have. A book, a novel, a comic book, a screenplay, a magazine article, or life story to which you own the film rights are all "source material" when you're selling. What matters is whether you have something this company will get excited about.

You've probably figured by now that I'm not telling you how to get an agent, or even a manager. That's because, in today's climate, you're unlikely to find a suitable representative unless someone refers you. On the other hand, many companies will talk to you without representation. So why not call the companies first? If you get an offer you can usually then get an agent, manager, or lawyer interested in representing you.

Why should you pay a representative if you've done all the writing and selling? Because that's how Hollywood works, and hopefully they will get you more money and a better deal.

Perhaps you think you can get by with sending a query letter or even an email. It could be that you can, but most of the people in town I know who do the most business spend a lot of time on the phone. If you live far from Hollywood, you can still call inexpensively via the Internet (see www.vonage.com or a similar company if you don't know about Internet-based phones).

Even if you become a successful screenwriter and are invited to explain why you should get a rewrite job, you'll still have to pitch your ideas verbally, so you'd better get used to using this approach. Pitching isn't that difficult, but too many people don't engage their brain before making contact. I once watched a person who helped write a book about pitching actually do a pitch to some executives. He failed miserably and I wondered how he could not have observed the obvious—that he hadn't interested anyone fifteen seconds in. He tried to flatter them and entertain them, and as a result didn't have time to fully explain his story. You don't have to fake enthusiasm or friendliness; this is a town full of actors so people are used to that. Being genuine and businesslike generally works.

Here's an inside fact about Hollywood that you can use to your advantage. People in this town have a dogged insistence that you spell their name correctly, so you can use that when calling. Let's say you don't know the proper spelling of someone's name or are unsure of his or her current address. You're trying to reach the director of development (the person who will listen to what you have to offer). So you call the office.

"Hi. I wanted to check the spelling of Jackie Onasty, your development exec."

"Jackie O is no longer with us."

That's if you had the right name in the first place. Let's say you didn't and you heard:

"Huh? We never had anyone by that name."

Maybe they did, maybe they didn't. The person could be new, but usually with that kind of answer it's a person who's been there awhile.

"Oh, I see. So who is your development exec now?"

"That's Walt Dizzy. Should I put you through?"

Or maybe you don't reach such a friendly receptionist and you get a challenge:

"Who is this?"

In that case, just tell them your name and that you're a writer hoping to get them interested in a project. They'll either put you through to the right person or try to make you go away.

Or maybe they won't offer to put you through, but will tell you how to spell Walt Dizzy. Any time you get a name, make sure you have the address correct. The good ones will even offer you their contact information.

"Hollywood's a place where they'll pay you a thousand dollars for a kiss and 50 cents for your soul."

—**Marilyn Monroe**

"Dizzy. Spelled like it sounds?"

"Usually." (There's one in every day.)

"And you're still at 123 Forest Lawn Drive?"

You might not have to introduce yourself when you call. Hollywood people are such sticklers for proper spellings of their names and current job titles that phone calls come in all the time from assistants making sure the information is correct before a letter or party invitation goes out.

The important thing is to get through to the person who will determine whether or not to look at your property. If you get a bad reception when you call and/or someone tells you immediately that they don't accept unsolicited material, you have a few choices:

1. That person might just be having a bad morning or bad day, so you can try a little humor. If he or she says, "We don't accept unsolicited material," you might respond: "So how could I get you to solicit me?"

2. If humor and friendliness don't work, do you really want to be doing business with them? Remember, birds of a feather flock together. People rarely hire people who don't share a similar mind-set, so if you get a jerk on the phone, he or she could be working for a jerk.

3. If the person is reasonable when you explain that you don't have an agent (we're assuming you got past the "we don't take" warning), he or she might let you sign a release or send something in via a lawyer. Some will insist on a "recognized entertainment lawyer" which basically means "is located in L.A. and regularly does business here."

4. You can just wait a while and the troublesome person might be gone from the office—if not later in the day, then later in the week, or in a few months. In this business, you must have patience.

I've even used different voices if I was convinced that I wanted to work with a certain company. I'll call up, find out who the right person is, and get the address down on paper if I don't already have it, then call back using a different voice (after waiting a while).

"Hi. Walt Dizzy, please."

"Who may I say is calling?" You'll get that or some variation.

"Skip Press."

They'll either say "Who?" (I get that a lot) or "Will he know what this is regarding?"

I could be coy and fake it, but usually I don't. I don't generally try to get around gatekeepers; I try to work with them. Why? Because they have a job, most of them want to keep it and/or make a good impression, and why should I cause trouble for them? Friendliness and honesty works. So if the person I'm trying to reach does *not* know why I'm calling, I explain, and then hope I'll get put through.

Here are a few more tips:

1. Don't call at 1:00 Pacific Standard Time, because that is when most people go to lunch (not noon).
2. I try not to call in the morning because that's when a lot of people make calls. (Of course, they're on the phone all day.)
3. Executives work late but office personnel often go home earlier. So if you call after 5:00 p.m. sometimes the executive will personally pick up the phone.
4. I try not to call anyone on his or her cell phone unless that person or an assistant gave me the number. People are fairly protective of their phone numbers in Hollywood.
5. I never call people at home unless I'm certain they will not be offended by it. If I do, I'll say something like "I hope you don't mind my calling you at home."

If you think you're not good on the phone, practice an imaginary call in the mirror, or call a friend. Or if you just can't do it, get someone to make calls for you. I know of one screenwriter who never sold a thing until his wife started posing as his manager (using her maiden name) and her skills as a salesperson. Using the phone is a Hollywood art, so you should try to master it.

What Do I Say, Skip?

When you get through to a director of development, a story editor, a creative executive, or whatever title that company uses for the person who fields incoming projects, you'd better know as much as you can about that company. One reason I've sold a lot of different things (not just scripts) is that I don't waste people's time. If they do horror movies, I don't try to sell them a romantic comedy. I try to find out something about every executive I call, or at least about the company.

When you pitch your project to an executive at a weekend pitch fest, you're only allowed five minutes to get it across. That's about all you'll get in an initial phone call, so you'd better know your logline well, and be able to answer questions about it without much hesitation.

The last script I had optioned was called *Alien Creeps*. It's a science-fiction comedy with a contemporary setting in a small American town. I knew the executive I pitched it to, and here's roughly how the conversation went.

Exec: "Hey there. How you been?"

Me: (Pleasantries exchanged.)

Exec: "So whatcha got for me?"

Me: "A script called *Alien Creeps*."

Exec: "Good title. What's it about?"

Me: "Some aliens are using humans as lab rats. If they're successful they'll use the whole planet."

Exec: "Great. Send it over."

He optioned the script, and I'd used the same pitch to get other top people to read it.

Sound too simplistic? Here's another pitch that almost got me a deal with Sean Connery's company. I happened to know the director of development, whom I hadn't seen or talked to for a year or so.

Exec: "Hey Skip, how you been?"

Me: (Pleasantries exchanged, I congratulate him on his new job.)

Exec: "So here's what we're looking for. (He explains; generally what Sean Connery is looking for is the type of movie he has always done.) If you know of anything like that, give me a call."

Me: "Matter of fact, I know of something right now."

Exec: "Oh yeah? What is it?"

Me: "It's a true story of how an MI-6 agent stopped the Russians from launching and winning World War III."

Exec: "No shit!?" (He knew me well enough to know I wouldn't make that up. As you can see, I got his attention.)

Me: (I explain the story, how I came to know the now retired agent, and briefly discuss the events.)

A week later, the retired agent and I were in the offices of Fountainbridge Films at Sony pitching the story to the development exec and Sean Connery's partner. We thought we would probably get a deal but extenuating circumstances kept that deal from happening.

Naturally, it doesn't always go that well over the phone, but in each instance I was prepared to quickly describe what I had to sell. I could have made the same pitch to someone face to face at a pitch event and explained the entire story in five minutes.

Now, are you thinking I can do this because people know my name and I know people? Even if I don't know people I'll use these methods, and then more often than not I'll get to know them—*if we click*.

It's important that you trust your instincts and notice when there's "chemistry" between you and anyone you're pitching to. In a people-centered business, resonating personalities are a large part of success.

Unfortunately, these days all too many people want to do everything via the Internet, and they can get lazy that way. I once told a client of mine via email that maybe his script would work at Icon, Mel Gibson's company. Their listing in one of my books was at Paramount. He wanted to know where they were now. He couldn't find them in an online database to which he subscribed. They're at Fox, I typed back. I sent him a copy of an article about them moving to Fox. So he searched an online database I recommend, ShowBizData.com, and found no phone number

*I made mistakes in drama.
I thought drama was when actors cried. But drama is when the audience cries.*

—Frank Capra

listed. I'd told him to call Icon, since no way in heck would they list an email address (Mel Gibson gets a few queries). Call Fox, I said.

I got another email. He tried, but "couldn't get anywhere with their phone tree." Sigh. My client was in Michigan, so I called the Fox switchboard and got Icon's number. The operator sounded a little grumpy so I played the fool. I made her laugh when I groused I wasn't having any luck with Icon's phone number because I woke up that day and saw an idiot in the mirror. She laughed and told me that no one was in the Icon office that day. She also explained that she hadn't had her morning coffee and was grouchy herself, so I wasn't an idiot.

"Big important me" who she didn't know got access by simply being friendly and honest and maybe having a little self-deprecating humor.

So I emailed the number to my client. He emailed back—was that Fox's number or Icon's number?

Idiot! Why don't you call and find out?

I didn't say that. I thought it, but I didn't even reply. And that's the kind of reaction he would've gotten from a producer's office by displaying such laziness.

Use the phone and you can get past the gatekeeper, but please use your head as well.

Can a Letter Be Better than Fax, Phone, or Email?

If you get someone on the phone and they like what they hear, they might ask to see your script or book or novel. They might also ask for a "one-sheet," a single-spaced synopsis, which you could fax, email, or mail them. That would be good enough for me. Here's how I approached one company that didn't know me from Adam.

I've long thought that my friend Sol Stein's *The Best Revenge: A Novel of Broadway* would be perfect for Michael Douglas. It's about a successful Broadway producer who wants to do his pet project that no one will finance; the guy is broke and has to turn to the son of his dead father's Mafia friend for the cash. At one point I aspired to produce the movie myself, but one day in 2003 I resolved to try to get Douglas to read it. Douglas had wanted to option something of mine fifteen years before, but the deal fell through. I had talked to Douglas on the phone, but never met him in person. I got the contact info on his company, Furthur Films, at both Universal Studios in L.A. and New York. I called the New York office first, since Michael Douglas lived there at the time, making it much more likely (I assumed) that he'd want to do something that would be filmed there. I made sure I had the right fax number, the correct spelling and title of the executive I wanted to reach, and faxed a one-page letter about the novel, describing it in probably twenty-five words, and added some rave reviews about the book that were about ten years old. In the close of the letter I said I thought Douglas would be perfect for the part, and he'd never played anything quite like it.

The next day I got a call from the executive, whom I had never met. He agreed with me that Douglas would be perfect for that kind of role, and asked if I could get the book to him. I got one to him immediately.

The executive didn't ask if I had an agent, or if my friend had one. Since it was a well-known novel, however, he knew he wouldn't take a chance of wasting time like he would with a book, novel, or screenplay from an unknown. I did my research and didn't waste anyone's time with something that wasn't his or her kind of thing.

You might be thinking that doesn't help you, if you don't have a name or something published. I disagree. I used the same approach when I started out. I would call, describe what my script was about, and they would ask to read it or not. That applied with both agents and producers (there weren't many writers' managers when I started). One producer who didn't buy a script of mine, but agreed to read it after a phone call remembered it fifteen years later. The same goes for a top agent who agreed to represent me based on a script he wanted to read after a phone call.

When I approach someone today, if for some reason I don't call and want to use email or regular post, here's what I keep in mind.

You have to get them to open a letter or an email. If my New York agent gets an email from someone he doesn't know, he wants to know who referred him or her. That person's name needs to be written on the outside of an envelope, or in the *subject line* of an email. For example: "Referred by Skip Press." Otherwise, an intern might not open the email or pass it on. In an office, query letters might even get thrown in the trash unopened. While preparing this book I was referred to an agent by his brother. A week later I emailed his brother about not hearing from the agent. The brother sent me a phone number and I called. "Oh," said the agent, "I delete all emails from people I don't know."

If someone in Hollywood wants to hear from people via email, they'll let you know. There are a number of Web sites and services that put writers in touch with producers in that manner, but unfortunately most of those producers are young and don't have any money to spend. That's why I prefer calling established people and following up with a letter or email if necessary, before I send over the project itself.

If you send in an unannounced query letter via post, it won't help you to have illustrations on the envelope or any such cuteness. They'll either open it or they won't. Some companies can get touchy and will return things unopened, even letters. Some will stop a fax from coming in if they don't know the originator. So don't get clever and send a registered letter to someone who doesn't know you. If you send an email unannounced, you'd better tell them what it's about in the subject line, such as, "Western you might like."

Of course, if you called first, you'd know how to approach all these things, wouldn't you?

Getting Inside the Reader's Head

However you manage to get your project inside a company for consideration, it's fairly certain that it will be given to a reader for coverage. We covered what that is, and what a coverage form looks like, in previous chapters.

There are two types of readers. One type is on staff in the production company. In addition to everything else they do, which might include answering phones while being known as "director of development," they could read as many as thirty scripts in a week. A reader like this might one day become a producer within that production company. Thus, if your property is "found" by them and becomes a profitable movie for the company, they help their own career while helping you. The second type of reader is someone hired by the company to read a property and provide an opinion, using the coverage form.

Producers treasure readers whose opinion they can trust. I've known of freelancers who live across the United States who get scripts via Federal Express or email and who fax the coverage back to the producer, or email the form in a Word document. This type of reader is usually paid $50 to $100 per covered script. Most of the readers like this are aspiring writers and they rarely give a "Recommend" to a project because if the sentiment isn't shared or a project gets made and fails, they could lose their job.

> *"I read part of it all the way through."*
>
> **—Samuel Goldwyn**

This brings us back inside the company and another problem that most aspiring writers don't know about. Many Hollywood companies seek free labor. Interns abound. Unlike union readers and people on staff, interns don't get benefits, or sick days, or paid vacations. The same goes for freelance readers. So how are interns a problem? Well, as I mentioned in the last chapter, a large percentage of them are trust fund babies, rich kids who grew up in show business or want to be involved, and they are supported outside the business. So they might not be in as big a hurry as a staff person to find a project they can produce, which would bring them a bonus. And they might have very different social tastes than you do.

Even so, worthwhile projects are hard to find. One fellow I know, who became a successful author and screenwriter, found only one worthwhile property while reading for a major producer over a couple of years. I think of that every time I see a rerun of "Walker, Texas Ranger," a show that producer helped produce. When the show was airing on CBS, I repeatedly watched it because it was simply the best thing I could find in its time slot on Saturday night.

You'll hear a lot of Hollywood advice about the importance of "the first ten pages" of a script (including in one of my own books). But that doesn't mean readers will stop there if they don't like your work. Generally, they will read the entire screenplay unless they are told it's okay to bail out after the first act if they find the writing lacking. Otherwise, how can they intelligently comment about structure, themes, arcs, and the beats of each act?

The secret is getting them to keep turning the pages. It is a given that you will understand good structure and proper format. What you might not know is that just as you need to qualify whom you try to sell to, a reader (staff or freelance) also tries not to waste his or her boss's time. One reader told me that she thought it was her job to "protect" her clients, that her reputation was on the line if her clients ever felt they were wasting their attention "on material not up their alley."

In years of explaining to writers what development executives want to see from people, and what they don't want to see, the basics have rarely varied.

- Writer blunders such as typos and overly lengthy screenplays are poison; ditto cliché characters.
- A staffer might read a dozen or more scripts on the weekend. After a while, they gloss over action and read dialogue to follow what's going on, so make it interesting.
- You won't have to worry so much about readers skimming if a great story compels them to turn the pages.
- Although some say there are no new stories, readers want them. (Don't we all?) They want to go somewhere new, see something unusual, via your pages.
- Stories that fit within an established genre are much easier to sell.
- If the story is predictable, you're sunk.
- International audiences are a major consideration. Hardly anyone

wants a movie that won't "travel well." Crossover from North American to European, Asian, and other markets is very important in the day of the $100 million studio feature.

- Storytelling quality and style can get a writer work, even if they don't buy that particular project.

If you move to Los Angeles and want to work in the entertainment business, be prepared to take a pay cut of at least 10 percent from a similar job in any other industry. That's what you pay for the privilege of being in show biz. It's yet another reason to have empathy for that unknown person you call about buying your property. So have patience. If you submit a property but don't hear from a company within six weeks, a short reminder phone call, email, or even postcard might not hurt. Even the least important person in an entertainment company has a lot to do.

And guess what? Those are often the people who show up to field pitches at pitch events. There's an old Hollywood saying that you see the same people on the way up as you see on the way down. You might as well treat them right.

Getting Inside the Development Process

Let's say the reader comes back with a "Consider" on your project. The director of development reads it and likes it, and gives it to her boss and he likes it. It's a small company with only three people in the office. They want to make a deal with you. If this was an independent producer, that would probably mean you'd only get a token $1 (to make it a legal contract) for an "option." For many writers starting out, any deal's better than no deal, so they take it. How can you find out if they'll offer you a paid option? Ask them if they have "discretionary funds." Companies housed at studios are usually there because they've made money for the studio or the studio has invited them there to make money for the studio, which usually means the studio will finance the development of projects. (Some companies might simply have a housekeeping deal that only pays for an assistant and an office.) So agents and managers from all over town are calling those companies, and they might not have time to talk to you. Or they might. There's no set rule about that. It's completely up to the people running the company.

Maybe you'll get lucky and end up working with a company that is attached to a studio. Even if it's only an independent production company, the development process will be about the same.

I've been through the process as a writer but never as a producer, so I talked about it with Rona Edwards and Monika Skerbelis. Together, they teach "Introduction to Feature Film Development" at UCLA Extension and are co-authors of the book *I Liked It, Didn't Love It: Understanding the Film Development Process*. Edwards, whom I met when she was a director of development, has had projects made and/or have been in development with many of the major networks and studios including a script deal at ABC, movies at CBS, ABC, NBC, Hearst Entertainment, VH1, HBO, Phoenix Television, Edward R. Pressman, Motor City Films, Warner Bros., and Wilshire Court. Skerbelis is a former Vice President of Creative and Executive Story Editor for Universal Pictures' story department. She spent ten years overseeing the story department and developing a number of screenplays including *Black Dog* (1998) starring Patrick Swayze. Prior to that, Skerbelis was Story Editor for Twentieth Century Fox.

I asked them why so few writers understand how the development process works.

Rona: That's very simple. There's never been a book written about the development process. We teach people how to take development notes or give them. It's also for people who want to be a development executive or studio executive. Or it's for an actor who has a production company.

Monika: It's important that people understand what is coverage, what is development, and who are the players involved. It used to be that studio story departments just filed coverage alphabetically by title, by numeric system. Now it's all computerized. Readers email their coverage to the studios. There are databases they use.

Rona: And don't forget the tracking boards.

Monika: The tracking boards have changed the way new scripts are sent out. Then there's also how to find new ideas.

If you've never heard of tracking, it's an analysis of the worthiness of any given project that is floating around Hollywood for purchase. Directors of development, VPs of development, creative executives, and story editors congregate online to discuss available projects and available writers.

Via email and online chats, trackers attempt to follow every property circulating at top production companies, TV networks, and studios. By cooperating among one another, trackers can often get the jump on buying a hot property. In the fall of 1997, producer Steve Stabler optioned the rights to Ben Queen's black comedy spec script *One Track Mind,* about a tracker who gets a hot script from a writer who is murdered and tries to pass it off as his own, since the writer has no friends or heirs. One problem: the trackers are onto him . . . .

The movie never got made, but it shows you the kind of aggressive attention that goes on in tracking. The practice expanded into the broad public as trackers realized that they could make money pre-screening material for producers by charging writers trying to break into Hollywood. Sadly, the only company I've ever known that has managed that with major producers is ScriptShark.com under the direction of Ryan Williams, the former director of development for Sean Connery. Another company or two has claimed great success, but I generally have never heard of the companies mentioned and never see the movies named.

Back to hands-on development. I asked Rona and Monika how they teach people to develop a project into a movie. Where does it all start?

A good film script should be able to do completely without dialogue.

—David Mamet

Monika: We have a way of finding an idea. We have our students find an article, an idea. And then we have them structure it on two pages, by title, by genre, theme, premise . . . .

Rona: Don't forget the logline.

Monika: . . . the logline, where it takes place, when it takes place. Then go into the structure, act one, act two, act three. Do a paragraph on each act. I do it today. When I'm reading the newspaper I think, "that's a great idea, I'm going to run this down." And I put that in my file. It could eventually become a story later on. It sits there in the back of your head. Then one day you think "What about that story idea?" and you go to the file and you've got something to work from.

Rona: When we teach people how to do this, we're demystifying the whole development process. People don't know about development. They hear about that word but they don't know what it means. So we're going to try to take the cover off of it.

Monika: Being in development is also for people looking for work in the film industry. Maybe they are great with homework and write great essays, so maybe reading is work they want to do? They love books, they love writing.

In discussing what it takes to stay in the business, Rona made the offhand remark that a lot of people who leave Hollywood become shrinks. Monika nodded enthusiastically.

Monika: I had a story analyst, she was reading at nighttime because she was going to school to become a shrink. She ended up coming back. I know a lot of people in this business who have become shrinks. Like Connie Chaplin who was at Paramount.

So I wanted to know what the people who stay in this business have that the people who leave don't.

Monika: Passion. There's nothing else out there that really interests me. If I love what I'm doing right now, what else would I want to do? There's nothing as exciting.

Since I knew both women had spent a long time in Hollywood, I wondered aloud about how the business had changed. What they had to say might tell you something about how overworked a production company staffer might be.

Monika: One thing that is predominantly happening is that jobs that paid execs six figures, such as a VP of development, now hire three people for that same amount of money.

Rona: There is also a shrinkage due to big companies buying things up. The anti-trust laws don't seem to be in effect. The TV movie business is virtually dead. The competition is fierce. They tend to buy from the same old people and in my opinion get the same old product. So diversity is gone. I think it used to be edgy in the studio system. All the studios had small specialty arms. `

So where does that leave someone who has a property to sell to Hollywood?

Rona: You need to find a producer. You can't go to a studio, but you never really could.

Monika: It's always best to find a producer who's passionate about the material, who will work with you on it.

Rona: You're not going to get big bucks right away.

Monika: You may, it's not impossible. There are some producers who have money for options, but most producers don't have discretionary funds any more.

Rona: So if you find someone who is willing to work with you, likes your material, and can get passionate about it, don't think you should get paid to do that unless you are a Writers Guild member. A writer should be willing to work on something with a producer who has faith in him. I always say the film business is a collaborative effort. If a writer can't write collaboratively, he should be a playwright. The business is about rewriting and working with other people, and you will be rewritten.

Monika: That's the bottom line.

Rona: That doesn't mean you won't get solo credit, but you will be rewritten. That's the nature of the beast. But if you become a playwright, the Dramatists Guild is very clear. You cannot change one thing, one comma, without the playwright's permission.

So there you have an example of what people think who have actively developed many projects. Now let's go over what happens when a script receives a "Consider" from a reader, or even the rare "Recommend" and what a producer or head of a production company does with a property they acquire.

What a Deal Really Means

The process of development can be confusing to people new to Hollywood. After a company makes a deal on a property, it will be rewritten and polished until a director, stars, and financing are secured. You may do the rewriting; you might not. What will they rewrite? They might change the location to take advantage of co-financing opportunities in some foreign country. Then they'll rewrite the story, followed by the dialogue. When shooting begins, actors may want to rewrite dialogue on the set, having put together enough background on their characters so that they feel comfortable saying, "He wouldn't say that." Directors will have their own ideas about the script, and sometimes they can hurt a script.

Dialogue might need to be changed to suit a rating the company wants. For example, in 2001 the director of the movie *Hardball* was forced to remove more than twenty uses "of a certain curse word" so that the film could be released with a PG rating instead of an R, according to the *Los Angeles Times.* Foul-mouthed pro baseball players? No, the movie was about a Chicago Little League team in which the members spout four-letter words. Since the story was supposedly based on an actual team, the team's coach denied that the team used offensive language and accused the studio of perpetuating racial stereotypes of black children. As a writer, you don't usually have to think about such things, but the production company does.

Generally, the whole movie rides on the shoulders of the script. Thus, when millions of dollars are on the line, movie executives try to cover all the bases, and get a number of writers to rewrite the screenplay. Sometimes the process takes so long that it is referred to as development hell.

It can be a complex process. If your script doesn't pass muster going up the ranks, maybe a film of your screenplay won't please the public, and the producer could lose the deal with the studio. Your property might not get made, and if money has been invested in it, but the studio doesn't want to make it, they might put it in "turnaround." That means you could get the property back, or it might cost you money to get it back (so the studio can recoup its investment). I know one author whose book was purchased (not optioned) for several hundred thousand dollars. The studio will probably never make the movie, and the amount spent on the book probably ensures that no one will buy it from the studio, because the subject matter of the story doesn't fit today's feature market.

The Pitching Never Stops

People in Hollywood rarely spend money on a property unless it's a high-profile project. That could be a hot script around town, a pre-publication novel that looks like it could be a hit, or anything else that seems to have a large degree of interest to the public.

The thing you have to know is that while you have to sell your project to an agent, manager, and producer, the selling never stops. You pitch to development, they pitch to the boss, the boss pitches to someone with money, and if that is an executive at the studio, the executive might have to pitch to the greenlight person (who writes the checks at the studio).

That's why it's important that you have a great logline that can be easily repeated, hopefully eagerly. Terry Rossio and Ted Elliot, two very successful screenwriters who maintain a great Web site for writers at www.wordplayer.com, believe that your logline and/or pitch needs to generate hallway buzz after you've shared it. It's the Hollywood equivalent of word of mouth around movie theaters and at the office.

One of the better pitchmen in Hollywood, who also happens to be a fine screenwriter, is Dan Gordon. I watched Gordon do a pitch for an audience at the first pitch fest put on by Carlos de Abreu, the proprietor of the Hollywood Film Festival. Basically, Gordon told a compelling story with emotional impact, beginning, middle, and end with a nice twist, and it happened to be a true story. The pitch took about twenty minutes, and he admonished the audience never to let anyone make them take less than twenty minutes for a pitch.

Of course, I knew Gordon made a number of deals while playing golf with executives, which can easily take more than twenty minutes, but having such an ideal captive audience is a luxury most writers will never have. I didn't tell Gordon that no one there for the pitch fest would have more than five minutes to sell his or her project to an executive there, so Gordon's "twenty minutes or nothing" exhortation was useless in the framework of the pitch fest.

Still, Gordon's dictum is illustrative of the hubris and conflicting information that abounds in Hollywood circles. He is great at pitching and selling, but I can only hope you get in a position some day not just to have people read your material, but to get to pitch it to them at length as well. Here are some facts about pitching, which I feel, if applied, can save you money and headaches.

1. Access is everything. If you can pick up a phone and call someone, or email someone with a short query and get a reply, you have access.

I like a film to have a beginning, a middle, and an end, but not necessarily in that order.

—*Jean-Luc Godard*

You don't have to send flowers on birthdays, attend their kid's bar mitzvah, or come by the office tap-dancing naked and carrying Godiva chocolates. What matters is that someone will listen to you. Then you can tell them about your project. And here's the big non-secret—you don't have to pay for access at pitch fests and the like. You can simply use the phone book and/or various Hollywood information directories to find people.

2. You can gain access to anyone. Really. The main thing people in Hollywood—a town filled with overly-ambitious egos—care about is whether or not you are going to waste their time. And since it takes a phony to know one, if you try to fool anyone about what you have to offer, you'll get seen with X-ray eyes rather quickly. On the other hand, if you actually have a truly commercial, interesting, well thought-out, entertaining story to tell, and more stories where that one came from, people who matter can sense it and will help you.

That's it. That's all you need to know. Good luck. Call me, we'll do lunch.

What? You want more? Gee, am I good at pitching?

Because of my books and the fact that I teach a screenwriting course available in almost 850 outlets, mostly colleges and universities, on three continents, people tend to think that I constantly circulate in Hollywood to keep up with people.

I don't, but I do read the trades regularly—*The Hollywood Reporter* and *Daily Variety*. If I read the trades religiously, I would probably be an agent or an aspiring development executive who works until 8:00 at night and reads screenplays all weekend. But I have a life and a family, so I only read the trades regularly, meaning every day. I also mostly read them online, particularly after I subscribed to *Variety* online. If I ever need to see if someone has been mentioned in an article, I simply search the Archives section and start reading.

Another secret I have is knowing where to look. Someone has a Web site? I look up the registry on Whois and get phone numbers and addresses. You don't know Whois? Every site that sells Web domains lets you search their registrations. One site I use to search for people's information is www.samspade.org.

The Internet aside, I often use the phone book. Some people are just not on the Web, as I'm sure you've found.

My kind of approach also works in person, if you're genuine and friendly. There are numerous producers and directors I've gotten to know over the years by simply walking up and introducing myself. Then, when I finally send them some material (not always immediately), I remind them of our meeting. And I make sure that the material is good enough not to embarrass me and is the kind of thing they're likely to be interested in. Remember what I said about not wasting people's time?

And how do you know who is likely to be interested in what? The key to accessing anyone is just this: You have to do your research. You need to look up their credits on IMDb and anywhere else you can find. Read articles about them at the online trades sites, even if you have to pay for articles. Look them up in the *Los Angeles Times* archives. Study the kinds of movies they've done, because more likely than not they'll do the same kinds of movies in the future.

Don't try to sell a romantic comedy to Wes Craven. You probably shouldn't try to sell anything to Wes Craven, anyway, because he writes. I once tried to sell something to Woody Allen, which was complete folly. You usually need to find producers who do not write.

The really important part of making pitches is telling people what you have to sell once you have their attention. Whatever it is, even if you think you have lightning in a bottle, other executives might not immediately agree. But one day you might get a "Recommend" and be on your way to a deal that is announced in the trades. "Jane Screenwriter's deal is $200,000 against a million, and the Big Movie Company is very excited about being in business with her."

Translated, that means Jane gets $200,000 now, and after all the rewrites and polishes and casting and funding and everything else, on the first day of principal photography (when they actually begin filming), Jane gets the rest of the $1,000,000.

Too bad she won't get to keep it all. She'll have to pay her agent 10 percent, her manager 15 percent, her lawyer 5 percent, and her tax bill. But hey, that's a set of problems I wouldn't mind having, how about you?

If you never get to a place like that, but you feel you have a movie that must get on screen, maybe you need to make your own movie. We'll go over the possibilities in the next chapter.

CHAPTER

7

The Independent Route

Wake up!

—Spike Lee, in more than one movie

Most aspiring screenwriters don't make it past the first act of a career. To illustrate what I mean, let's compare the normal structure of a Hollywood movie and the protagonist's actions to the way beginners approach Hollywood. Here are the first two important items of Act One:

Big Opening. This could be something as simple as an idea that moved them so much they sweated out the writing of a screenplay, the optioning of material, and the like. Whatever moves them toward Hollywood with something to sell.

And that's as far as most people get, the first step. They write one script or try to sell a book or novel to the business, and then when it doesn't work out, they give up. Or, they write a lot of screenplays and keep making the same mistakes. So while they think the next one will be their big break (read: Big Opening), they never get started.

Here's what they're missing, which is step two:

The Shaping Force. This is my own discovery, an item that arrives in the middle of the first act in the good movies, and there's usually a hint or two of it before it firmly arrives. My students learn it can be anything: a concept (time in *Cast Away*, 2000); a mentor (Obi-Wan in *Star Wars*); an object (the Ark of the Covenant in the first Indiana Jones movie); a lover (the non-Greek suitor in *My Big Fat Greek Wedding*); or even a villain (the alien in the *Alien* [1979, 1982] movies). The Shaping Force is what that movie is about. Sadly, most people who approach Hollywood don't know what *they* are about. Thus they don't carry the passion necessary to break through all barriers and show that they have that unique voice the town is always seeking.

Accordingly, and unfortunately, most aspiring screenwriters don't have a Shaping Force to their career. Those who break through do have a Shaping Force, which could take the form of a teacher, an epiphany about writing, or even a decision to move to Los Angeles and not give up. The lucky ones write a special screenplay that appeals to as many people as possible with a concept that is simple, easily stated, and reflected so well in the title that anyone gets it, such as *Ghostbusters* (1984).

Writing a screenplay like that can be a transforming event. It can get you hired to write and rewrite screenplays before your own script is ever filmed. This happened with Wesley Strick and *Final Analysis* (1992) and also with a writer Strick helped, David Ayer who wrote *Training Day.* After writing a great script, a writer is propelled from being just another peddler of used paper to someone Hollywood producers can profitably exploit.

It's the entertainment *business*, remember?

Problematically, not many writers write a script with profit potential and move on to be A-list screenwriters.

So then what? How can someone make a breakthrough and get that Hollywood career they want?

In my screenwriting courses, we examine the Midpoint Change in Act Two, an event in which the protagonist does something very dramatic that might threaten his or her very existence. This change transforms the character and allows him or her to meet the challenge of the final struggle in Act Three. Think of Tom Hanks knocking out his abscessed tooth in the middle of *Cast Away* (2000). The screen then goes black; when we fade back in, Hanks is transformed and able to easily survive on his island.

I've found that the most popular elements of film storytelling are applicable to a career. After all, current screenwriting conventions took a long time to evolve, and thus the key elements of hit movies today are based in Aristotle's *Poetics,* Shakespearean themes, Freudian psychology, Jungian imagery, and Joseph Campbell's myth study. I believe Hollywood movies are so popular with audiences because they speak deeply to our human experience and hopes for a better life. And so I began to apply the elements in the "story matrix" that I teach to my own life.

My own Midpoint Change was to begin focusing on my own work and quit wasting time helping people who didn't appreciate it, no matter how much they were paying me. When I took this leap of faith, I began receiving unexpected boons:

A number of time-wasting people exited my life.

My student population doubled.

A producer expressed a desire to make a deal on three of my novels.

My literary agent extracted long overdue royalties from one of my publishers.

A new friend produced a demo of a radio show I wanted to do at no cost.

In the inexplicable film world, cowardice increases in relation to the amount of money invested.

—Peter Ustinov

I got the rights back on four of my old books, which offered tremendous re-marketing possibilities.

It's interesting what happens when people realize that you are passionately committed to your endeavors. I've seen others take that approach over the years and produce career breakthroughs. My friend Michael Rymer once turned down an offer from Nicole Kidman to buy his script *Angel Baby* (1995). She wouldn't let Michael direct it, so he took it to his native Australia, got it financed, and after making the movie, his career opened up tremendously. His most recent project was a TV miniseries of *Battlestar Galactica*.

Any number of filmmakers I have encountered, beginning with Richard Donner, have told me that their determining factor in making a movie is whether they want to see it on screen. Because of this passionate commitment, they'll do whatever it takes to get the movie made.

How many screenwriters have such a level of conviction to something they've written? They should, because people like that get taken seriously. Consider this quote from Mencius, probably the third most popular Chinese philosopher (after Lao Tzu and Confucius):

> Men for the most part can mend their ways only
> after they make mistakes. Only when they are frus-
> trated in mind and in their deliberations can they
> stand up anew. Only when their intentions become
> visible on their countenances and audible in their
> voices can they be understood by others.
> —Mencius, Book VI Kao Tzu, Part II, 15

Have you been frustrated in trying to sell a screenplay? Getting yourself on the talent radar screen of Hollywood might ultimately mean making your own movie. The majority of the finalists at the Sundance Film Festival in 2004 were films made by people who had seen their scripts repeatedly turned down in the Hollywood development process. The director of the festival made a point of this when first talking with the press about the chosen few.

In our digital age, movies don't have to be expensive. *Tarnation* (2003), a Sundance hit, was originally edited on an Apple computer using the Apple's free iMovie software. The total reported cost of making the documentary (a biographical pastiche of the life of the film-maker Jonathan Caouette) was $218.32. Caouette mixed narration with snapshots, answering machine messages, Super-8 movies, and video diaries, all drawn from nineteen years of his life.

So what's stopping you?

The main point is that to get through your own Midpoint Change so you can conquer your own Second Act. As a screenwriter, you need to focus on your own strengths and hew to them vigorously. Every producer's assistant, when pressed for what the producer is really looking for, will say, "An original voice." But guess what? They get more excited watching movies by new filmmakers than they do reading scripts.

Filmmaking is impressive. It's one thing to know the market. It's great to know screenplay theory. It's fun to take weekend workshops, even though they might be hard on the bank account. Your original voice, however, is a pristine domain where no one may trespass. If you are certain of it, if you display clarity and distinctive style, that voice can transform people's lives.

Most screenwriters are rewritten. If you make a movie from your script, though, you can preserve your voice. So, where do you start?

Short Yourself Out

I often lecture to groups and appear on Hollywood panels. More often than not, I advise people that to make a mark as a screenwriter they should make their own movies. Even short films can make a major impact. I hadn't spoken to an actress friend, Lisa Blount, for years, and then I watched her, her husband, and their business partner receive an Oscar in 2002 for best short film. (See www.ginnymule.com for details). Wow, I thought, I really should make my own movie.

If you have to

have a job in

this world,

a high-priced

movie star is a

pretty good gig.

—Tom Hanks

I read books like *Digital Guerrilla Video* by Avi Hoffer and studied the three-CD interactive film school package by Rajko Grlic (www.interactivefilmschool.com). With my Apple Powerbook, I knew I could at least do a rough edit of a digital feature and burn a DVD. I read *iMovie2: The Missing Manual* by David Pogue, the *New York Times* electronics columnist (see www.pogueman.com). I digested Erica Sadun's *iMovie 2 Solutions: Tips, Tricks, and Special Effects* (www.ericasadun.com). I knew all about Apple's QuickTime Pro (www.apple.com/quicktime—it's a cross-platform tool). I began going over old home movies converted to video, thinking they could be edited to make short films that could be ported to QuickTime, burned to a CD or DVD, and sent off.

I even considered making a documentary of my life since becoming a father. Then *Tarnation* (2003) came out. Someone beat me to the home movie approach!

Back to the drawing board for me. I started making short films. It's easier to make a short than a feature. With a short you can show your style. Producers and studio execs will readily look at original short films on a Web site or even via email. Now that broadband Internet is a given in Hollywood, you can quickly show someone what you're capable of producing. Contrast that to how long it takes to get them to read a screenplay.

A great short film can work wonders. A former student of mine won the first Sundance Online contest, and was quickly hired by a major California entertainment company. The team that created the genius short "405" got a U.S. network TV deal (see www.405themovie.com). And why wouldn't they? There were four million views of their film on ifilm.com within sixteen months.

Short animations can also propel careers to the heights. As I mentioned in an earlier chapter, the movie *Undercover Brother* (2002) originated on a Web show created using Macromedia Flash, and so did *South Park*. If you can't afford that software, take a look at *Wildform Flix Pro* (www.wildform.com). As advertised, it allows you to "edit, crop, convert, and post your video on the Web in minutes," and it is indeed "the only software available that can automatically turn a video into a vector-based animation." Shoot your short with a camcorder and use Wild Flix Pro to turn it into an animated Web show. It's similar to the technique used by Richard Linklater in *Waking Life* (2001).

And how about this—what if you shot a truly great screenplay from a script you wrote, and sent someone an email with a Web site link for watching it? Put yourself in an executive's shoes. Which would you rather do, read a few pages, or see actors on a screen?

"Filmmaker" Sounds Better Than "Screenwriter"

Why not get rid of some of that frustration? You're writing scripts, you're coming up with great scenes, but no one sees them. Why not figure out some way to make a movie? That's what *Project Greenlight* (www.projectgreenlight.com) was all about, and the contest and show are still running. Perhaps it prompted actor Kevin Spacey to start his own contest to find the next great filmmaker via www.triggerstreet.com, with funding from major sponsors. (They also look for screenplays, so check out the site.) No matter where you live, it's easy to keep up with the latest possibilities via the Internet. It's easier to stay motivated when people are actually getting things done, not just hoping something (their script) will get done.

When it became clear to me that people who make movies (as opposed to writers) get most of Hollywood's attention, I began to attend events like the LA Digital Video Show (www.ladvshow.com). Preparing to make my own movie, I took a weekend workshop on directing from Guy Magar, an American director who graduated from film school in London. (See www.actioncut.com for more information.) At the Action Cut seminar, I heard a story that reminded me of the value of doing whatever it takes to get your vision on screen, no matter what. Magar told the group how Kevin *"Clerks"* Smith had his no-budget feature turned down repeatedly by festivals. So Smith paid an entry fee to a festival in New York, and was assigned a slot at midnight in the middle of the week. He expected and got a handful of people in the audience, but one of them turned out to be an insomniac who was a scout for Sundance. This led to the pickup of the film by Miramax and the rest is Smith's career.

I'm sure you know the story of *The Blair Witch Project* or Robert Rodriguez's *El Mariachi* (but don't believe that story about doing it for $7,000). One of the best films I've seen in recent years was *The Poor and Hungry* (2000), which won Best Digital at the Hollywood Film Festival. With a total budget of $20,000, it was shot on a consumer camcorder in black and white with unknown actors, and was exhibited on a U.S. cable channel.

If you have a character-driven screenplay that might be rejected by production companies because of its perceived lack of commercialism, shooting the movie might be your ticket to Hollywood.

You don't have to travel to Hollywood to learn to be a filmmaker. In the U.K., the Lo-to-No Budget Filmmaking Weekend Masterclass presented by Raindance founder Elliot Grove offers: "One weekend to learn how to shoot, edit, and direct your first feature cost-effectively and develop a plan for submitting to film festivals and distributors." The writers, directors, or producers of *Lock, Stock and Two Smoking Barrels* (1998), *Waking Ned Devine* (1998), and *Memento* (2000) all attended this intensive seminar before making their first films. In other words, all of these people at one point made a leap of faith. They picked up a camera and learned how to edit. They didn't wait for someone else to spend millions to put their vision on a thirty-foot-high movie screen.

Hollywood Reality 101

If you're "only" a screenwriter, you can make a nice living. Until you become a filmmaker, however, you won't fully understand how movies work. These days there's little excuse. For under $10,000, you can buy a

digital camera and the computer hardware and software to make a feature-length movie. Did you know that Spike Lee used a $1,200 con-
sumer video camera to shoot his feature *Bamboozled* (2000)?

Then there's editing, which teaches story flow in a way that no
screenwriting class can match. According to Norman Hollyn, USC professor and the author of *The Film Editing Room Handbook: How to
Manage the Near Chaos of the Cutting Room*:

> Editors and writers deal with the same issues—char-
> acter arc, storytelling, suspense, pacing, etc. Editing
> is rewriting. Story construction is the hardest thing to
> learn without actually making a movie, putting it up
> on the rack, and seeing what falls off the axles.
> There are elements of story that *don't* need to be
> told because it can all be done in performance and
> nuance, and there are points that absolutely *cannot
> be omitted*. Filmmaking is the process of guiding an
> audience to feel a movie in a way that you, as a
> filmmaker, want them to feel. Leave out one crucial
> detail ("that character is the other character's
> sister," or "he actually saw him fall on the ice") and
> you let the audience write its own movie—for better
> or for worse. Tell the audience too much and it will
> be way ahead of you, without anything to do except
> think of tomorrow's laundry list.
>
> What the writer can learn during the editing
> process is what he or she already should know—
> storytelling. However, much as the writer needs to
> learn how to write a script to sell it, the writer
> should also know how the *rewriting* of a movie (for
> that is what editing essentially is) can tell a story in
> this non-written medium. Editing, rather than pro-
> duction, is the best way to learn this.

You don't learn editing by reading about it. You have to do it to see how scenes cut together or don't. Believe me, your screenwriting will change. You can lie to yourself about your screenplay, but not what you see on film.

The Story before Your Eyes

Putting together a film can also help you develop tools to use if you need to pitch something to sell it. By the time Alfred Hitchcock made a movie, he often felt bored with it. That's because he had so thoroughly planned it out in advance, meticulously creating "storyboards" for each camera angle and scene. If you've never seen a storyboard, think of a crude cartoon (but better than stick figures). Software like StoryBoard Quick (www.powerproduction.com) allows you to draft out scenes easily and can be very effective in creating presentations that will sell investors on investing in your film.

When you approach telling a story visually, it helps you in Hollywood. If you've ever seen a PowerPoint presentation in a work environment, you might groan at the idea of using it in a Hollywood context, but some successful screenwriters use a similar approach. (And hey, you can email a PowerPoint presentation, can't you?) In a column called "The Wind-up & the Pitch" on the excellent Wordplay site (www.wordplayer.com), Terry Rossio explains how he and Ted Elliott presented their *Zorro* story to Amblin Entertainment (Steven Spielberg's company prior to Dreamworks). Using cards to cover the 18–21 major sequences of a film—with each sequence having a name—they were "forced to simplify the story and emphasize (or in some cases even 'discover') the major elements of the story. These cards were attached to a board to use as a visual aid for the presentation. Rossio and Elliott were relieved to see that by using it, all the people listening to their story looked at the board, not them. They had never used the board before and weren't sure how it would be received. Then Spielberg saw it and said: "This is great. This is how all movies should be pitched."

A novelist sits over his work like a god, but he knows he's a particularly minor god. Whereas a director making a small movie is a bona fide general of a small army.

—*Norman Mailer*

If you've ever studied what sells in Hollywood, you've probably noticed that a lot of comics and graphic novels are purchased to be made into movies. Recently, Japanese manga has taken the town by storm as well. Think of it this way. Aren't all these things just elaborate storyboards? Screenwriters are ultimately trying to get pictures on a large screen. Anything you can do to get that process started can only help you. If you can't do a comic book, do a storyboard. You'll be closer to making a film, and you might even have a presentation that will help you sell a screenplay.

Getting Down to Basics

Approaching Hollywood as a filmmaker can greatly increase your chances of being taken seriously. I won't bore you about recommended equipment because I could write an entire book about that, and others have already done it better than I could. What matters is that you do whatever it takes to get your script upon a screen. When you have that determination, people will go out of their way to help you. When a member of my Yahoo! discussion group announced his plan to make his first feature, I did a free script evaluation for him, continued to give him advice, and people in the group contributed financially.

Speaking of money, the main thing you'll find yourself concerned with (if you're like most of us) when you make a film is financing. To that end, I recommend one book most highly to learn all about film production and financing, worldwide. *Producing for Hollywood*, written by show biz veterans Paul Mason and Donald L. Gold (look them up on www.imdb.com), is the best thing an aspiring producer can read. Richard Donner, the producer/director of the *Lethal Weapon* (1987, 1989, 1992, 1998) movies, said, "There's no set corporate ladder in the world of Hollywood producing . . . these guys show you how to take the elevator."

Whether funded or broke, there is a buoyant spirit rampant

among digital filmmakers. For example, Eric Colley put up an excellent Web site, www.indieclub.com, as a public service to help others get their films made as cheaply as possible. No matter how much enthusiasm you have, however, you have to do things professionally. I've been involved with a number of productions and seen a number of homemade low-budget movies. When they fall short it's always because of deficits in one or more of the following categories:

1. Script—Unless you improvise your scenes (which has been done in many indie films and on TV shows such as *Curb Your Enthusiasm*), you'd better get the script right. That could include having staged readings, lots of rewriting, and watching many similar movies for tips.
2. Direction—You can take the aforementioned Action Cut workshop, Dov S-S Simens' similar two-day school (see www.webfilmschool.com for the live version and other possibilities), or simply learn by doing. Or you can attend a longer program at a film school. More on that later.
3. Acting—Don't buy into the conventional wisdom that you need names to sell a movie. You don't, if the movie is good enough. If your actors aren't good or excellent, though, you're sunk.
4. Sound—Badly recorded dialogue and/or sound effects mentally divorces an audience after a while. The greatest script, direction, and acting on earth won't matter with bad sound.
5. Lighting—These days, people expect to see good lighting in any movie. It behooves any beginning filmmaker to put in extra study on lighting. John Jackman's *Lighting for Digital Video and Televison* covers all the basics well. See his site at http://greatdv.com/index.htm for more info.

There are so many people making digital movies these days, there's no excuse. What information you can get in books, on CDs, DVDs, or online, you can get in a relatively short and affordable curriculum. Here are some examples of places in southern California.

L.A. Resources

With apologies to great filmmaking programs around the U.S. and the world (which would fill a large book), this is a book about Hollywood. I write what I know, and I've been here two decades, so maybe I'm biased. If you have a make-it-happen-now attitude like me, you might not feel inclined to enroll in a four-year program. Two-day basic workshops can be excellent, but you won't learn all the specifics you need.

In Los Angeles, filmmaking can be an around-the-clock endeavor and more great moviemakers are here than in any other place in the world. So it can be daunting, trying to figure out where to learn. That's why I recommend the following two programs for people who want to learn filmmaking hands-on. They both take a similar approach.

The L.A. Film Lab (www.1421e9k.com): Conceived as an incubator for 1421/E9k Entertainment, the Lab supports and showcases the achievements of emerging filmmakers "after guiding them through the process of creating a high quality calling card."

The calling card is what it's all about. Just as you need a great sample script to show people what you can do as a screenwriter, in filmmaking you're only as good as your last movie, whether it's a short or a feature. Corey Blake and his partners, Jesse Biltz and David Cohen, have produced eighteen short films and three features, winning prizes at the Texas Film Festival, the San Diego Film Festival, and getting their films into more than forty festivals. Their yearlong course emphasizes a feature film approach in creating quality short film projects. According to Blake, "Students gain four years of experience in a year's time and walk away with an amazing network and a tangible calling card that will assist them in procuring more work in the industry." In other words, a film they're proud to show.

The partners built their curriculum on the example of the Group Theatre of the 1930s. They team writers, actors, producers, and directors into teams to create short films in both Los Angeles and New York.

Classes meet weekly with guest lecturers and screenings alternating for an additional class period each week. Tuition for the full year's program is $1,200 for the Los Angeles Lab and $1,500 for the New York Lab.

Students learn insider information, such as how to keep a short film under fifteen minutes because that's what festivals prefer. Generally, says Blake, around fifty to one hundred people become involved in each project. The price of making a short ranges from $3,000 to $15,000. In additional to learning techniques, the Lab schools students on building a long-term career including the creation of public relations awareness of their activities. Most of the Lab's movies are shot digitally, but they will also work with 16mm or 35mm filmed projects.

The Lab is also partnered with the Los Angeles Short Film Festival to showcase some of the Lab filmmakers in a monthly series at the Arclight Theatre in Hollywood.

In short, the L.A. Film Lab is a great idea. You can reach them at (818) 980-0394.

The Los Angeles Film School (www.lafilm.com): Located in the former headquarters of RCA Records in Hollywood, this school was co-founded by former Universal Pictures president Thom Mount and offers a faculty of highly qualified professional filmmakers. They cover cinematography, editing, production design, and sound recording, and students must complete four films to graduate. On their Web site they explain why students should pick their program:

> 5 Reasons to Attend the Los Angeles Film School:
> 1) Small Hands-on Classes
> 2) A Faculty of Professional Filmmakers
> 3) State-of-the-art Facilities
> 4) Keep the Rights to Your Films
> 5) The Cost of Education (We want to build your career, not your debt.)

I first learned about this school when appearing on a panel

there. Afterward, the panelists listened to pitches from people in the audience, and I was astounded that every single person who spoke to me had a commercial story. They were all students at the school.

When I investigated the school's Web site, I discovered an advisory board that includes multiple Oscar-winners as well as an old friend of mine who is on the Board of the Academy of Motion Picture Arts and Sciences. The quality of the students' pitches suddenly made sense.

The school has an eight-month Feature Development Program. Students' films are seen by dozens of Hollywood companies, and top agencies have signed students. To complete the program, students are expected to have a polished final draft of a screenplay, a finished short or set of scenes ready for screening, a marketing and positioning strategy, a fundraising strategy and final budget, a casting and attachment strategy, and final pitches that will attract investors. The one catch is that the school wants individuals who have film school and/or professional experience.

Students work in teams of two or three, functioning as writer, director, or producer. The cost of the program is $15,000, and tuition is charged per team (two-member teams $7,500 each, three-member teams $5,000 each). International students must pay an additional $1,000 in tuition.

Although I haven't attended the school, its students and faculty alone assure me of its quality. Sound good? Call (323) 769-2487 or email info@lafilm.com.

The Chill of Reality

It might seem that once you have a film ready for exhibition, hitting the road to film festivals would be a good idea. After all, the Academy Foundation of the Academy of Motion Picture Arts and Sciences has a Film Festival Fund that was established by the Academy's Board of Governors. The truth is always a little different in Hollywood. Unless you win at a

*The embarrassing
thing is that the
salad dressing
is outgrossing
my films.*

—Paul Newman

major festival such as Sundance, being a festival winner might not mean much. There are thousands of festivals, both virtual and real. Who can keep up with all of them? It's much like winning a screenwriting competition. People in Hollywood know the main ones: Nicholl, Heart of Film (Austin), Chesterfield, Scriptapalooza, Final Draft, and so forth. Unless the competition takes place where people in the industry are reading the scripts in play (quarter-finalists on up), it's really a bit of "so what?"

Although people have been sending me DVDs of their independent movies for years, such films have always been made with unknowns and are generally relationship movies. Professionals take a different approach. They think in terms of genre films, which have a more attractive classification than drama. When Jeff Monahan, a WGA screenwriter and SAG actor who teaches at Carnegie-Mellon University in Pittsburgh wrote to me about a horror project, I knew he was onto something.

Tom Savini's Chill Factor is an anthology horror series being distributed direct-to-DVD over the production company Web site. "Instead of waiting for permission from a studio or production company," Monahan told me, "we've created our own studio. We're producing, writing, directing, acting—using union talent—and making the stories we want to make the way we want to make them. Our number-one concern is quality, and since we're our own toughest critics, we're very confident. We were approached by cable networks after airing the trailer for the very first episode, so who knows where this goes. Check it out at www.tomsavinischillfactor.com."

Making a genre film can be important. Although comedy is hard, I would make that before a drama any day, and wouldn't hesitate to film a horror movie with the right script. Perhaps you saw *Meet the Parents*? No, not the one with Ben Stiller. I'm talking about the original one, from Chicago. That's right, there was an original, and that film was bought by Universal and remade. Even if your movie doesn't get wide distribution, you could make a lot of money by simply selling it to have it remade.

Perhaps by the time I write my next book I'll have directed my first feature. By the time you read it, I hope you will have made a movie, too. Meanwhile, here are some Web sites that might help get you started.

Filmmaking Resources via the Web

AFCI / Association of Film Commissioners International (www.afci.org): A global resource for production and a network of worldwide film liaison professionals

Apple Computers (www.apple.com): The best software for short film viewing on the Web is QuickTime Pro. Factor in Apple's iLife movie and photo suite, the Final Cut editing products, and ease of use, and Apple is living on the cutting edge.

Atom Films (http://atomfilms.shockwave.com): One of the leading sites for showcasing short films

DV.com (www.dv.com): A very useful magazine with a great newsletter and several useful online forums. They also put on excellent video expositions.

DV Café (www.dv-cafe.com): A multitudinous collection of sites beneficial for anyone getting started in digital video

Film Arts Foundation (www.filmarts.org): One of the nation's top resource centers for independent filmmakers, which includes a film festival, exhibition, education, grants, fiscal sponsorship programs, and equipment rental facility. They also publish *Release Print* magazine.

Hypnotic (www.nibblebox.com): Originally founded by former NBC executive David Bartis to incubate college filmmaking talent, this company's programs have reached more than one billion consumers worldwide. They produce shows like "The O.C." on Fox and are experts at "branded entertainment" (see the site for an explanation).

Ifilm (www.ifilm.com): A short film showcase offering many other products including the Hollywood Creative Directory

Independent Feature Project West (http://ifpwest.org): This not-for-profit service organization provides "resources, information, and avenues of communication for its members: independent filmmakers, industry professionals, and independent film enthusiasts." With six chapters located in Chicago, Los Angeles, Miami, Minneapolis/St. Paul, New York, and Seattle, the group offers programs that help members make connections, and find out who's who, who's buying, who's financing, and who's making what features, shorts, and documentaries. It has nine thousand filmmaker and film industry members, publishes *FILMMAKER: The Magazine of Independent Film,* and puts on an annual film festival.

Motion Picture Association of America (www.mpaa.org): Formed in 1945 in the aftermath of World War II, this organization represents the Hollywood film industry globally and provides the ratings on movies. See the site for an explanation of how your movie might be rated.

New Filmmakers Los Angeles (www.newfilmmakers.com): Executive Director Henry Turner says his goal "is to present the most challenging new, unsigned independent films to both industry professionals and film fans, away from the high-pressure atmosphere of a film festival, in what is the finest venue in California—Cinespace." (Cine-Space is L.A.'s only digital theater supper club at 6356 Hollywood Boulevard.)

New Venue (www.newvenue.com): A personal favorite with a FlickTips page that every aspiring filmmaker should read

The Orphanage (http://theorphanage.com): Founded by the supervising visual effects artist at George Lucas' Industrial Light and Magic, this company's Magic Bullet software makes digital video look like film

Pixies (www.pixieawards.org): The "Oscars of the Internet," named after the term "pixel" for Web movies

RESFEST Digital Film Festival (www.resfest.com): A showcase of the best of digital filmmaking

Shockwave (www.shockwave.com): The site for Flash animations and Flash player downloads

StudentReel (www.studentreel.com): A place to broadcast your work online using QuickTime

Studio Systems (www.studiosystemsinc.com): Excellent source for information and research for the film and television industries with its ScriptLog submission, project feature, and Hollywood film and contact information service

University Film and Video Association (www.ufva.org): An organization offering membership and college information, including $4,000 production grants and $1,000 research grants to those who qualify

Videomaker (www.videomaker.com): To keep up with the digital and computer world, this is my favorite. It offers a free monthly email newsletter for video production enthusiasts and sponsors video expos around the country.

See You in the Credits?

It might seem to be a Herculean task to go from screenwriting to film-making, but plenty of people have done it. It takes a lot of study, a lot of practice, and learning what works, but in our digital age it's a lot easier than it was when everyone had to shoot on film.

There's another thing to be considered about becoming a film-maker. If you do it successfully, you would be a lot more attractive to the medium where most of the money is made in Hollywood—television.

I'll tell you why in the next chapter.

CHAPTER

8

The Realities of
Television

I find television very educational. Every time someone switches it on, I go into another room and read a good book.

—Groucho Marx

Television has long been the pot of gold at the end of the Hollywood rainbow, but lately things are changing. The last time I wrote a book about selling to Hollywood, the Writers Guild of America was fighting with the producers, networks, and studios and threatening a strike.

As I write this book, the Writers Guild of America is fighting with the producers, networks, and studios and threatening a strike.

C'est la Hollywood. The fights and strikes are almost always about money. This time, the arguments are over revenues from the DVD sales of television shows such as *Friends*. The writers are cut out of the profits; they get paid for reruns on TV, but not for DVDs. Only the writer/producers have that luxury.

It's getting tougher to be only a writer in television, and not just because of the increasing emphasis on the writer/producer. Ageism seems to be getting worse, too. After a certain age, you could be pushed out of the loop. Ageism prompted some writers to file a class-action lawsuit against more than fifty TV networks, studios, production companies, and talent agencies, alleging that they had been "graylisted" after age forty (see www.writerscase.com). Some of these writers had Emmys and all had a long list of credits. Following that suit, a fifty-three-year-old writer for the show *Reba* filed his own suit, claiming he was fired because of his age.

A young writer might think, "More room for me!" Maybe not. Current American television is not a pretty picture. In the last couple of years, scripted shows have been falling by the wayside as reality television takes over. Reality shows might have writers, but most of these writers are not covered by Writers Guild of America agreements. Why so many reality shows? The bottom line; they're cheaper to make and the talent are usually amateurs who are not members of the actors' unions.

These recent trends spell trouble in Tinseltown because the majority of the members of the Writers Guild of America, west write for television. TV has been Hollywood's golden goose, but for writers it has been producing fewer and fewer golden nest eggs. Even mega-writer/producer David E. Kelley (*Ally McBeal* and *The Practice*) turned to reality television in 2004 with a true-life version of his ABC drama *The Practice*, after swearing in print he never would do a reality show.

Are You Ready for Primetime?

It's difficult for a mere writer to make a career breakthrough in prime-time television. The person television executives care most about is the showrunner, that special person who can write a script, polish it, work with people, actors, directors, and crews, and get a show delivered on time. To become one of those, you have a few options:

1. Get on the radar with a movie you've made and sell a show to TV as a proven creative entity;
2. Get a staff job on an existing series, move up to co-producer, and take over when the show creator moves on to other projects;
3. Work as a staff writer on a hit show and try to sell your own show at the same time;
4. Create a hit show in a country outside the U.S. and sell the remake rights to a U.S. company;
5. Do something unusual such as creating a hit in another medium that can transition to television;
6. Sell a series idea to an existing producer who has a track record (this is generally only possible with reality television).

Whatever route you take, you probably need to live in Los Angeles or another television center such as New York or Toronto. There are always exceptions, but rarely in primetime. I was a staff writer for a UPN network show that was filmed in Minnesota, but it was a morning kids' show. Writers living in other states sell screenplays for TV movies and to other markets, but the primetime writers generally live in the Los Angeles area.

One way you can break in is by taking the educational route, and on a studio level at that. Here follow two programs that might help you break into primetime television. In both cases you'll need to be in Los Angeles.

The Walt Disney Studios/ABC TV Fellowship Program
(www.abcnewtalent.disney.com/html/writmain.htm):

Fewer than a dozen writers are selected each year for the program at The Walt Disney Studios and ABC Entertainment. The Fellowships are available in both the feature film and television areas, and no previous experience is necessary. If they like your writing sample and select you, you'll receive a salary of $50,000 for a one-year period, and you'll also receive round-trip airfare (coach) and one month's accommodations. Even if you are a member of the Writers Guild of America, you're eligible for the program. WGA members should apply directly through the WGA's Employment Access Department by calling (323) 782-4648. Others should read the details at the Web site, where you can find a long list of the accomplishments of successful graduates including the very talented Gary Hardwick (1990–91), who wrote and directed *The Brothers* (2001) and *Deliver Us from Eva* (2003).

Warner Bros. Writers Workshop

(www.warnerbros.com/writersworkshop): Studios may copy each other in movies, but the Warner Bros. Writers Workshop couldn't be more different than the Disney Fellowship. While its stated objective is "to develop talented sitcom or drama writers," they don't spend any money to do so. Rather, they charge $495 for either the one-hour drama workshop or the comedy half-hour version. Similar to Disney, you must submit a sample script "based on a one-hour drama or half-hour comedy that has aired during the previous season." Still, the program has a good reputation and you won't spend as much time learning the basics as you would at Disney. See the Web site or contact:

Warner Bros. Writers Workshop Director

300 Television Plaza

Burbank, CA 91505

(818) 954-7906

writersworkshop@warnerbros.com

On the probable chance that, like most of my readers, you are not living in southern California, let's go over how to get a long-distance education in television before deciding whether or not you want to make the big move.

The TV Writer

Before he retired, Larry Brody was a showrunner and producer. He had a long track record in animation as well as "normal" shows, and somewhere in his busy career he found time to be a screenwriter and novelist, too. I recommend his book *Television Writing from the Inside Out* before any other book on writing for TV. One reason is that Larry maintains a very active Web site at www.tvwriter.com that offers a plethora of resources for aspiring television writers, including a contest and busy online forums.

The main reason I recommend his book, though, is the content that gives the reader a thorough grounding in all types of TV writing. For example, if you're an aspiring screenwriter you probably know that producers want to know what a movie is about by the middle of the first act or so. In television, it's the norm to let the audience in on the movie by page three, after the teaser that opens a show. "Believe it or not," writes Brody, "there's a good reason for this. Historically, audiences will go with you just about anywhere—as long as they understand the general direction." Brody covers all parts of teleplays with copious examples of actual scripts. He even includes scripts from shows in other countries, such as the long-running *Nikola* from Germany. From pitch meetings to delivering on assignments, everything a TV writer needs to know is in this book. Brody even shows you a sample of his own résumé.

The last time I discussed the TV business with Larry he remarked on how it had changed since the time he had started in 1968. Back then, he said, there were only about four thousand members in the WGA, and fewer than half of them considered themselves TV writers. Shows did twenty-six episodes per season, and just about every episode was written by freelance writers under the direction of a producer who knew every facet of production. With that kind of supervising producer, breaking in was much less difficult than today. Age discrimination was rampant then too, but it was directed against writers who were considered too young.

If writers ever realize how important they are, they'll take [Hollywood] all over.

—Attributed to Columbia's Harry Cohn and other studio heads

Ah, how the pendulum has swung.

Brody believes that any writer approaching the Hollywood TV business should have a portfolio with at least four scripts—a feature and three spec episodes for a current series. Instead of contacting agents directly, he believes you should contact anyone who might know an agent, because the best way to get an agent is to be referred.

He has a lot of other useful advice for writers, which is why he started TVWriter.Com. He told me: "I wanted to give back to the medium I love—television. I'm hooked on TV. I'm moved by TV. And I've been very fortunate in my relationship with TV. I've had a lot of success, but have never forgotten how rough it can be out there for a beginner. So I'm trying to give back the help I got from people like Harlan Ellison and Gene Roddenberry, as well as other, lesser-known writer/producers such as Bill Blinn and Phil Saltzman, who saw a young man with potential and believed in him enough to teach him and give him a break. I want to teach others and give them their breaks. It's the right thing to do."

If you're serious about getting started in television, start with Larry Brody's book and Web site. You'll save yourself a lot of time and puzzlement.

Animated Facts

A great many Hollywood writers break in by writing for children's shows and/or animation. One reason that has been traditionally true is that writers for such shows are paid much less than primetime writers who are Writers Guild members. It used to be that the WGA's collective bargaining strategy did not include animation. Writers for animation belonged to the Cartoonist's Guild, and comprised only about 10 percent of the membership. The Animation Writers Caucus of the WGA, founded in 1994, has changed that landscape. While some Hollywood companies are signatory to (working under agreements with) the Cartoonist's Guild, many are also signatory to the WGA. All the network primetime animated shows are covered by a WGA contract, and most animated pilots and animated feature films are done under WGA contracts.

That doesn't mean Hollywood companies are necessarily happy with the situation. Many would rather not deal with the WGA, and thus avoid paying residuals and doling out benefits to animation writers. When Nickelodeon refused to give the writers of *SpongeBob SquarePants* a WGA contract, it landed in a seemingly endless arbitration battle. Given the showdown looming between the WGA and producers as I wrote this book, I don't expect any easier going for companies such as Nickelodeon. The WGA decided to put off a strike until contracts expired for other unions. If the Screen Actors Guild supported the Directors Guild and the Writers Guild, Hollywood animation companies would grind to a halt and be forced to deal fairly with everyone like the writers for Nickelodeon. If they did not, the companies wouldn't have professional actors to do voices. If you want the latest news on animation writers and unionization, read about the WGA's Animation Writers Caucus at www.wga.org.

Since you're now informed about some problems with Nickelodeon, I should also tell you they do have a development program for new animation writers. To learn about their fellowship, contact:

Nickelodeon

Writing Fellowship Program

231 W. Olive Ave.

Burbank, CA 91502

(818) 736-3663

www.nick.com/all_nick/fellowshipprogram

According to their site, "This program stems from Nickelodeon's commitment to encouraging meaningful participation from culturally and ethnically diverse new writers. We will be offering Nickelodeon fellowships in live action and animation television. The program consists of a paid training phase, as well as two subsequent and conditional development phases . . . . No previous writing experience is necessary."

Just as writer/producers are the "heavy hitters" in primetime that mere writers aren't, an animator who also writes and/or directs is more in demand with animation companies. If you think you might be interested in that route, spend some time cruising around the Animation World Network at www.awn.com. Offering resources such as *Animation World* magazine and the book *How to Succeed in Animation* by Gene Deitch, this site is the Hollywood cornucopia for anyone interested in animation.

If you want to succeed in animation with a Hollywood company, the fact is you'll probably have to live in southern California. In the words of Porky Pig, "That's all, folks!"

Changing Faces of Television

Although I know what I've personally observed and dealt with in television over the years, I never trust only my own opinion about such a broad subject. That's why, when putting together this chapter, I wanted to go back to people I had previously interviewed to get their take on the current state of television. I started with a TV movie producer who has maintained a steady course and never changed his email address in the nearly ten years I've known him.

Mr. TV Movies

When I first met Marc Lorber, he was actively looking online for scripts from other AOL members. He wouldn't do that these days because he's become a lot more successful, producing TV and cable movies with such companies as Alliance-Atlantis, Disney Television, Hearst, Jaffe/Braunstein, and the Konigsberg Company. After a stint at Hallmark Productions, he was head of television at Phoenix Pictures, then became the last VP of Development & Production for Carlton America, the Hollywood office of a major British company. Now an independent producer of TV movies and series, Marc is also a consultant for overseas production and distribution companies, with such clients as London's Working Title, for whom he sold their first wholly U.S. television movie, *A Tale of Two Wives,* airing on the Oxygen Network.

When I checked back in with Marc, he was working on another film for Oxygen as well as scripts for the Lifetime Network and ABC Family Channel. He told me that these days, the only way an independent TV producer can survive is to align with one of the major distributors or become part of one of the major networks or studios.

"Not many production companies make TV movies regularly anymore," Marc said. "There are just a handful remaining strong. Otherwise it's all individual independent producers."

Because of the current market, he passes fairly easily and quickly on most of the material that crosses his desk. To make a decision, he asks himself two questions about any project:

1. Does it personally interest me? (Of course, it has to be commercially viable.)
2. Do I think I can sell it somewhere in the current marketplace?

Having dealt with Marc on many occasions, I know that if he sees no place to sell a project, he'll pass, no matter how much it personally appeals to him. He's very realistic about the latter half of the phrase *show business.*

He's unusual among television producers in that he'll accept short email queries from writers that might lead to a further submission of a longer synopsis and/or the actual completed, edited, and polished script.

"If a writer writes me that he has an agent," he says, "I want him to send the material through his agent, manager, or known entertainment attorney. It's just one greater step of protection for us. Still, I do accept short emails."

Another thing he'll do is try to keep a writer on board any project he sells, giving that writer at least a crack at the first revision or the first draft. Writers don't have to be Writers Guild members to sell him a project.

One thing that surprised me is that he hasn't lost his enthusiasm for TV, despite the changes in the marketplace. This holds true even when working with beginning writers. In fact, he still encourages people to work in television.

"Television is a fantastic training ground because you can often get credit and money and involvement faster than you can in features— if the project goes forward—and we normally are moving forward or are dropped in a quicker fashion that most features. More people will see a television movie or cable movie, even a poorly rated one, than everything but the top features in a year. If you want your message or your entertainment to reach the largest number of people, television is the widest medium. Records, books, features, newspapers—nothing reaches more people than television."

He believes that writers should tell the movie they want to tell, and to take all notes with a grain of salt. Everyone, he says, will have notes and changes, thoughts and concerns. The perfect property is "one the network will buy, that I can afford to produce well for the budget I'm given." The perfect writer is one who takes notes easily "but fights to a point for what they're passionate about, writes as quickly as possible dependent upon the project and its needs, is flexible, and knows good coffee houses."

As in the feature film world, TV producer Lorber will start with anything that grabs him and that he thinks is saleable. That includes articles, plays, news stories, whatever. From an unknown writer he prefers a finished script or a novel. He's had success with unknowns. He got an email from a writer who had heard him speak at a seminar, and subsequently he sold her script to Lifetime.

Despite the unquenchable enthusiasm I've seen him display over the years, Marc says that his business is harder these days. "The major broadcast networks are either not making telefilms or making far fewer of them," he told me, "so the real breadth of opportunity—admit-

I hate television. I hate it as much as peanuts. But I can't stop eating peanuts.

—Orson Welles

tedly often for fewer dollars and a smaller stake in ownership—is at the cable networks."

It doesn't matter if writers know about things like TV "Q." TV producers know who is a star and able to greenlight a project by being attached, and even then it varies depending on the network. In other words, don't try to do the producer's job.

You can reach Marc at TVMovies@aol.com.

Independent Features to Small Screen Reality

Terence Michael began his career by breaking into a studio. He simply walked onto the lot at Warner Brothers and stepped into the first production office he found. That office was the Donner Company, and he got a job interning for Lauren Shuler-Donner, producer wife of producer/director Richard Donner. Terry subsequently took a class at Pepperdine University from ICM agent Bill Robinson called "How to Enter the Film Business." In that class he learned that in Hollywood things like educational background don't matter much, that it's all about dealing with people.

He went on to work for producer Gene Kirkwood as Director of Development and, once he knew enough about the business, he found some investors, formed a corporation, and put together a movie starring Stephen Baldwin and Mary-Louise Parker. Sounds impressive, but at the time those actors "didn't mean anything to people" and the project "about four talking heads" never got made. He changed gears, "went the film festival route, raised money from foreign pre-sales, put together budgets with a little from a studio, some from private investors, some from banks," and ended up making his first independent feature. He still uses the following formula for taking a screenplay from option to film:

1. Find a great script;
2. Fix it until no one can pass on it;

3. Meet with as many directors as possible who can attract a cast of bankable actors;

4. Get the cast, which is difficult with no financing, but give them opportunities they don't usually have;

5. Get at least half the budget from foreign sales companies, who say "yes" with a check for video rights and the like.

Terry has always liked new writers because he feels they have a fresh eye even if, conceptually, their work contains elements that need to be honed by established writers. I contacted him expecting him to be making yet another independent feature. I was surprised to discover he had ventured into television.

"Although I never thought I would do TV (nothing against it, it's just an entirely different industry)," he explained, "I fell into it through interesting circumstances. First of all, two films that I made with writer/producer Richard Finney ended up on TV, even though we had full intentions of making them as large feature films. But they ended up on The Disney Channel and Lifetime, so that was a start."

Finding the production process identical to theatrical films, he decided to do some work with TV producer Yann Debonne, who was creating alternative television programming.

"It was basically documentary-type television—but sexier," Terry said. "What he did really appealed to me because where I deal in fantasy and fiction all day, he deals with real people, real ongoing problems in their lives, and real issues. Most of that kind of programming has turned into reality TV, but as a producer that just opens up the avenues of places to put product. I've now done three TV projects, which twenty years ago would have been documentaries, but are now fun, light, informative shows. NBC's *The Road to Ironman* is a perfect example. We profiled three athletes who were training for the famous triathalon race in Kona, Hawaii. I got to learn how these incredible athletes balance daily lives, yet put their bodies through the challenges of swimming 2.4 miles, biking 112 miles, and then running a marathon-length race, all in under fifteen hours! I would never get that opportunity in the film world. In film, we just make it up."

I wondered if Terry would advise someone wanting to break into the business today to start as a reader like he did. Obviously, it would be very difficult to simply walk onto a studio lot, but where should you start?

"Be an assistant to the position you someday want," he answered. "Period. It will all unfold naturally from there. And if you don't like who you're working for, find someone you do like. That makes all the difference. In hindsight, I wish I had stuck it out more and worked my way up a bit. I was very impatient and jumped off on my own too early, which threw a three-year learning curve at me, with nothing happening during those years." He laughed, thinking about it. "It was excruciating living in my parents' garage and answering the phone 'Terence Michael Productions.'"

In learning how Terry had moved into television in such a seemingly effortless fashion, it showed me once again how people who survive in Hollywood find creative outlets no matter how the market changes. If you want to read more about Terry and perhaps follow his activities, surf www.terencemichael.com.

The Entrepreneurial View

When I met the writing/directing/producing team of Martin Kunert and Eric Manes, they had just sold a TV pilot to CBS based on the FBI's Hostage Rescue Team. At the time, their TV show *Fear* had been airing on MTV since February 2000 and was the #2 show on the network after *The Osbournes*. Martin and Eric met in film school at New York University (NYU), where Martin gave up medical studies and Eric gave up business. Since the time we first met, I've spoken on panels with them and have never failed to be impressed by their prevailingly entrepreneurial attitude toward the entertainment business. Like Terence Michael, they did whatever it took to get their first movie, *Campfire Tales* (1997), on screen. The story of how their TV show came about should be a lesson for any screenwriter who has ever thought of working in television.

When I caught up with Martin anew, he and Eric were in the midst of a unique documentary. A financier approached them wanting ideas for a special project. They decided to distribute three hundred cameras to the population of Iraq so that the citizens could interview each other about the changes in the country after the fall of Saddam Hussein. The purpose was not to make a news program, but simply to see what was on the minds of Iraqis in their day-to-day life. Martin was gushing with enthusiasm about the project.

"We see graduations, birthday parties, artists working. There's some footage from an Iraqi short film festival. In one film an Iraqi is having a daydream that he's watching TV and the news comes on. It's September 11, 2001, and news of an attack on the World Trade Center. The news then cuts to supposed news footage that shows a plane flying toward the building when suddenly the building just goes *whoop* and moves out of the way and the plane misses it. A few seconds later another plane, *whoop,* and the plane misses! It's just the guy's daydream. We have Iraqis interviewing other Iraqis asking what do you want for the future? How's your life? What do you want to say to the world? We discovered many unique things."

Once they had a budget in place, they worked with a friend who is a former marine to distribute the cameras. Though the cameras are NTSC format, not the PAL standard used in Europe and Iraq, they still thought they would lose about half of them.

"We thought we would have to pay people to do it," Martin said, "but everyone was willing to do it for free. No one had been willing to listen to them. They got to express themselves. There is an organization similar to a Museum of Tolerance in Baghdad. We agreed that in five years we would donate all our footage and become a part of the national archives.

"We got shocking stuff out of there. A bunch of former prisoners under Saddam's regime got some of the cameras and they started taping what they went through, such as having electrodes wired to their penises or having their eyeballs cut out. A guy's hand was cut off because he was caught with American dollars in his pocket. They're talking about this and they're joking around! They say 'American' and 'Abu Ghraib,' that's torture, that's abuse? It's nothing. They say, 'Hey I'd love to be fondled by a female guard!'"

Word of the footage spread quickly, and Dateline NBC made an offer. The BBC tried to buy them out. Not going for instant satisfaction, they wanted to finish a cut and get it out to the Toronto Film Festival, then get the documentary into some theaters.

"The main thing is to get it onto TV," Martin said, "and so through our agents we already are in touch with the major networks. We need to put together a promo piece and show others what the heart of the project is, as did the French documentarians who reported the fall of the buildings on 9/11. We want to secure a time slot and just broadcast it. Our goal is not to make money on this, but to just get it shown."

While putting the project together, Martin and Eric found out that Iraq is the most culturally diverse country in Asia, only second to India in demographic differences. I was told this when I asked him what Iraqis thought about the war. He chuckled at the question.

"When people ask what an Iraqi thinks, it's like asking what does an American think? It's hundreds of different viewpoints. The country has three or four major languages. There's no one viewpoint. We have all these different languages on tape. There's Arabic and Turkmen, Kurdish, two different varieties of Iraqi. That country goes back ten thousand years. It's Babylon. There's a village where people still worship blue pheasants, yet Abraham was born in Iraq."

I asked Martin what he would do if he were starting his career today. Would he go about it any different way? He told me he would be more entrepreneurial.

"Ultimately you just need to go out and make films. After a while, getting agents and such, you get kind of cynical. Like I'm going to rely on my agent to get me jobs. One of the lessons we learned

Why should people go out and pay money to see bad movies when they can stay at home and see bad television for nothing?

—*Samuel Goldwyn*

recently was that you can't do that. You just have to be as entrepreneurial as possible. It's very easy to wait for my agent to make a phone call. The phone calls come in enough so that you're making a living, but you're not really progressing. It's crazy. That's why we make films, make TV shows, whatever we think is a good idea."

The team never particularly intended to venture into television. Their MTV hit *Fear* was conceived as a film.

"It was basically a film about the shooting of a pilot episode of a *Real World* type show on this island and it turns into *The Shining* and everybody is screwed. We were pitching it around town and MTV heard about it and they said why don't you make it into a real TV show? And that sounded even more interesting."

As a lesson for someone wanting to create a show for Hollywood, the point about Martin and Eric's experience is that they had made *Campfire Tales* and were thus welcome to pitch new, similar movies to companies. After they began telling people about their next proposed movie, someone at MTV heard about it and had the idea to make a reality show. Perhaps this could be seen as a lucky accident. In reality, they made their luck by creating a good reputation with a successful movie they wrote, produced, and directed.

I asked Martin about the changing face of television and how someone might break in, given the current environment. He was pensive for a moment.

"I know that reality shows have killed off a lot of TV, and that sitcoms are really suffering. So people should just be resourceful. If you can't write on a TV show, create a reality show. There are more networks out there than ever, and they're all trying to create programming. I wouldn't say go out and make your own version of a reality show, though. You just have to find a way in. The idea that you can write this great spec screenplay and suddenly make a million bucks might not be the way. I think statistically you have a better chance of winning the California lottery. So why waste time writing a script? Just buy a lottery ticket."

Martin told me they were also putting together two feature films.

As if that weren't enough, they were also doing a rewrite of a romantic comedy for Warner Bros. I wondered how they could get a writing job like that when most of their known work had to do with horror and action. (In addition to the fear-based projects, Eric directed *3000 Miles to Graceland* [2001], while Martin directed *Renegade Force* [1998].)

"It was because they had a romantic comedy already written where the hero was great but the action and suspense and other stuff needed improving. So they hired us more for action and suspense and because in one film we had a very twisted villain. That's what we brought to the project."

Just don't get the idea that the job came easily. Few of them do in Hollywood. It took six months of back-and-forth exchange of ideas between Kunert, Manes, and executives before they got the job. And although Martin is certain they could never have gotten into television or made some of their movie deals if not living in southern California, he feels you can still have a Hollywood career without living here.

"My agent told me about a client in Wisconsin. Twice a year he sends him a script. Sometimes the script is great and he sells it and the guy makes enough money to keep living in Wisconsin. And even if it doesn't sell, he's made enough money off the last project to stay in Wisconsin."

Although he stays incredibly busy, Martin told me that to really get your career into high gear you need to spend a lot of time networking in Hollywood. Unfortunately, neither of them are good at putting on a social face to schmooze (as it's known in Tinseltown).

"I don't think either of us are very comfortable at being fake friends for the sake of promoting ourselves," he said. "We hang out with people we genuinely like. Whether it's a group or buddies, whatever. It's not enough, and it kind of hurts us. Other people who are more successful are much more aggressive on a social basis. Some of these guys are such smooth great talkers, they talk themselves into a project and before that project falls apart or tanks, while it's in progress they get a second project going.

"We just write and network any which way we can. People are looking for new writers all the time. Some folks outside Hollywood have this misconception that you sell the first project and it's gravy from there on in. No. You have to sell the next one. You have to jump over a higher hurdle, then a higher hurdle. People come in and think how do I make a connection, it's so hard. You gotta figure it out, because if you can't do this you won't be able to do any of the other stuff. Luck is opportunity plus preparedness."

I dream for a

living.

—*Steven Spielberg*

Martin Kunert and Eric Manes were prepared when the opportunity came to create a show for MTV. They learned filmmaking at NYU, then learned Hollywood by living here and working the town. If you have TV aspirations, don't discount the way they began in feature films and then segued to television.

These days, it is not at all unusual for someone who makes a successful independent feature to move into TV. In case you're wondering why so many filmmakers make that transition, consider the fact that if a series runs for three years or longer, you're almost guaranteed to become a millionaire.

If, that is, you're entrepreneurial enough to do more than simply try to sell screenplays.

More Television Resources

Living in a television center, such as Los Angeles or New York, is almost mandatory for a television career, but the following Web sites might help you learn more about television career possibilities.

Academy of Television Arts & Sciences (ATAS): At www.emmys.tv you'll learn how the prime-time Emmy Awards are voted on by the ATAS membership of twenty-six television peer groups. The organization's counterpart in New York is the National Television Arts & Sciences (NATAS). NATAS administers news and sports Emmys, and via affiliated chapters in major cities awards Emmys for local programming. NATAS and ATAS work closely together on the daytime Emmys. The NATAS site is at www.emmyonline.org. The Emmys are also international in scope; see www.iemmys.tv for information on The International Academy of Television Arts & Sciences.

Classic Sitcoms: Search for your favorite episode by title, guest star, writer, director, key phrase, or airdate at www.ilovelucy.org

Hidden DVD Features: Since you're spending so much time watching television you need something to chat about, right? Take a look at dvdreview.com/html/hidden_features.shtml

Humanitas Awards: At www.humanitasprize.org you can learn about this prestigious prize given to encourage "those who create contemporary media to use their immense power in a humanistic way, to enrich as well as entertain their viewers."

Independent Film Channel: Follow the path of noteworthy independent films to television at www.ifctv.com

Jump the Shark: A look at how good TV shows go bad and when they do at www.jumptheshark.com

Reality Television Show Directory: Learn just how much reality shows dominate American TV at www.realitytvlinks.com

Sitcom Format 101: If you are determined to write situation comedies, at www.deadpan.net/sitcom you can learn the proper script format for shows you probably want to write.

So You Wanna Pitch a TV Show?: Sitcom writing is covered at www.soyouwanna.com/site/syws/sitcom/sitcomFULL.html. You'll find links to scripts and a lot of other stuff. *So You Wanna Pitch a TV Show?* will tell you what to do, once you've written that script.

Superbowl Ads: Equal time for the folks who bring America its greatest sporting event at www.superbowl-ads.com

Talk Shows: By its own billing, "The Biggest Dysfunctional Web site on The Internet" is at www.TvTalkShows.com

Television Week: Check out www.tvweek.com for the magazine that covers all aspects of modern television.

A Note to the Wise

One of my readers discovered one day that by simply calling the SciFi Channel he got through to the director of development and was able to pitch a few story ideas over the phone. Due to the continuing expansion of cable television, smart writers know that once a channel becomes profitable it wants to create its own programming. That often begins with a movie made for that channel, usually with a budget of $3 million or under. If you can write that kind of movie and it fits with the overall theme of a cable channel, you might make a sale.

Yes, even as just a screenwriter.

Each of these channels has a Web site, often with contact information. I won't try to list them all here, because by the time you read this there could be twice as many sites.

If you want a career in television, you can probably get one. I don't see anything replacing the medium any time soon.

Except of course, video games, which I'll cover in the next chapter.

CHAPTER

9

Bigger Than Hollywood: The Video Game Industry

It's my belief that players play games—large games, anyway—to have an experience that they cannot have in the real world. The thing to do first, then, is imagine the nature of that experience.

—Ernest Adams, author of
Break Into the Game Industry:
How to Get a Job Making Video Games

The North American video game business grosses $10 billion annually according to Doug Lowenstein, the president of the Electronic Software Association (ESA). That figure, which includes money spent on hardware, is more than doubled worldwide, with annual sales of more than $25 billion. Lowenstein told a crowd at the 2004 Electronic Entertainment Expo (aka "E3", see www.e3expo.com) that revenues of game hardware and software did not even include money spent on online gaming. That's a lot of eyeball time, and Hollywood's new kid on the block has changed the neighborhood.

The gaming business has passed Hollywood's movie business in economic terms, and it took away its core demographic in the process. It used to be that the phrase "males eighteen to thirty-four" was the movie audience everyone wanted to reach. Now that is the core group of game players. The average gamer is twenty-nine, and guess what? A third of gamers are women.

That's bad news for moviemakers and bad news for network television, whose ratings go down year by year as executives wonder where the viewers have gone.

The good news is that, even though writing and creating video games may be something you know nothing about, there is an ongoing confluence of games and movies, and you might be able to get in on the action as more than just a player.

I've been to countless Hollywood and publishing events over the years at the Los Angeles Convention Center, an imposing structure just south of downtown. The Convention Center offers spacious halls, decent restaurants, and ample parking. Usually it does, anyway. During the 2004 E3, parking spaces were at such a premium I had to pay $40 to park at a garage across from the Convention Center. The event was the tenth anniversary of E3 and the event attracted tens of thousands of people involved in the interactive entertainment industry, with the top companies exhibiting their newest products, and attendees participating in "three days of thought-provoking workshops and seminars." I thought I'd landed on some planet in the "Star Wars" galaxy and entered the largest video arcade in the universe.

I had a meeting at the Expo with Flint Dille and John Platten, two of the three writers of the Xbox game "The Chronicles of Riddick: Escape from Butcher Bay," whose story is a prequel to the movie starring Vin Diesel.

I began to realize how big video games had become when I started hearing from more than one producer who quit making movies to produce video games. Why, I wondered, would they do that? Then I learned that a mainstream game could cost $10 million to produce, with a staff of perhaps forty people making the game. Double that crew for the "Riddick" game, which might've cost twice as much if the game had not been made by Swedish game developer Starbreeze (www.starbreeze.com). In other words, making a video game is like making a movie in terms of personnel and cost.

The great thing about games is that they can spring from any aspect of a movie and don't really have to make much sense within the context of a film. With the "Riddick" game, the story is a prequel to a movie story sequel that started with the film *Pitch Black* (2000). Hope you can follow that.

As I toured E3 2004, I felt like I had landed in another universe that was a cross between a *Star Wars* city and a high-tech convention in Las Vegas. Suddenly, I got why all the producers I knew had left moviemaking for gaming. Hollywood is largely about money, and there is a *ton* of money in games.

Let's look at some figures. As of this writing, the average Hollywood studio movie budget is $108 million. Roughly double that figure for promotion and you'll have an idea of how many tickets have to be sold to make a studio feature profitable. In contrast, a $10 million- to $20 million-budget game has a more active word-of-mouth public. Gamers might rent a new game to play every day while seeing only one movie a week. This makes video games *very* profitable, and producers have far fewer production costs and locations than on even a small-budget movie.

Where Games and Hollywood Meet

I met the creators of the "Riddick" game via Richard Leibowitz, the President of Union Entertainment. Rich is partnered with Sean O'Keefe, the President of Union Films, and their games and movies company may be unique in Hollywood. Union was founded to give equal importance to video games and features, and business is booming. (See www.unionent.com for more information.)

If you're a screenwriter looking for another outlet for your creativity, you might be wondering how easy it is to get into this booming business. I wondered, too. After a tour of Union's offices and a note-taking lunch, I emailed Rich a list of questions to get an idea of what goes on in a company that could be a model for *all* major production companies in the future. Here's a look at how Union caught the big wave of the confluence of gaming and film.

Skip: *Does Union Entertainment ever take on a new writer or content creator? If so, what goes into the decision to sign that person?*

Rich: Writers and creators of intellectual properties are critical to films and games alike. Union Entertainment presently manages several accomplished writers and a limited number of highly skilled content creators. We are extremely selective in our management choices. On the production side, Union is open to anyone— established or not—with a great concept or script on which the Union team can collectively decide to get behind.

Skip: *Please tell me something about the background of yourself and other principals of the company.*

Rich: Prior to forming Union, Sean was a senior producer at Artists Production Group, the feature film production arm of Michael Ovitz's Artists Management Group (AMG). I represented many world-class video game development companies, following stints at Paramount Pictures and Rysher Entertainment.

Skip: *What can you tell me about the merging of film and games that is going on, and what prompted you two to put together what could be a one-of-a-kind company?*

Rich: Both creative and financial factors are driving a collision between the two mediums. On the creative front, Hollywood always needs new ideas, worlds, and characters, and the game industry attracts the best creative talent in the world. Conversely, the film industry has the storytelling expertise that games historically have lacked. Union was formed to bridge the game creators and filmmakers.

On the financial front, increasing game budgets demand that publishers work on licenses with broad market awareness. Co-releasing films and games guarantees a major marketing push behind the franchise.

It is worth noting, however, that not all great films are great ideas for games (*American Beauty*, 1999) and not all great games make good films (*Gran Turismo*, 1998). Because of this, Union is structured so that both divisions can work independently on the best franchises in their respective medium.

Never treat your audience as customers, always as partners.

—Jimmy Stewart

Skip: *How do you folks assess whether a property should be a game first or a movie? Do you ever go for both possibilities at the same time?*

Rich: If both the film and the game divisions believe in a project creatively, then we almost always begin development of the film and game concurrently, cross-pollinating the best talent in both mediums. This not only leads to superior story and characters, but also synchronizes the development cycles for day-and-date release. It is worth noting that because the game production cycle is longer, it will often seem like we are leading with the game. However, the story will have already been developed by a Hollywood screenwriter.

Skip: *Just how busy are you in an average day?*

Rich: To give you a better idea about what the seven-person team at Union is working on: (a) Union Management currently represents nearly a dozen developers, content creators, and writers,

(b) Union Games is in various stages of development for more than thirty projects, and (c) Union Films is producing more than two dozen movies while, at the same time, writing two original scripts of their own. You can say we keep pretty busy.

Skip: *You told me over lunch that video games are moving from a $10 million, forty-person operation into a $20 million, eighty-person operation. Does that mean the big players like Electronic Arts (EA) will be able to spend small players out of business?*

Rich: Yes, and in many instances, that is already the case. I think the best way to understand the path of the game industry is to look at it as analogous to Hollywood. In much the same way that Hollywood has been stratified with large studios at the top surrounded by several smaller niche-based production houses, it would not surprise me to see an industry dominated by a relatively small number of the large publishing houses—the EAs, the THQs, the Activisions, and a few others—while leaving room for the smaller, niche-based publishers such as Steam with its *Half-Life 2* (2004) licensing model.

The major difference between the Hollywood model and what is happening in the game industry, is that Hollywood organically evolved over a period of roughly eighty years, whereas the games business is maturing at about eight times the Hollywood pace.

Skip: *Are there any current trends going on in gaming that you think might dominate, such as ascendance of female leads, Xbox online playing, and the like?*

Rich: Of course, technology is always improving, which allows games to move ever closer to reality. From the content side, the dominant trend is to develop and release games and films simultaneously.

This latter point indicates the greater respect and consideration games are garnering from their Hollywood counterparts. The involvement of talent such as John Woo, Vin Diesel, and Robert Rodriguez—and the success of companies such as Union—emphasizes some of the ways the two communities are truly merging. Also, as game and film budgets continue to balloon, studios and publishers are looking for ways to piggyback on each other and release properties across the two mediums and take advantage of the same marketing expenditures.

Two more trends I'd note here: (a) games will become increasingly more non-linear and open-ended, which augments players' game-play options and involvement in the game's "world"; and (b) the popularity of online gaming will continue to grow as broadband technologies proliferate.

Skip: *Are there any more factors that people new to the industry might want to know?*

Rich: The increasing budgets in the game industry will create two more global trends worth pointing out: (a) game companies will look to make fewer gambles and therefore will become more selective with regards to their projects and talent; and (b) we are bound to see a proliferation of co-financing models as publishers look to offset some of their financial burdens and spread their risk across more properties.

I hope that gives you a good overview of what is going on in southern California gaming. With the largest game company in the world located just down the beach from Union Entertainment, you can be assured that Hollywood and gaming will be associated in a big way for years to come.

Multi-Faceted Game Creators

While it's great to get an overview of the gaming business and know about companies such as Union (I'm sure there will be many others by the time you read this), what really matters is how you go about getting into gaming. That means learning basics, then seeing if your talents translate to the medium.

It also means meeting the people. Gaming is as much a people business as the film industry. Here's a perfect example. I was managed by the aforementioned AMG of Michael Ovitz. I'm now managed by The Gotham Group, which like Sean O'Keefe, spun off from AMG. My introduction to Union Entertainment came from Peter McHugh at Gotham Group. Through Rich Leibowitz, I met Flint Dille and John Platten, two of the three creators of the "Riddick" game. Their company, Bureau of Film & Games (BFG) was formed "to create and develop intellectual properties that become franchises across multiple media." In short, if it can't be big, they're not interested. Considering their backgrounds, such aspirations are not unrealistic.

When I got together with Flint and John at E3, BFG had the following games in production or release: *Batman: Rise of Sin Tzu, Mission: Impossible, Crimson Skies, Red Ninja, Dead Rush, Tribes Vengeance, Constantine,* and *Scooby-Doo 2005.* Three of their properties have been optioned for films, the most prominent being *Backwater* (an original survival-horror property), which Dimension Films had optioned. Dille and Platten were attached as producers, with the script being written by Kevin Williamson (*Scream,* 1996) and Jim Gillespie (*I Know What You Did Last Summer,* 1997) attached to direct.

In case you're thinking these are young Turks, be advised that Flint Dille's credits go back twenty years. He's written just about everything you can think of, from comic books to animation to television to "Dungeons & Dragons" games. He even worked on *Scooby-Doo* (2002). Since it was obvious that he could float freely across disciplines, I asked him if it mattered in which medium a property is first launched.

"It doesn't matter at all. If the core idea is strong, the project can start anywhere and port over to different media with ease. For example, we all know *Spider-Man* started out as a comic book, but has flourished as a television show, a movie, a toy line, and a video game. When *Spider-Man* was created, comics were one of the few places you could do a superhero property, but that isn't true anymore. If *Spider-Man* came out today, it wouldn't matter much what medium it debuted in."

I found John Platten to be an equally experienced producer knowledgeable in all aspects of production: budgeting, breakdowns, scheduling, personnel, post-production, and programming management. His comprehensive resume includes a seven-year stint at Universal Studios working on such TV shows as *Jake and the Fatman, Matlock, Perry Mason Mysteries,* and *The New Lassie.* John elaborated on the broad view of any project created by BFG.

"With each property we create we try and envision how it will be able to live in multiple media," John said. "Once we've got the initial idea down, and agree that it is something we are excited about, we immediately go through the process of trying to see it as a game, a comic book, a film, a TV series. If we are creating a family-friendly property, we try and think what the 'happy meal' prize from our movie will look like. If you can see that, you know that you have a concept with mass appeal. We aren't as concerned by which medium is the first out of the gate. Getting a film made is the most difficult, and usually has the longest development time to get greenlit, so if we can get a game up and running, we see that as beneficial to the larger franchise we are creating."

Given all the people who work on major games, I wondered if "too many chiefs" could hurt. Flint explained it: "Bad projects usually happen when there is a muddy, conflicting or shifting vision—when people on the project are fighting over what it should be. Too many players leave or join a team, an executive does the 'swoop and poop' (flies in, messes up a project, and flies out), or the people doing the project simply lose their vision of it."

John feels that problems can be circumvented by how people

Failure is inevitable. Success is elusive.

—Steven Spielberg

sign on to a project. Intermediaries and experience help: "We have great representatives, and their help and guidance is invaluable in getting deals. However, both of us have been doing this for quite a while now, and we have a pretty extensive network of decision-makers. For games, what we do is fairly specialized, and most of that work comes through personal recommendations."

I wondered if among all the hits they'd created or worked on, Flint and John had personal favorites. After all, I've seen many people in Hollywood surprised when one thing is a hit, then disappointed when something they were sure would be a hit was not.

"My favorite remains *Fear Effect* (2000)," John said. "It was a chance to try so many different things with story, character, and design. I also have a place in my heart for *Johnny Mnemonic* (1995),which was a glorious failure for a number of reasons. The game was really one of the first true pieces of interactive cinema. I still look on it fondly."

The question prompted much more reflection from Flint on what makes a hit and how flops occur.

"For me, there are a lot of projects I walked away feeling extremely good about. The video games that stand out are *Soviet Strike* and *Nuclear Strike* a long time ago on the Playstation 1. *Dead to Rights* worked out well (and is now in development as a feature film). I loved doing *Batman: Rise of Sin Tzu. Riddick* is looking good; *Constantine* could be great; *Dead Rush* has huge potential. As far as board games, I am especially proud of "Buck Rogers: Battle for the Future" and "Line in the Sand." Gary Gygax and I wrote some fun interactive novels (the Sagard Series). They did OK sales wise, and I've always wanted to bring that character back. *Transformers* as a TV show always had hit written all over it; our whole mission was to keep it going. Same thing with *G.I. Joe.* The movie was a hit on DVD. It went platinum instantly. In those days, nobody knew what to do with an animated movie.

"Usually, when you're working on a flop, you know it. Something goes horribly wrong in production and the rest of the process is a death march. I'd say it is a lot like the first line of *Anna Karenina*—'All great projects are the same, all rotten projects are rotten for their own reasons.' The thing that seems to be common with great projects is that they start with a vision and the vision never changes; it gets refined, expanded, edited, but the initial impulse is reflected in the final project.

"All of that having been said, every project hits rough spots. I've yet to work on a game that doesn't have to be shortened. The design documents are always too ambitious. Also, some projects, which seem to be in horrible shape, snap into focus.

"I've got some projects I wish would come back to life. I designed *Hyperwar* with John Warden, the architect of the air campaign in the first Gulf War and it went into submission around the time our third publisher died underneath us. John and I have a project at EA that we wish would come back to life called *Dead Center*. It would make a great movie as well as game. What can you do?"

Given his lengthy response about projects across so many years and media, I asked Flint if he had any suggestions on how someone new to the business might break in. Was it even possible for a screenwriter to make the leap?

"Frankly, it takes a long time," he said. "You have to be a hybrid game designer and screenwriter. That means you must study both disciplines, as both John and I have. That being said, there will be hundreds of movie tie-in games written in the next few years, and somebody will be writing them."

John was even more encouraging and instructive in the process of gamewriting:

"This may sound counterintuitive, but I believe that it is actually a little easier now than in the earlier days of game development. The game industry has come to realize how important quality storytelling, compelling characters, realistic dialogue, and so forth is to their titles. It used to be that designers or even the receptionist would write the stories. But now, when you have major Hollywood talent involved and budgets that can match or exceed some small films, the need for professional writers has become obvious.

"The same basic storytelling skills that make a good screenwriter make a good gamewriter. However, there is a unique 'skill-set' that you need to write for games. In general, game narratives are fast-paced because you are using the story not as an end in itself, but to support another component of the experience that will have the dominant role . . . the gameplay. You may write a brilliant character study that goes on for five minutes, but no matter how genius it may be, the player is going to start trying to figure out how to button past it within thirty seconds, because his expectation is to play the game. Narrative sequences need to keep the player engaged, so they usually happen at major plot points. The game is what happens between them. Dialogue may have to convey hints to the player about how to meet an objective in the game, remind you of characters that you won't see again for a couple of levels, establish the tools you have at your disposal, and so forth. And it all has to be done in an elegant way that makes the entire experience feel unified and seamless.

"The difference between traditional screenwriting and gamewriting is in understanding the unique needs of the talent, the developer, and the publisher within the game development process. As the game business matures, the same innate understanding of story structure and characters that writers use in traditional media will become more valued. The opportunities will be there for people who have taken the time to study games and are able to transfer their skills to game scripts."

The first game scenario I saw at Union Entertainment was *Backwater* from Dille and Platten. Although a script for a game might run two hundred pages or more, the document I saw reminded me of the days in Hollywood when treatments were being purchased, with illustrations for key elements of the proposed movie. Supposedly, New Line was sold on *Backwater* by seeing the sketch of the villain alone.

If you want to sell games and know any comic book artists, better give them a call.

"*Backwater* was initially created as a survival/horror game pitch,"

John told me. "However, as we do with all our game ideas, we scripted both a key cinematic and about ten minutes of gameplay. By that, I mean that we wrote a narrative description of the game experience within screenplay format. This allows us to communicate our vision for the game, which may include some complex concepts, into something that is accessible to producers and executives. On *Backwater,* this scripted sequence included introducing our main villain, our heroine, and the mythology of the horror experience we were creating. So while it was tailored to gaming, there was plenty within the document that looked like a script to the film industry. And this is what Dimension responded to, as they were looking for a new horror franchise, and were able to see elements that excited them within the game documentation."

Flint teaches game design at a school in southern California, and he and John were developing a book (or maybe two) on the subject when we got together. What struck me about both men was the breadth of their knowledge across many fields, not just in media. Flint, who has a degree in ancient history, feels that he patched together his knowledge of gamewriting slowly, but thinks that in the future learning the craft will become easier.

"The discipline is beginning to define itself," he said, "but the basic premise doesn't change. Prepare. Learn your craft. Practice your art and learn things, even if you don't see any relevance at the moment. Learn them simply because they interest you. It never occurred to me that ancient history was going to be a good career choice. I was just fascinated by it. You have to prepare yourself any way you can."

The E3 I attended has a hugely international flavor. While it might not be so easy to break into writing Hollywood movies from outside the United States, that is not true with video games. Consider the BFG experience:

"In the past year," John told me, "we've worked (or are working with) developers in Sweden, the U.K., Canada, and Japan, as well as developers located in two other states. This is pretty common. Game development is global, and with teleconferencing and email, we can virtually go wherever the job takes us. It's our experience that gamers speak a universal language, regardless of where they are located. Unlike features, where you see very distinctive styles depending on where the film was made, in games this is usually not the case."

I found almost four hundred exhibitor profiles with names, full contact information, and descriptions in the back of the Official Exhibit Guide of the 2004 Expo. They ranged from 1C Company in Moscow (http://int.games.1c.ru) to Zoo Digital Publishing in Sheffield, U.K. (www.zoodigitalpublishing.com). The Guide was published by Prima Games (www.primagames.com).

You'll also find plenty of useful information by visiting www.gamasutra.com. There you'll learn about "The Art and Science of Making Games" and things like "How to Break into the Video Game Industry" conferences put on by The Game Initiative (www.thegameinitiative.com).

In his address at E3 2004, Doug Lowenstein said that handheld and mobile gaming was the new frontier ahead. He spoke about a *Star Wars*–like smartphone with global positioning capabilities and wireless gaming as well. Since I haven't yet seen a device quite like that, I could only wonder what kind of games could be developed for it. With $25 billion on the table each year, though, I'm sure it'll be figured out by the next E3.

If you make it to southern California for that event, you'll see more games and meet avid gamers from every continent. I apologize in advance for what you'll have to pay for parking. And if you sell a game, I hope you don't have an executive in charge of the project who does, as Flint Dille would say, a "swoop and poop" on you.

Now let's look at yet another aspect of how the southern California entertainment business has become a crossroads of international activity. Although it has a prominent sign and a very real geographical location, Hollywood is a state of mind, one that encompasses creative people of all lands and cultures.

CHAPTER

10

Hollywood
Around the World

What in fact has been created? An international community. A perfect blueprint for world order. When the sides facing each other suddenly realize that they're looking into a mirror, they'll see that this is the pattern for the future.

—"Number Two" (actor Leo McKern) in The Prisoner (1967)

For years, I've been telling people that Hollywood is as much a state of mind as it is a geographical location. On a daily basis I'll hear from someone who has read a column I wrote for *Scriptwriter* magazine in the U.K., or a reader of one of my books in Russian, or a student in Australia, Italy, Japan, or another country. As I began writing this book, I sent an email to a friend, asking for an interview. I thought she might be back from the Netherlands, where she had been scouting locations, but she'd come and gone. When she replied to my message she was working on a production in Shanghai, a place she said was "becoming the new back lot for Hollywood." Then she came back to southern California and I thought we'd get together, but she had to leave for that festival in Cannes, France.

This type of story is not an isolated instance in my life. There's no telling where I'll find one of my Hollywood friends, week to week. Thus, I don't have to count on news articles or television to learn what's going on in international filmdom. I get the straight opinion from "my peeps" (that's "people" in urban slang).

All the Hollywood professionals I know have a lot in common with the aspiring screenwriters I hear from. They all love movies and want to make a living making them. And the most prominent movies in the world generally originate in Hollywood. That's why so many amateurs I've known who have achieved Hollywood success have generally only done so after spending time in L.A. I don't hesitate on advising them to come here because I know they'll have a better chance. When their talent matches the needs of the town and they commit themselves to at least a trip to Hollywood, there's a chance for a breakthrough.

This chapter will cover Hollywood's foreign connections, but it's not only for international readers. Good film stories work in just about any culture, and some great movies can *change* local culture. My favorite story of Hollywood influence came from a Tunisian filmmaker. He went into a mud hut in the middle of Africa and gasped when he saw John Travolta in a white suit and classic disco pose. It was the poster for *Saturday Night Fever* (1977), a movie the hut's owner thought was fantastic.

Hollywood filmmaking differs from filmmaking in other places only in the way the stories are told. I don't ask people outside the U.S. to conform to Hollywood standards, but I insist they be aware of them. Conversely, I try to tell my North American readers and students as much as I can about what goes on around the world. I talk about Hollywood basics, but I might also mention a film by Luis Bunuel, Federico Fellini, Akiro Kurosawa, Luc Besson, or John Woo. Hollywood is always open to new ideas, and what most ordinary moviegoers don't realize is that, increasingly, many of those ideas come from outside the United States.

Any person starting out in film, no matter where he or she lives, needs to keep the international audience in mind. That includes not just knowing what non–U.S. audiences like, but watching movies made outside North America. I'm not sure I needed to look inside the lives of Scottish heroin addicts as I did watching *Trainspotting* (1996), but I certainly enjoyed taking a look at a lonely middle-aged man in Japan via Sofia Coppola's *Lost in Translation* (2003). And for pure cinematic vision and thrills, I've seen few Hollywood films in recent years that matched *The Fifth Element* (1997), *Run Lola Run* (1998), or *Crouching Tiger Hidden Dragon* (2000).

If I were trying to break into Hollywood today, I would make a point of watching as many foreign films as possible. I would even read books about screenwriting from other lands. Yves Lavandier offers useful insights in the French-language *La Dramaturgie* and (unlike some screenwriting gurus) is also a writer/director. If you look up his *Oui Mais . . .* (2001) at http://imdb.com/title/tt0246278 you'll see that one viewer thought this was the best movie about therapy ever made. Of course, we don't know if this was posted by Mssr. Lavandier's cousin, but if the movie is that good, why not remake it in English?

Who knows, a foreign film might inspire you enough to create a billion-dollar franchise. That's partially what happened to George Lucas, who drew from many influences to create *Star Wars* (1977); the main one was probably the Akira Kurosawa film *Kakushi toride no san akunin* (aka *The Hidden Fortress*, 1958). Lucas even considered the star of that movie, the late great Toshiro Mifune, to play the Master Jedi Obi-Wan Kenobi. And it's not just foreign movies that have great influence for U.S. filmmakers. The "Jedi" name came from the Japanese words "Jidai Geki" (period drama), a TV soap opera set in the days of the samurai warriors.

So let's take a quick tour of the film world of today; maybe you'll get some great ideas that I'll be enjoying over popcorn a few years hence.

The saving grace of the cinema is that with time and patience and a little love, we may arrive at that wonderfully complex creature which is called man.

—Jean Renoir

Ailing Europe, Healthy Russia

Cinema attendance within the member states of the European Union was down an estimated 5 percent in 2003. While video games and other distractions might explain some of that decline, European movies haven't exactly been breaking new ground. I say this despite a year 2000 one billion Euro fund for film and television projects by companies in the European Union. When MEDIA Plus, the European Union group responsible for development, production, and promotion of European film, changed its guidelines to provide funding only for slates of films, it took away incentive from independent filmmakers who often think of only one project at a time. Of course, that's the kind of thing that happens in places where people prefer a government-guaranteed market over a free market. The European approach seems to be increasingly concentrated along socialist lines, and great film has rarely been created under such atmospheres.

After the war in Iraq began, French enthusiasm for American film seemed to concentrate only on those American filmmakers and actors who were the most vocally opposed to the Republican administration of George W. Bush. This culminated in Michael Moore winning the Palme d'Or, the top award of the Cannes Film Festival, for *Fahrenheit 9/11* (2004). (Naturally, it didn't hurt Moore that fellow American self-styled rebel Quentin Tarantino headed up the Cannes jury.) It's too bad that so much French attention seemed to be caught up in political matters, because French cinema of recent years could use substantial improvement. Except for occasional masterpieces such as *Le Fabuleux destin d'Amélie Poulain* (simply *Amelie* in the U.S., 2001) by Jean-Pierre Jeunet, or anything by Luc Besson, the great tradition of innovative French filmmakers is suffering.

Meanwhile, the German market, previously a force unto itself regarding consumption of Hollywood product, became a morass over the last few years when some of its largest media companies fell into financial difficulty. Things still aren't exactly booming in Berlin; in fact the soul of Germany seems depressed. In May 2004, German President Johannes Rau claimed that Germans were suffering from "collective depression" with little faith in their government and a fear of the future.

Nevertheless, any English-speaking person hoping to sell a property to anyone in Europe is probably best attempting a German sale over any other country in the EU. Andreas Gruenberg (see www.gruenbergfilm.com) brokers North American writers to Euro companies, as does Script House (see www.scripthouse.de). Another possibility, if you have a film story based in Germany, is Nordmedia Funds GmbH, a joint media company of the German Federal States of Lower Saxony and Bremen. With a budget of around 10 million Euros per year to create more productions in Lower Saxony and Bremen, they offer script and project development possibilities and much more (see www.nordmedia.de).

German companies also have a substantial presence in Hollywood, most prominent being Constantin Films, which buys controversial projects like *Pope Joan,* the story of a woman who ruled over Christendom in the ninth century A.D. (the book sold three million copies and was a German bestseller). Just don't try selling Germans on Nazi content; it's still a sore point with most of the country's residents.

Veteran readers of my books may recognize that the European information offered here is pretty much the same as what I reported in my last book. There is, however, now a much better "one-stop shop" to find information about film, TV, and video activities in Europe. The European Audiovisual Observatory at www.obs.coe.int offers much worthwhile information, including ever-important data on European intellectual property and media law.

The most excitement in recent European cinema has come, surprisingly enough, from the new wave of filmmakers in Russia. What a little freedom can do, eh? Or maybe it's my *Complete Idiot's Guide to Screenwriting,* Russian version? (A little joke there, indulge me.) When Andrei Zvyagintsev's *Vozvrashcheniye* (*The Return,* 2003) won the

Golden Lion at the Venice Film Festival, international film critics lauded the type of kudos reserved for Russian film pioneers like Eisenstein. This independent film, the first from the Siberian director, was made with a budget of only $405,000 and earned a 2004 Golden Globe nomination in the foreign-language film category.

According to *The Hollywood Reporter*, the collapse of the USSR in December 1991 forced filmmakers to find their own sources of financing and removed restrictions on subject matter. Russian appetites for homegrown films skyrocketed, and four of the nation's ten highest-grossing movies in 2003 were first-time films from local filmmakers. As of late March 2004, *Vozvrashcheniye* had been sold to more than sixty-five territories for minimum guarantees of $1.3 million. A three-time return for a first-time director? Not bad in any land.

A fascinating collaboration between French and Russian filmmakers led to the movie *Est-Ouest* (*East-West,* 1999), co-written and directed by Régis Wargnier. Set in 1946, it is based on Stalin's invitation to Russian émigrés to come back to the motherland. Stalin then orders a shipload of arrivals from France victimized, and only a physician and his family are spared execution or prison. Distributed in the U.S. by Sony Classics, the film was nominated for an Academy Award for Best Foreign Language Film. Read about it at www.sonyclassics.com/east-west/director/interview.html; the director's description of events is a blueprint for anyone wanting to film in Russia.

Additional European (and African) Web sites follow. Don't be surprised if they're not written in English, but you can always translate whole Web pages via AltaVista's Babelfish at http://babelfish.altavista.com/babelfish/tr.

Association of German Screenwriters aka *Verband deutscher Drehbuchautoren* (www.drehbuchautoren.de)—A professional organization; site in German

Association of Italian Cinema & Television Writers aka *Scrittori Associati di Cinema e Televisione Italiani, SACT* (www.sact.it)—Site in Italian

> *We all steal but if we're smart we steal from great directors. Then, we can call it influence.*
>
> **—Krzysztof Kieslowski**

Cineuropa (www.cineuropa.org)—A cornucopia of European film information

Companies in Film (www.filmbyen.com)—A collection of links and email addresses to top Scandinavian film companies

Danske Dramatikeres Forbund (www.dramatiker.dk)—The Danish Playwrights and Screenwriters Guild

European Film Academy (www.europeanfilmacademy.org)—Home of the European Film Awards

EuroScreenwriters & European Film (www.euroscreenwriters. tsx.org)—A simple site with many helpful links

Euroscript Consultancy (www.euroscript.co.uk)—A script development company working in ten European countries to provide "one-to-one development programmes, international workshops, and a biannual Film Story Competition encouraging original new screen and TV ideas from new and established writers"

Euro VR (www.eurovr.com)—Virtual Reality panoramas of places in Europe using QuickTime VR technology

Federation of German film and Fernsehdramaturgen VeDRA aka *German Cinema* (www.german-cinema.de)—Official trade association for the promotion of the export of German films

Italian Writers (www.sceneggiatori.com)—The first Web site for Italian screenwriters (in Italian, of course)

Futureshock (www.futureshock.co.za)—Internet information specialists offering writing jobs and resources for writers that include the South African Writer's Network

The English Manner

While English filmmaking might not be booming, it's not for lack of trying on the part of writers and filmmakers. Scriptwriting opportunities are diverse in the U.K. and it's not uncommon to see original "one-off" programming or limited-run TV series. The unfortunate thing is that the British Broadcasting Company (BBC) tends to provide most U.K. scriptwriting jobs and filmmakers' orientation leans toward the publicly funded. It used to be that various ITV franchises broadcast original teleplays or telefilms on a weekly basis. The BBC was known for its *Play for Today* series, contemporary dramas reflecting changes in British society, as well as the "Film of the Week" which was more wide-ranging and adventurous. BBC shows have no commercial interruption, while ITV shows have commercials mid-program and at the end. That meant the ITV shows had a clear two-act structure. You don't see as much violence in U.K. television, but you see a lot more openness about sex, so it's a different scene than American TV.

Story editors in the U.K. have traditionally been hungry for new writers and material, and many who started in TV went on to film careers, like their U.S. counterparts. The English film industry, however, never seems to be able to move into high gear, despite the great competency of its writers, talents, and crews. So most of the opportunities remain in television and, more specifically, the BBC. If you're interested in working for them contact:

> BBC Recruitment
> PO Box 7000
> London, England W1A 6GJ
> Phone: 0870 333 1330
> Textphone: (020) 7765 1192
> Email: Recruitment@bbc.co.uk

They also have regular talent competitions, all of which are copiously explained at www.bbc.co.uk/talent. If you'd like a good overview of how people begin writing for the BBC, you'll find a great deal of information on this site.

In the last five years, London has also become a hotbed of instruction for hopeful writers and filmmakers from all over Europe. This has led to a groundswell of independent filmmaking. A good acquaintance of mine, Charlie Harris, freelanced for the BBC before moving on to documentaries, TV drama, and features. His directorial debut, *Paradise Grove* (2003), came about after he and some fellow writers put together the London Screenwriters Workshop (www.paradisegrove.co.uk). Now renamed Screenwriters Workshop, it puts on events that are regularly attended by writers from across Europe. Charlie once clarified for me what he thought was the difference in American films and their English counterparts:

"It has been said that a typical American film has one act where the hero is stuck and two acts where he tries do something about it (and succeeds). A typical British film has two and a half acts where the hero is stuck and half an act where he tries to do something about it (and fails)! More seriously, differences in structure seem related more to the genre or subject of the film than to the country of origin.

"What I notice is that American films, whether mainstream or indie, tend to be much quicker to establish the essentials and move into story. It's noticeable that when I show examples of character development from U.S. movies, I often find myself showing the title sequence! Two clips that I like to use are the openings of *Tender Mercies* (1983) written by Horton Foote and directed by Bruce Beresford, and John Sayles's *Passion Fish* (1992). Neither are exactly fast-moving films in the conventional sense, but both have firmly established the situation and the basics of their central characters by the time the final title has faded off the screen, allowing the story to get under way with minimum fuss. European films (I include British here) tend to be more indulgent. However, there are excellent examples of exceptions to this rule."

Differences aside, an officer of the Writers Guild of Great Britain once told me that the real problem in the U.K. was a lack of quality scripts. He blamed that on not having "a proper film industry, just a few jobbing producers." Which meant, of course, that it was very hard to make a living in the U.K. as a screenwriter. Given the quality of many English films in recent years and the plethora of workshops offered there and in Europe by both American and European instructors, I tend to believe the quality of U.K. scripts has risen greatly.

The best overview of the U.K. and Euro screenwriting scene that I've encountered is described in the book *How to Make Money Scriptwriting* by Julian Friedmann. It's available at www.amazon.co.uk and at the Screenwriters Store Ltd. (www.screenwritersstore.co.uk). I'm a columnist for Julian's bimonthly magazine, *Scriptwriter,* and am consistently impressed by what my friends across the Atlantic have to say. Julian, who is also an agent, told me at one point that there are "ten thousand film scripts doing the rounds in the U.K. at any one time," yet only around one hundred movies made in the U.K. each year. While that could be depressing to think about, it's not that much different, ratiowise, than in the U.S.

Writing movies set in the U.K. and working with British filmmakers and writers has appealed to me for a long time. Shortly before writing this chapter, a British friend sent me a screenplay she'd written based on a jointly created treatment. By the time you read this and send me an email, we may have sold it, so I'm typing with crossed fingers. If you have similar aspirations, here are a number of Web resources that might help you navigate the U.K. film and TV scene.

BBC Education Learning Zone (www.bbc.co.uk/education/lzone/master/links.shtml)—Offers some links to American schools as well

Breaking Down The Door Of The U.K. Market (www.screentalk.biz/art027.htm)—Excellent article by Matthew Ogborn, a working U.K. screenwriter

Directors Guild of Great Britain (www.dggb.co.uk)—Union for British directors across all media

Mandy.com Film/TV Jobs (www.mandy.com)—Jobs all over the world, including the U.S., from a U.K.–based site

Media UK (www.mediauk.com)—Independent media directory for the U.K. with extensive links and discussions

Netribution (www.netribution.co.uk)—Extensive U.K. film news, features, statistics, and festival information

New Producers Alliance (www.npa.org.uk)—Training, advice, and networking for emerging filmmakers with a free weekly email newsletter

Raindance (www.raindance.co.uk)—A production company, a festival of independent film in London, and year-round training in low-budget filmmaking

Rocliffe Forum (www.rocliffe.com)—Script showcase connecting established industry professionals with emerging writers and filmmakers

ScreenLab (www.screen-lab.co.uk)—Development and executive training for directors, producers, and script editors

The Screenwriter's Store (www.screenwriterstore.co.uk)—Purveyors of screenwriting software, magazines, and books

Screenwriters Workshop (www.lsw.org.uk)—Seminars and workshops for screenwriters in cinema and TV, run by writers for writers

Life is a tragedy when seen in close up, but a comedy in long shot.

—Charles Chaplin

Talent Circle/UK Filmmakers' Network (www.talentcircle.co.uk)
—The U.K.'s only completely free resource for the community of
emerging independent filmmakers, crew, and artists

UK Arts (www.artshub.co.uk)—Collection of resources for
people who work in the arts; offers news, jobs, and events

UK Film Council (www.filmcouncil.org.uk)—British govern-
ment-backed agency for film in the U.K.

Writers Guild of Great Britain (www.writers.org.uk)—Surprisingly, membership could be open to U.S. writers with few credits, thus
enabling them to in effect be members of the Writers Guild of America
via cooperating agreements

Writersroom (www.bbc.co.uk/writersroom)—The BBC's New
Writing Initiative

Writing for Performance (www.writing.org.uk)—Web site by
Robin Kelly with lots of tips for writers, particularly sitcom writers

Blame Canada

One of the first things Arnold Schwarzenegger wanted to accomplish as
governor of California was to stop "runaway production" from the
Golden State. To that end, he appointed Hollywood buddies Clint Eastwood and Danny DeVito to help figure out ways to keep more movies
in California. That's not easy, because in my last book I reported that
fifty-plus features were made in Toronto and Montreal in the summer
of 2000. Production has not slowed down since, and the reasons are
simple:

a. More value for the money with the Canadian dollar weaker than its U.S. counterpart;

b. Ample crew and talent in Canadian production centers; and

c. Direct financial remuneration for filming there.

One producer who was filming a TV show explained to me that every time he completed a project in Canada, he was handed a check for 18 percent of the budget. Contrast that to California, where you might get union fines and workman's compensation insurance costs that would *add* 18 percent to the budget. Top that with more expensive filming in California, and it's not hard to understand why people film in Canada.

The main creative consideration in Canadian production is "Canadian content." Canadian federal tax incentives instituted in 1996 allow rebates of up to 25 percent of labor costs and can cover as much as 12 percent of a film's total budget, providing that a certain number of key people in the production must originate from Canada. If you're a Canadian writer, you benefit. Otherwise, you might discover that our screenplay suddenly needs rewriting by a Canadian screenwriter. Fortunately, Canada has produced a number of talented actors, and crews in Canada are highly competent, so "Canadian content" is a good thing, except for American talent that get cut out of that loop.

It's been estimated that more than a third of the films made in North America are filmed in Canada. Partially because of that, when filming *Mystic River* (2003), Clint Eastwood insisted on shooting in Boston rather than a Canadian pretender city. His move was applauded by the Film and Television Action Committee (www.ftac.net), which is a Los Angeles–based activist organization working to halt runaway production.

While Canada has enjoyed many fat years thanks to Hollywood producers, it might have trouble in the future due to Hollywood backlash and Governor Schwarzenegger's efforts to keep production in California. Runaway production is such a hot topic it caused an upset in an election at Local 600 of the International Cinematographers Guild. Gary Dunham was elected president of this prominent Hollywood labor union by a 52–48 percent margin over Stephen Lighthill. Dunham stressed the need for confrontation over runaway production that included more than simply waiting for federal legislation.

Despite problems that might arise over production, Canada is doing well. It is the world's most "wired" country and Canadian film-makers continue to impress. The winner of the Best Foreign Film Oscar in 2004 went to Canadian Denys Arcand for his French-language *Les Invasions Barbares* (aka *The Barbarian Invasions,* 2003). And now that I mentioned that, here's a little story about the open nature of Canadians.

A client of mine wrote a script that was quirky, human, touching, and had French content. "You need to get that to Denys Arcand," I told him. I even chased down the contact information for him. Did he do it? No, because he is not a professional and does not live in Hollywood and doesn't know that you have to act on instincts and advice from Holly-wood veterans.

The next week, Arcand thanked the Academy as he accepted his Oscar. Five minutes later I got an email from my friend. It started out, "Damn!" Now, most directors would then be out of reach, unwilling to talk to mere mortal screenwriters after winning an Oscar, wouldn't you think? Not in Canada. The next week, after waiting for some hoopla to die down, I called Arcand's producer and talked to her assistant. Within a couple of days, she was reading my friend's script as a possible project for Arcand.

In addition to being friendly, Canadians love movies as much as their American cousins. Attendance at Canadian movie theaters in 2003 set a record of 125.7 million, according to Statistics Canada. The figure was 5.4 percent higher than the last survey of Canadian moviegoing habits. The government agency pointed out that attendance rose despite the fact that the number of screens fell by 284 due to theater closings.

I admit a fondness for Canadians; I've actually never met one I didn't like. And since a reviewer for the Writers Guild of Canada said one of my books was the best of its kind, I will not "blame Canada" no matter how many songs the creators of *South Park* write (and hey, hosers, the tune got nominated for an Oscar, didn't it, eh?).

To find out more about what goes on in Canada, check out the following sites:

Canadian Broadcasting Company (CBC) (www.cbc.ca)—The big gun of Canadian TV and radio

Canadian Film Festivals (www.cs.cmu.edu/Unofficial/Canadiana/CA-filmfests.html)—Collection of links to various festivals

Canadian Lawyer Index (www.canlaw.com)—You'll need a lawyer to help you figure out Canadian content and possibilities, and there are 65,000 listed here.

Société des Auteurs de Radio, Télévision et Cinéma (www.sartec.qc.ca) —French language screenwriters in Canada (and there is no Anglais version, mon frère)

The Writers Guild of Canada and the Canadian Screenwriters Collection Society (www.writersguildofcanada.com)—An excellent site featuring the smartest book reviewers in North America. The Resources page features advice for new writers, and links to Canadian agents, lawyers, development funding, film and television festivals, and various industry links. I can't stress enough how well put together these links are. If you have a script set in Canada and can't get anything going via this site, you'd better rewrite that script.

All Roads Lead to Hollywood

The last time I wrote a book about selling foreign projects to Hollywood, my Argentinean producer/publisher friend, Jose Levy in Buenos Aires, was trying to sell the English rights to *El Guarante*, his miniseries, which was the most successful in the history of his country. I helped him select an agent (CAA), listened to offers he received, provided advice, and steered producers his way. I even talked to him about writing an English-language novel of the book, and I did all of this for several bottles of excellent Argentinean wine, because Jose is a thoughtful, talented, sincere, and funny friend. David Hasselhoff was talking to Jose about buying the English-language remake rights back then. Three years later, he's still talking to Jose.

That is not uncommon for Hollywood which, unfortunately, too many of my international friends have to learn by experience. I try to tell them that "Hurry up and wait" is a phrase to remember when dealing with Hollywood, but all too many people think that they're going to change the way things normally go because their project is special.

If you write books about a wizard in training named Harry Potter, maybe your project is special, but guess what? The powers-that-be at Warner Bros. had to be convinced that the books would make profitable movies, even with multiple Potter titles topping the *New York Times* bestseller lists!

Despite the barriers thrown up by Hollywood, it remains the ultimate destination for filmmakers around the world, and the competition continues to expand. In 2004, eighty-nine countries were invited by the Academy of Motion Picture Arts and Sciences to submit their top films for consideration in the Foreign Language Film category for the seventy-seventh Academy Awards. That didn't necessarily mean each country would submit an entry, but in 2003 a record fifty-six entries were submitted for consideration in the category.

Winning an Oscar is one thing, but in our digital age where technology continually levels the playing field, Hollywood no longer has a stranglehold on moviemaking technology. In fact, so much of its product creation is farmed out internationally, people in other countries advertise in the U.S. for talent! For example, in April 2004 I was astonished by an ad from *Resource Manager, Today Jobs India* seeking "Design

Experts of 2D and 3D Animations and Faculty for Multimedia Courses." I wasn't completely surprised, given that the Indian film industry makes more movies annually than Hollywood, but the ad was a bit of culture shock.

Yet another shock came when I read in the *Times of India* that a new Spider-Man movie was being made, except Peter Parker was being replaced by a young Indian boy named Pavitr Prabhakar. As the Indian Spider-Man, Prabhakar would swing through Indian landmarks like the Gateway of India and the Taj Mahal. Spider-Man's nemesis, The Green Goblin, was to be replaced by Rakshasa, an Indian mythological demon. (See http://timesofindia.indiatimes.com/articleshow/744273.cms for the full article.)

For years, Asian films have greatly influenced Hollywood film-makers, and Asian audiences have eagerly consumed Hollywood movies. Australian actors and filmmakers have done extraordinarily well in the U.S., as have their British cousins. The ideas flow back and forth, which is exactly how it should work in an American culture made great by its melting pot of citizens. For writers trying to figure out what Hollywood will be buying, though, it helps to know what is currently hot. To answer that, you can usually look to that which is firing the imagination of young people. These days, a lot of that content is coming from Japan.

I'm not talking about "Pokémon," but I am talking about some-thing similar. On April 30, 2004, a *New York Daily News* business head-line proclaimed "Boom time for manga books" and explained how the reading passion of some New York members of Meetup.com was "Japanese manga—edgy, graphic novels with translated storylines steeped in mystery, fantasy, and the surreal." It wasn't only New York where this form of Japanese comics is popular. At about the same time, two titles by San Francisco–based Viz Communications, "Naruto Vol. 3" and "Rurouni Kenshin Vol. 4," became the first graphic novels of any type (not just manga) to make it onto national bestseller lists. The books made it onto the *USA Today* Top 150 list of adult trade books.

That doesn't mean everything was rosy for Japanese comic art

The length of a film should be directly related to the endurance of the human bladder.

—Alfred Hitchcock

225

and animation creators. In May 2004, *Asahi Shimbun* in Tokyo reported that Japanese animation companies were facing extinction as studios cut back on animation budgets and turned to overseas competitors in South Korea and China where labor costs were lower. So while American consumers were enjoying Japanese product, "runaway production" was threatening the Japanese artists. Problems for creatives are much the same all over the world.

Wherever content is being produced, if I had to make a bet about artistic influence on Hollywood in the future, it would be hard to bet against the Japanese. In June of 2004, Lucasfilm and Japanese start-up animation company Anime World Osaka agreed to co-produce an upcoming animated feature, *The Tiny Fairy Mirun* (aka *Chiisana Yosei Mirun*). George Lucas would act as executive producer of the film, with the $18.5-million budget provided by Anime World Osaka. The plot? "A fairy comes to Earth and communicates to others with the aid of a crow." (I don't write this stuff, I just report it.)

To learn more about American involvement with Asian content, I spoke to producers Jennie Lew Tugend and Lauren Weissman, both women with impeccable Hollywood track records. They had formed a partnership to do business with Kadokawa Shoten Publishing Ltd., the largest entertainment conglomerate in Japan. Kadokawa has an entertainment division that has a distribution unit, a film production unit, a film financing unit, and video games, as well as the film library of Daiei Film Studios, the biggest and oldest studio in Japan. All of Akira Kurosawa's films are in the Daiei library, which is comprised of more than sixteen hundred film titles. In addition to the existing Daiei titles, Kadokawa produces six Japanese films each year. It publishes twelve to fifteen new books each month, and is a large source of manga and anime titles. How they came to be involved with the conglomerate can serve as a lesson to anyone hoping to do business with a Japanese company.

"During the Japanese bubble economy," Lauren explained, "a lot of the companies came to Los Angeles and had international marketing divisions here. At that time in Hollywood I was known for my ability to develop scripts that would package easily with A-list talent. So I had three Japanese companies talk to me about developing screenplays for them. One of them was Nikkatsu and the head of the international division was a man named Shinya Egawa. I developed three projects for them and then added a fourth, one I brought to them. The fourth one was *Dance with Me* (1998), which I later produced. After the bubble economy in Japan burst, Nikkatsu went bankrupt, so Shinya went back to Japan.

"Eventually, he and I got involved in three different companies together, and I developed with Shinya and his colleagues in Japan a friendly and professional relationship, which is crucial to the Japanese. They have to learn to trust you over time, and I won that trust over fifteen years. So when Shinya finally landed at Kadokawa as the head of their entertainment division, he called me up and said, 'Let's export low-budget films, up to $10 million each.' They would finance half of these proposed genre films because Kadokawa is known for its genre titles. We did an exploratory research journey through Hollywood to find partners, and that's when I met Jennie, whom I had heard of and known of throughout her career."

"I was doing low-budget films," Jennie added. "The company was called Capstone Pictures, and we had a business plan to do blocks of low-budget movies, co-finance them and so forth. The first time I met Shinya, I kept the brochure about Kadokawa and thought, 'This is interesting.'"

Hurry up and wait. A year passed, then Lauren's mother became ill and Lauren dropped everything to care for her. By the time Shinya called Lauren again, almost two years had gone by. In the meantime he had sold the remake rights to *The Ring* (2002) to New Line via an Asian film scout named Roy Lee. When Shinya asked Lauren if she was still interested, she immediately thought of Jennie and asked her to be her partner. Of all the people she had considered working with in a Hollywood/Japanese venture, she wanted it to be Jennie.

"It was a gut thing," Lauren told me.

"And the timing was right," Jennie added. "Because of the time that had passed since I first met Lauren, Capstone Pictures had made a movie and closed its doors. I was looking for a new venture."

"What Jennie and I have in common is long-range planning and short-range deliverables," Lauren said. "What we didn't know was the amount of exhaustive work it would take to mine a foreign-language library that was Eastern rather than Western. It was a critical factor, and it is also why people are interested, popping up all over because Western culture is now becoming old stuff. Eastern culture is what Western culture is looking to for innovative ideas."

"And young people are probably the most open-minded to literature from elsewhere," Jennie explained. "Young people gobble up the Japanese manga and the style of dress, hip language, whatever is perceived as cool. The Japanese pop culture is perceived as cool by young people here. So when the mangas and the graphic novels and the anime came over here it was young American kids who supported it and eventually it had to get the eyes of Hollywood, which is always looking for what's hip and what's cool."

Lauren added that at the core of these creative products from young Japan is a universal concept of storytelling. "It's all about a good story. And right now the flavors are thrillers and horror and supernatural horror. Japan is a culture that is rich in supernatural lore. Therefore, it emerges in their films, very much like *The Ring*. Curses, ghosts, demons, not necessarily Christian, and it comes out in a very different way. So in the beginning, since everything was in Japanese, we had to have them suggest titles and loglines and let us research them. It is such a huge library! We took around one hundred movies and hired translators and watched them, word by word, stopping, going back, and trying to figure it out. And out of those we found a handful that we felt would be viable to an American market."

"Actually there's more than just a handful," Jennie said. "We assembled a portfolio to show a sampling of a library of titles we thought could be reinvented or adapted to the Western marketplace. Our first selection was ten movies, ten novels, ten manga, ten comics, ten anime, and some video games."

Naturally, I wanted to know what barriers might be present in trying to Westernize classic Japanese stories. I asked if there were any basic differences in how the stories were told.

Jennie smiled and I knew I'd touched on something. "Some of the Japanese films don't have a third act," she said. "They're great storytellers, but their structure in many cases is very different from our typical three acts. So in many cases we invented a third act, being honest with the material of course, or putting a different spin on it. It might have been a really good story, but at the end of it we put a little modern American spin on it while maintaining the integrity of the property. Our portfolio was assembled after months of work and getting it to the point that we could walk in and a Hollywood buyer would get it, because a picture is worth a thousand words. We have loglines and graphics and brief paragraph descriptions, so they can see at a glance that this library has horrors, thrillers, comedies, classics, musicals, and great mythological stories. And the Daiei library, coming from the oldest studio in Japan, goes back over fifty years."

To package the properties for presentation, Jennie and Lauren's approach is to do whatever is necessary to sell the product. If they feel that the story is better by having a writer attached to provide a more fleshed-out version of the English version, they do it. If a director or a writer/director's vision is necessary to sell a product, they find the right person. If it seems certain stories would be performance-dependent, they bring an actor on board.

What Lauren had to say about writers for these projects might be reassuring for anyone who is long on anime knowledge but short on writing credits.

"You need a writer that the studio has confidence in," she said. "Although I have to say that the studios' trends right now are to get the younger talent all the way across the board. That's because they're cheaper."

Jennie agreed that youth can help in such a market.

"We might discover in our day's work a young writer who is a Japanophile who has always loved a certain story or character or creature or whatever in the Japanese folk library or whatever, right? And that's the person who's going to bring the most enthusiasm into a room because he's known it since he was nine years old. He's always wanted to tell this story, he knows exactly what to do, and his youth and his enthusiasm will get you excited in the room. So that's the other side of the more seasoned writer with a track record. They both are viable."

I wanted to know how they went about finding the kind of young writers like they had described.

"We go to a variety of places," Lauren said. "In our search to find translators we found a bunch of very interesting Japanese or half-Japanese kids or American-Japanese just back from Japan who are in Los Angeles. All of them are flocking to us to help us do this stuff. Then, in our travels through the studios we found some people who knew more about our library than we did! They're avid manga and graphic novel admirers, and they introduced us to projects in our library that we are now going out to sell. There are so many anime addicts out there, especially in the studio system. A lot of writers have been into this material for years. They tell their agents and their agents contact us. Or when we contact the agents and tell them who we are they say 'We have the writers for you.'"

"The territory has been broken," Jennie added. "*The Last Samurai* (2003) set a precedent as a commercial movie, and a lot more similar projects will start to emerge. It is a global industry at this point."

Lauren agrees. "Hollywood still is the leader, but as much as Japan wants to work with the U.S., Hollywood wants to work with Japan. You'd be shocked."

"And China, too," said Jennie. "We have a presence there, and we're going to have a stronger presence. What is interesting is what's coming out of China itself, their productions and stories. It's not the China of lore. When you look at a picture of kids in Shanghai today they are talking on their cell phones on the treadmill in the gym. This is a different time. So China is also going to be interesting for us, too."

I thought of how ironic that would be, given that I had known Jennie for twenty years and that her family had come over from China.

The ladies explained how they planned to make movies for the American audience in China, using Japanese stories. How much more international could it get? And despite what I'd read about troubles for Japanese animators, Jennie and Lauren were producing an animated kids TV series in Japan for an American audience. I asked why in Japan, instead of Korea?

Lauren shrugged. "Because we have such good deals."

Well, I thought, that's how it goes. So much for American writers, with those hundreds of Japanese classics floating around. Then Lauren told me of a story brought to them through Random House in New York. They took it to Kadokawa and got a deal to produce it as a franchise feature film in China.

"It doesn't matter where it starts," Lauren said. "There is always going to be a demand for aesthetically pleasing films that surprise and nourish people and make them want more. It's all about supply and demand. For anyone just starting out in the business, however, I would advise them that you cannot go into the business these days thinking of art first, because you won't be in the business."

Jennie agreed, and elaborated. "That's because these days you have what, seven studio buyers? If you pull your own plug on a project over art, you have nowhere to go, you're going good-bye. Now it's a business more than ever."

About a week after I met with Jennie and Lauren, I read in *The Hollywood Reporter* how Japanese publisher Kadokawa Holdings had agreed to invest $100 million in DreamWorks SKG to take a 2.83 percent stake in the studio. The deal also gave Kadokawa exclusive rights to sell DreamWorks films, videos, DVDs, and other products in Japan. Kadokawa expected sales of about 3.5 billion yen ($32 million) from selling DreamWorks content in the year starting April 1, 2004, and 15 billion yen ($138 million) the following year. An article in *Variety* the same day revealed that in March, Kadokawa had secured a majority stake in Japanese film distributor and exhibitor Nippon Herald Film, making the Japanese conglomerate even bigger. Now I understood what

Hollywood . . . was the place where the United States perpetrated itself as a universal dream and put the dream into mass production.

—Angela Carter

Jennie and Lauren had meant when they hinted during our meeting that they had some pretty big deals in the works.

While someone new to Hollywood would need a miracle to get into a position like Jennie Lew Tugend and Lauren Weissman, and perhaps years to develop the trust of major players in another country, it can be done. At least for now, it helps to know how "the next big thing" in Hollywood often comes from outside the city limits, and just how much work goes into making it all seem like such a natural idea.

With filmmakers from New Zealand dominating the Oscars in 2004 and cultural films like *Whale Rider* (2003) showing the worth of indigenous cultures to international audiences, expect a lot more great films and film ideas from the East. If you're already a fan of such product, you might not need the following links to explore. If you're not, you might be delighted at what you can find.

Australian Centre for the Moving Image (ACMI) (www.acmi.net.au) —Established in 2002 to provide a new cultural institution in Victoria dedicated to the moving image in all its forms

Australian Writers Guild (www.awg.com.au)—Pro organization for writers of film, television, radio, theatre, video, and new media

Bollywood Online (www.indiafm.com)—A site to help you keep up with the prodigious output of the Indian film industry

Golden Harvest Entertainment (www.goldenharvest.com/eng/index.asp)—English site of Asia's most well-known entertainment company

New Zealand Authors and Writers (www.nzwriters.co.nz)— Open to writers of every genre, published or unpublished

New Zealand Writers Guild (www.nzwritersguild.org.nz/about/about.html)—A nonprofit association for pro writers

The Best International Screenwriting Competition

And now something for my international readers alone, since American writers are not eligible. Would you like to know about a contest where a very high percentage of the winners actually see their screenplay made into a film?

That's the Hartley-Merrill Prize. It began in 1989 when Dina Merrill and Ted Hartley attended the Soviet-American Film Summit in Moscow in the midst of *perestroika*. They wanted to do something for writers there, so they established a screenwriting competition with a cash award of $10,000.

The competition started off with a bang. Irakly Kvirikadze, the first Hartley-Merrill Grand Prize in 1990, was nominated for the Best Foreign Oscar in 1997, for his film *Les Mille et une recettes du cuisinier amoureux* (*A Chef in Love*). Roughly three quarters of the winners have had their scripts made into films.

Current Executive Director Debbie Vandermeulen works with the ministers of culture in countries across the globe to find great scripts. Any country can get involved, and the Hartley-Merrill is constantly growing. Competitions held in the individual countries usually receive between 100 and 125 entries, and the winning screenplays are translated into English (when necessary) and forwarded to Los Angeles, where an international jury picks the top three selections. The awards are announced at the annual Cannes Film Festival, with a gala in Los Angeles each June. The grand prizewinner is invited to be a part of the Sundance Writers Lab, airfare and accommodations paid. With cash prizes in the U.S. in addition to the money a participant can win in his or her home country (an average of $5,000), this poses quite an opportunity for someone to come to Hollywood in a big way.

To be eligible, a writer cannot have had more than one feature film made as a writer, although he or she can have more than one of other film credits. American judges are top Hollywood "players" and the competition attempts to set standards and formats for writers worldwide.

For more information or to see if your country participates in the contest, see www.hartleymerrillprize.org or contact:

Debbie Vandermeulen
Executive Director
Hartley Merrill Prize
RKO Pictures
8675 Hayden Place
Culver City, CA 90232
Phone: (310) 558-9167
Email: foundation@rko.com

For those of you who live in Los Angeles, Hartley-Merrill and RKO Pictures have something to offer you after all. It's called The Story Project and is also administered by the able Ms. Vandermeulen. It's about mentoring inner city kids in writing. And if you don't think that will give you a big prize, I can't help you.

Back to Hollywood

I hope this chapter has given you at least some idea of screenwriting opportunities around the world and the international filmmaking scene. Obviously, I can only scratch the surface; it would require a full book to adequately cover this media world we live in.

Or maybe a library.

Speaking of which, there are still some areas that haven't been addressed. About a wheelbarrow full of tips, actually—and you might need all of them to sell to Hollywood. I've been acquiring them for almost two decades, so I hope you'll let me unload some on you.

Turn the page and help me out, okay?

CHAPTER

11

Hollywood
Road Map

Silent Bob, we're going to Hollywood.

—Actor Jason Mewes as "Jay"

in Jay and Silent Bob Strike Back (2001)

Along Sunset Boulevard in Beverly Hills, people stand by the side of the road bearing signs advertising "Maps to the Stars' Homes!" It's been that way for decades. When I first arrived in this town I was naïve enough to think that I could get one of those maps, find the address of a movie star I admired, send that star something I'd written, and get a response. Why not? I've always felt a kinship with people who made the movies, and I thought my sheer enthusiasm and interesting stories would win any star over. Maybe I'd seen too many rags-to-riches movies.

I didn't have to use an address from one of those maps. I quickly learned that, in this people town, by simply networking, I could find Hollywood professionals who liked my stories. Because I tried to write things that I thought the public would want—not simply something that pleased me—I found readers particularly receptive to me. Some of them even expressed relief that it was nice, for once, to read a new writer who wrote commercially.

Once I had some success I learned that very few people achieve the big career-making deal that you read about in the Hollywood trade papers. I learned that a breakthrough for a writer can be years or decades in coming and that many people only get one shot at glory.

Then I accidentally got into the Hollywood advice business and my advice turned out to be popular. Because of my Hollywood Rule #10—*The rules in Hollywood change all the time*—writers around the world continued to ask me about this or that. I responded to tens of thousands of emails and phone calls for free. I explained why people had moved from companies, why there was a new address and phone for a producer, why certain agents were not worth contacting unless you were a working writer. I wanted to make sure that no writer reading my book got lost in a Hollywood dead-end the way I had too many times.

Now here we are. You're venturing on the road to success with a property to sell and I'm providing you with the best advice I can muster, which even includes the names of people who might offer you a deal. You might think of yourself as a student driver, but I don't have that extra steering wheel on this side of the vehicle. I can only guess where you're going. I've learned over the years that I can't possibly cover everything. I can only try. You only truly learn how this town works by traveling its roads, and I do my best to make it seem like you're here when I describe it. So, in this chapter we'll cover details, little things you'll need to take care of to give yourself the best chance possible for Hollywood success. If that doesn't do it for you, I'm sorry, I don't know everything about Hollywood, and the rules really do change all the time, just like the maps and the vendors on Sunset Boulevard.

Drive Safely

Earlier in the book, I covered ways to protect your intellectual property. You must take that seriously because these days, unfortunately, there's an ongoing trend toward theft, with a conceit that nobody really owns anything. That doesn't help people trying to sell intellectual property, and Hollywood pays the price. Music is downloaded from the Internet and no royalties are paid. Movies are pirated, with DVDs often for sale before the film screens in theaters. Thus, box-office sales can be miserable—so bad a movie will lose money. Here's an example of how that is affecting Hollywood. The DVDs distributed to members of The Academy of Motion Picture Arts and Sciences for Oscar voting have been compromised in the past, resulting in the Academy now endorsing a plan to distribute thousands of unique DVD players to its members. These machines use specially encrypted discs known as "screeners" that are digitally tailored to the owner. An invisible watermark is digitized to the DVD each time it is viewed. Within the pixels of on-screen images are more codes, so that if someone records the movie with a camcorder or VCR, the attempted theft will show up on the resultant image.

Now, in such an environment, would you think that young people (there are a lot of them working in Hollywood) who have grown up in an "everything on the Internet is free" environment would be more or less inclined to steal that property you worked on so hard and long?

They're more trustworthy, according to a 2001 study by the University of Maryland sociologists. The researchers found that Internet users "appear to be more open, tolerant, trusting, optimistic, and literate than non-users." But that's the Internet, and this is Hollywood, where some computer-illiterate older Hollywood executives believe their revenues are declining due to a thief mentality among the public. Maybe, just maybe, the problem could be what they're offering *to* the public, but don't try to tell them that. Such executives are cautious, fearful (not

*When you start
you want to
make the
greatest film in
the world, but
when you get
into it, you just
want to get it
done, let it be
passable
and not
embarrassing.*

—Francis Ford Coppola

entirely without reason), and more likely to try to obtain properties as cheaply as possible. If you have to spend a lot of money apprehending pirates and developing protective mechanisms, you don't have as much money to spend on talent and material. And seriously, it does cost a lot of money to deal with theft. So my advice to you is, when interacting with Hollywood, expect a climate of fear and mistrust until you find otherwise, and protect yourself each step of the way. This is particularly true if you are approaching Hollywood from outside town, using mass media such as the Internet.

It's a people town, and until they respect you as a person, you're nobody to them.

Follow the Main Roads

Here are a dozen tips that I hope will help you break in from wherever you are:

1. Write a *great* script, not just a competent one. Sorry, but when you're starting out you need to be a little more impressive—show something that gets you on the radar. Or, get a novel published that is easily defined within a genre and is popular with the public; it will probably catch Hollywood's attention.

2. Figure out which company/producer is most likely to make a movie of your project. Do thorough research on them using trade publication archives, IMDb searches, Web site research, and so forth.

3. Get the current contact information on these people via an online database, because locations and personnel change constantly. Do not count on books (including this one) for up-to-date contact information, because books are published months or years before today.

4. Learn how to pitch your project effectively, whether over the phone, via fax, via email, or in person. Presentation can be all-important in Tinseltown.

5. If you can't contact someone personally due to your location and/or financial circumstances, *call* them. Spend the money, even on an international call, because that will impress them and they'll be more likely to take the time to speak with you. If you're not in the U.S., tell them where you're calling from and that you'd like to send them something. Then describe it succinctly. If they won't take your project without a signed release, ask if you can provide one or if they can fax or email one to you. They won't think twice about faxing something around the world.

6. If you can afford to pitch here in person, do a Sherwood Oaks week-long event (www.sherwoodoaks.com). You'll be well cared for and will meet good people. Research the speakers and executives in attendance. Some pitch fests can be effective, but usually only if you know who you are talking to and what that company has done before you sit in front of them. Most fests provide a list of names and info on the companies before the event.

7. If you come here in person, forget the starry-eyed exuberance and gushy comments like, "This is so great being here!" Be friendly and professional, yet passionate about the story you're telling. Have *at least* two more stories ready to pitch with all the beats worked out. Then, if you hear, "We have something like that already, what else do you have?" you're covered. In most pitch fest settings you'll have only five minutes to get your pitch across, so be prepared.

8. Have business cards ready so that people can contact you. While some folks advise very simple cards with no graphics, I believe a picture of yourself helps Hollywood people remember who you are (a screenplay title might not). Any simple card would work, however. Don't expect anyone at a pitch to do anything with your card, but throw it away later unless they are impressed with what you present.

9. Don't expect people to take a script right there, or even a one-sheet synopsis. After hours of listening to stories, they usually want to get out of there.

10. If you don't hear from someone in about a month after contacting them, it's OK to do a follow-up phone call or email to inquire about the status. Personally, I wait about six weeks, and sometimes I get so busy it might be two months. Don't appear anxious. It helps you in Hollywood if you give no appearance at all of being "hungry."

11. If you have someone looking at a project, an agent won't care. If you have someone ready to make an offer on a project, an agent might care. Do *not* depend on agents.

12. Don't expect to succeed with any shortcuts. Forget every story you've ever read about anyone who broke in without a great piece of completed writing, or who wasn't already a successful writer of some kind. If you want to count on flukes, play the lottery and forget Hollywood.

When you are pitching something, it helps to have a concept that most people "get" very quickly. Here's an example of one I liked. I saw a posting about the following sale in *Publisher's Marketplace:*

> Film rights to Gerald A. Browne's SWISH HITTERS, about two East Hampton antique dealers who become the unlikeliest pair of Mob hit-men ever (think the *Queer Eye* guys meet *The Sopranos*), to Ruddy-Morgan Productions (*The Godfather,* 1972, and upcoming *Million Dollar Baby* starring Clint Eastwood and Hilary Swank), by Patricia Nelson at Kneerim & Williams.

Let's analyze why that one's so good. Everyone knows what a "switch hitter" is in social slang. The title plays on that and throws in a gay context with "swish." A mob "hit" (murder) is well known. The great playwright/screenwriter Neil Simon was fond of titles that seem familiar to the public; *Swish Hitters* fits that criteria. The "meets" in the description tells you a lot about the movie, if you're familiar with the two properties to which it is compared. That kind of comparison is very common in Hollywood. It's an obviously commercial property by producers who have rarely done anything but commercial movies. The *Million Dollar Baby* project (which has been retitled as *Rope Burns*) was written by a very commercial writer/director/producer named Paul Haggis with whom I started out with in Hollywood. (Just to show you that commercial producers usually try to be consistent in picking only commercial properties.)

If you create well-written properties like the one above, you will probably succeed in Hollywood. Unfortunately most students and people I hear from don't do that. Instead, they write about:

a. Values and things that matter (soap-boxing);

b. Things they are "passionate" about in stories that are not entertaining; or

c. Stories based on something they just dreamed up or were inspired to write because [fill in blanks here].

Too many of these people ignore what Hollywood buys on a day-to-day basis, then get flummoxed because they can't get heard or make a sale. That shows me they simply aren't paying any attention whatsoever to what Hollywood buys all day long, over and over, year after year.

For example, if you're writing a drama and expect to sell it as a feature, you've cut your chances greatly. On occasion there's an *In the Bedroom* (2001), but these kinds of movies usually get made in the independent arena by some crusading filmmaker who convinces good actors that mean something at the box office to get behind the project.

Let's contrast two vehicles with Jim Carrey to give you a better example. Was *Bruce Almighty* (2003) about values and things that matter? Sure it was, and it was a hit. But it wasn't preachy. Compare that to *The Majestic* (2001), which spawned all sorts of imitator scripts when it was in the pipeline to be made. Why did that movie flop at the box office? Because it was an "issue" movie about the HUAC anti-Communist trials in the '50s and most audiences didn't find it particularly relevant today. The movie was a Hollywood crusade, nicely made, beautiful to look at, but not in step with most of current American society, much less international audiences. *Bruce Almighty,* on the other hand, was a concept that people could get behind all over the world: *If you were God, what would you do?*

I started off in this town getting noticed, getting optioned, and getting sold because I usually had some kind of high concept at the core of what I wrote. Some examples:

Texas Rising—This one got the interest of Burt Reynolds (who should've done it, but turned it down), Clint Eastwood (the agent screwed up the written presentation after getting Clint's producer interested over the phone), Robert Redford (who did *The Milagro Beanfield War*, 1988, instead), and Michael Douglas (who wanted to option it, but the producer messed up the deal). It's about Texas seceding in modern times, a comedy.

Allure—A script about TV lingerie models who start getting killed as their dangerously sexy ads begin airing on TV; it sold over 250 other scripts read by the company.

South China Sea—A revenge/action story about modern-day pirates who kidnap the wife of the last guy they'd like to take on. A femme fatale is the leader of the pirates. It sold because of its location and investors in that area.

You must write about things audiences will care about seeing and/or things that fit what producers need. Good movies often revolve around a simple concept. Then there are demographics. Once I learned that "kids love it" is the element most often found in #1 box-office successes, I narrowed it down further (kids will go back and see a movie repeatedly, and tired parents will pay for the tickets). If you don't have children you might wonder how *Finding Nemo* (2003) could make $76 million in a weekend. If you're a parent you totally understand, and the film's concept—*a single dad does whatever is necessary to get his captured son back*—represents values you support. In that type of high-concept story, you can get across big themes while providing entertaining stories, and it's a Hollywood goldmine. Instead, too many people write scripts based on a weak concept. The stories are filled with things the writer cares about but the broad public isn't particularly interested

> *An audience is never wrong. An individual member of it may be an imbecile, but a thousand imbeciles together in the dark—that's critical genius.*
>
> **—Billy Wilder**

in. If a movie was made from their property, it wouldn't get people talking, lift them up for a couple of hours, give them an adrenaline rush of fear, or boost their serotonin levels from laughing so hard.

Here's a good example of a commercial writer. In May 2004, Twentieth Century Fox bought writer Andrew Klavan's spec script "Gideon" for mid- against high-six figures. The story is about "a young female artist who imagines evil figures so deeply that they cross over into her real world." Pretty easy to envision, isn't it? According to *The Hollywood Reporter,* it was the third Klavan project to sell in as many weeks. I'd say he's commercial.

In contrast, too many writers venture off the main roads of storytelling. That might be okay to do, even desirable, but when you're just starting out you usually have to stay on the more traveled thoroughfares if you want to reach that destination known as a sale.

Park Your Property Where It Belongs

There is no "one size fits all" screenplay. A TV movie is very different than a feature, and there are many different types of TV movies, dictated by their forum. For example, it used to be that every movie on the Lifetime cable TV channel was "women in jeopardy." Melissa Gilbert was so adept at those parts that if you got her committed to a script, it was a go at Lifetime (not true anymore, and now she's the President of the Screen Actors Guild). On occasion, I'll hear from writers who have history or military properties, yet it doesn't occur to them to approach the History Channel via someone who produces there. Turner Network Television makes movies based on books, but few authors I know have thought to seek out producers who work with TNT. It used to be that one production company, Wilshire Court, was the main conduit to the USA Network. Now, cable channels are fairly open to hearing directly from writers. As I was writing this book, I led a panel discussion with the head of development at the Sci-Fi Channel sitting next to me. He freely discussed what type of material he looked for, how to contact him, and he even met with writers afterward. Although Sci-Fi Channel is now under the NBC/Universal corporate umbrella, smaller cable channels have to take the approach I just described, because they can't afford A-list writers. You have to pay attention and understand details like this to effectively market to these outlets. That's what producers do, and often they use agents or managers or lawyers who know such details.

If you have a property that traditionally might appear on network television, the best place for it these days might be cable. In 2003, as reality programming was beginning to replace sitcoms on the networks, Oxygen bought *Good Girls Don't . . .* , a new sitcom centered on the sad sex lives of two young girls. At the same time, HBO was busy developing its own situation comedies. The catch with a show on cable is that it's usually a little more twisted (like *Six Feet Under*) or racy (like *Sex and the City*).

If you want to sell a feature, expect a slightly different story. Features fall into a couple of categories—studio and independent. A studio movie is usually a simple movie, story-wise. An indie can be all over the place, about anything that actors find appealing to portray or tout (such as a cause célèbre they're into). With indies and studio features in particular, you almost inevitably have to have a movie star attached before it will get funded. Even then, a studio might not, for example, fund a comedy with Rob Schneider in the lead role because Schneider doesn't do well with foreign audiences.

Here's another difference in the two types of features. If you write complex human dramas, where would you think your market would most likely be? In studio films, the complex human drama is often the subtext or B story of the movie (for example, the estranged marriage between Bruce Willis and Bonnie Bedelia in *Die Hard*, 1988). In indies, it's usually the A (main) story and often the only story, perhaps with various "shades" of the same theme, as in *The Anniversary Party* (2001).

In one-hour TV dramas, even the most "cheesecake" shows such as "Baywatch" (the most popular show in the world during its run) have an A story, a B story, a C story, and some times even a D story. If you don't understand story layering, or even terms like this, you'll be greatly handicapped, but don't be hard on yourself. A great many people don't figure this stuff out. They think there's some "magic formula" (like the right agent) that will make it all happen, and get them that million-dollar check from the Hollywood bank.

If you want to get on the Hollywood carousel and grab the platinum ring, the ticket is talent. There's a catch, though. The entertainment business, and the people who can write big checks, simply want the goods that they and the public believe are worthwhile. If you write a great script, you'll get noticed and talked about, but you'll get noticed and talked about within the context of where that script fits within the Hollywood industry. Notice I said "industry." That's how Hollywood runs.

Here's another layer—ratings. Do you know whether or not your script, if made into a movie as written, would get a PG-13 rating or an R? You should. It could mean a hundred million dollars' difference in profits. The movie *Dodgeball* (2004) was #1 in its opening weekend, beating star vehicle *The Terminal* (2004) starring Tom Hanks, Catherine Zeta-Jones, and directed by Steven Spielberg. In a bit of Hollywood payback, *Dodgeball* had been rejected by Spielberg's DreamWorks because DreamWorks executive Walter Parkes "couldn't see the movie" from the script. The script was changed before it was filmed at Fox so that it would have a PG-13 rating, much more favorable to a teenage audience. The version DreamWorks saw would have had an R rating, keeping a lot of kids out of the theater. If kids under seventeen stay away from a studio movie, that movie could be in big trouble.

Do you know what goes into assigning ratings? You can see how they are formulated at the Motion Picture Association of America site at www.mpaa.org/movieratings. If you wonder about your property's possible rating, search for movies at www.mpaa.org/movieratings/search/index.htm. You'd better know about this, because you might be asked, "So what would it be rated?" by someone at a production company.

In 1999, I did a study of what qualities were present in the most successful movies. I redid my study in 2003. Although it can comprise several factors, I found that if kids love it, a movie has the best chance of being a smash success. If you'd like to see the complex details of what I came up with, you can read about it in my *Complete Idiot's Guide to Screenwriting*, or send me an email request and I'll send you the study.

What They Expect at Your Destination

Hollywood people, who make a living giving the public what they want, think about the consumer. Sometimes I wonder if the people writing scripts I read actually think about the fact that the audience pays around $20 per person to see a movie, if you factor in the cost of a ticket, refreshments, and parking. After all, most people are caught up in simple struggles of jobs, housing, relationships, education, and family. If Hollywood executives with big salaries can think of this, why can't writers?

You don't get the full meaning of this until you're involved with this business regularly. Let's say you are not, and you can only reach producers via email. You'll have to be persistent. So here's a persistence story. I knew a producer named Al Burton who did *Charles in Charge* and many other hit shows. When he first arrived in Hollywood decades ago and went to the *one* person he thought might hire him and was told, no, sorry, not hiring, Al was stuck. He had about $10 in his pocket. So he went around the back of the TV station and started talking to people and got a job at the same place where he'd been turned down fifteen minutes before. You could use that kind of persistence in creative email. Title your post "Free Chocolate, You Pick, Really." Maybe they'll delete spam about making their penis bigger but they might read about chocolate. If you don't hear from them in a week, title it "Free Chocolate, I Wasn't Kidding." Then wait and try again, "What? You Hate Free Chocolate?" Many people will respond after the third missive, as long as you space them out just enough so they remember the previous messages.

The body of your email could read, "OK, I really am gonna send you some free chocolate, as long as you'll read my script. Think about it. You could lie to me about reading it and you'd still get the chocolate, wouldn't you? Of course, then you'd be a rotten Hollywood person, but most people I contact don't have the keen insight you're famous for, which is why I picked you. Here's my logline…"

I can't promise you that approach would work, but the light touch has been successful for me. Guys can seduce women with humor even if the guys are not so good-looking. Everyone sends jokes flying all over the Internet. So why not display some humor, personality, and persistence? They won't forget you and that's important. Just be persistent and not obnoxious and stay professional. Successful people are generally happy people, so why not act like one?

Once you've gotten someone to agree to read your material, make sure you know any special steps you need to take in getting it to them. When I was doing music in this town I often had to write "Requested Material" on a package to get my tape past mail screening. My New York literary agent won't open an email or a package unless it says, "Referred by Skip Press." Otherwise, his intern opens it and might not pass it on to him. See if you'll need anything like that written on your package.

Next, don't confuse the issue. When someone in Hollywood requests material from you he or she generally only cares about that one item. Nobody cares about everything else you have to offer unless it's an agent or manager thinking about how much they can make off you long-term, or a producer who wants a franchise that your material might provide. If they hear one idea and they say, "Ah, I might be able to sell that" or, "I bet I could set that up at Dimension," let them follow through with acquiring that project before you mention another. If they think fondly enough of you personally or are excited enough about the project in question, they could deal with it immediately, and often do. So why distract them with something else?

Highly successful producers recognize good material, while lower-level people either respond due to (a) their own personal prejudices,

Hollywood has always been a cage . . . a cage to catch our dreams.

—*John Huston*

(b) what's hot according to the buzz around town, or (c) something their boss tells them to find. Overworked lower-level people and busy producers often look for ways to compare your project to something already done and turn it down so they don't even have to read it. This makes it *highly* important to pick people that are most likely to like your type of material. When marketing, you need to think in terms of abundant promotion, because dozens of people might see a script before it's bought. You also need to know the types of things that will turn people off about a script. Here are some basics:

a. *Use Courier or Courier New.* When a script is bought for production, it is broken down for the various personnel to use in getting the film made (location scout, casting, special effects, and the like). When the script is written in a Courier 12 font, a movie generally works out to a minute per written page. When Courier New is converted to Courier the script shrinks because Courier New is a bigger font. I've heard a lot of complaints from readers about scripts not being in Courier, so use it.

b. *Beware of too much dark space.* When there are more than six to eight lines in a descriptive paragraph of a script, or if you describe what would be another separate shot in that paragraph, that's not good. Each paragraph should probably equal one shot. You don't write the shots out, but it's clear what they are from what you describe. Read *Some Like It Hot* (1959) and see how Billy Wilder and Izzy Diamond did it. Readers want short, easy, descriptive, and dialogue paragraphs that are not novel length.

c. *Don't worry about the trees.* The Nicholl Contest accepts scripts printed on two sides to save paper, but production companies and agents may not (although some big agencies send out dual-sided scripts). If someone gets a script and doesn't know that it's printed on two sides, they might assume it's too short and toss it without reading it.

d. *Simple is better.* Avoid fancy covers, any brads but brass ones (use two, not three), and don't embellish your presentation in any way that will distract people from reading your words. Submit the kind of script a professional submits.

e. *Learn to spell and type.* If your work has misspelled words and badly typed sentences, it might not matter how well you write. If you can't turn out a professional-looking script, hire someone who can.

f. *Don't think you own everything in your script.* You might have the best title that's ever been written, but copyright won't protect it. Once a title achieves sufficient public recognition it can be trademarked, but most screenwriters aren't in that position. So if you submit a script and a company later comes out with a different story, but the same title, you're probably out of luck.

g. *Make music if you wish, but not in your script.* It's fine to suggest music for a film, but don't insist on it. Licensing music for movies is big business, and expensive. If even a section of your script revolves around a popular song, it could cause a problem because the song is too expensive to license within the budget.

h. *Seek resonance.* When you impress someone at a company with your writing, that's a major accomplishment. Even if they don't make an offer on your property, chalk it up as a victory. These people have friends, and can spread favorable comments about you.

i. *Save people time.* Some people insist on a self-addressed, stamped envelope (SASE) with a submission, so that they can return a rejected project at the writer's expense. If you want to know your project has been received use a postal device such as a proof of delivery, or include an SASE postcard with some verbiage and a checkbox to show it was received. Most people don't mind something like that, and then you'll have a visual reminder to post on your bulletin board.

I've always had a simple point of view on submitting material. I think of what I would want it to be like if I were on the receiving end. What would make me comfortable, and give me the space to get interested? That's helped me make friends.

Word on the Street

By now you probably know that you can't believe everything that comes out of Hollywood, even if it's a "documentary." You shouldn't let what you read in the trades have too much influence on you. Here are some more things to be aware of, as you navigate your way through the marketing maze:

- Don't get seduced into the idea that you shouldn't write something because "it's already being done." That can backfire on you because you might have something better. Steven Spielberg told me during an interview that the *Hook* script was bought even though they already had another Peter Pan script ready.

- Even if a certain type of script just sold, yours might still sell. When some high-profile actor or director is doing, for example, a baseball pic, the other studios might want one of the same. Neurotic executives don't want anyone to top them or they could be fired. What if you have the other perfect baseball script?

- People lie to the trades. The trades unfortunately sometimes buy the lies. Nobody remembers the lies told in print or the announced projects that never happened. I first got wind of this when John Badham told a reporter from *Variety* he was doing a modern-day pirate pic just to give the reporter a scoop and get him off his back. This was after Badham had done *Blue Thunder* (1983) and was very hot. I know Badham lied because some producers who'd optioned a cowritten modern day pirate script of mine took it to him and he admitted what I've just told you. He said the first ten pages of our script were the best he'd ever read. Then he immediately did a bicycle pic called *American Flyers* (1985).

- Guess where most information databases get their knowledge? They sit there every morning and type it into the computer right out of *Variety* and *The Hollywood Reporter*. They also import text and data from other sites and assimilate it. How do I know? I've seen them do it, at several sites.

- Development people share information with each other on tracking boards. To cultivate this (and thus have access to the information), the information sites give them free access to the tracking boards.

In truth, Hollywood is a big shell game with hype flying all around. If you write a script with a good story that a major star would love to appear in, chances are it will get bought. On an important project, a production company might not tell anyone about it unless they just can't help it. Often when information about a sale reaches the trades, it's because the agent/manager who sold it wants his/her name in the news. There are people who actually worry if their name hasn't been in the trades in three months, and being mentioned in an article is free advertising.

Word on the street is different. That's often how insiders make deals and get jobs, but you probably won't be privy to it unless you actually live here, or are in contact with someone who does live here.

Are Those Bandits by the Side of the Road?

When you teach screenwriting as I do, a common question from novices is "Will they steal my idea?"

"Yes," I reply, "but you'll have to prove it."

If a studio finances a movie it might go through a dozen writers. Inexperienced writers often don't know this, and they also think their words are writ in stone. Many producers would like to drop that stone in the sea, save the basic idea, and get a writer who understands the collaborative nature of the medium to turn what they think is basically just a good concept into a script they can actually film.

Some producers steal, but usually that's only the low-end hustlers who will do anything to make a movie. The top screenwriters don't bother with low-enders so beginners often come in contact with that kind of producer first.

Even if you are a flexible writer who can take notes without taking a pill, you still might get stolen from, because literary pirates in southern California outnumber the oranges. (Just watch, someone will steal that line.) If you want a movie depiction of how Hollywood theft can happen, watch an old movie called *Hearts of the West* (1975). It's one of Jeff Bridges's best roles and you'll have a great time with the story.

In my own experience, I once had to hire a detective to find out if a cowritten script had been stolen. Maybe, he said, but couldn't prove it. Luckily, the movie in question, starring Gary Busey, did next to nothing at the box office, so what could we sue for? Often enough, a new corporation is formed to support a single movie, and if you sue you have to sue that corporation. If the Busey film was not profitable, what could I hope to recover with a lawsuit? We later sold the script outright for a nice price, which goes to show that Hollywood doesn't always require an original idea.

Another time, I was suspicious that a cowboy film I co-wrote with actress Linda Blair had been stolen as the basis for another cowboy movie that was unprofitable. Since it had been made by a billionaire (and Linda had personally handed him our script), all I did was have a conversation with the man's lawyer. I didn't sue, and a few years later, the same billionaire optioned some of my novels.

Here's another story I wrote about for the U.K. magazine *Scriptwriter.*

Shortly after meeting actor Michael York in the mid-1980s, I told him about a treatment I'd written that excited him so much he optioned it. It was a concept I'd never seen dealt with on screen about William Shakespeare's "Dark Lady of the Sonnets." What if young Will Shakespeare's self-esteem was shaky, I mused. What if he was ready to give up writing because he wasn't getting any respect? What if a former acting friend who had gone into wizardry showed up to cheer Shakespeare and encourage him to keep writing, because he'd gone through time and seen the impact Sweet William would have on Western society?

That was my story. To convince the budding Bard, the wizard friend whisks him to modern-day New York City, where Shakespeare promptly falls in love with a girl who becomes his Muse, sparks his writing, gets him going.

Michael York couldn't get anyone to fund the writing of a script on my romantic comedy treatment. I knew that one. Two people at International Creative Management in Los Angeles had previously optioned the story. The deal had been negotiated by Dan Petrie, Jr., an agent who went on to write *The Big Easy* (1987) and other films as well as become president of the Writers Guild of America, west.

My story, we can assume, got around town.

Fast forward to the fall of 2003 and a photographic exhibit by Pat York, Michael's wife, at the Academy of Arts and Sciences on Wilshire Boulevard in Beverly Hills. My wife and I were strolling around marveling at the photos when I saw, in close proximity to each other, shots of Tom Stoppard and Edward Zwick.

Respectively, the cowriter and director of *Shakespeare in Love* (1998), a movie which seemed to spring from the same idea in my treatment which had been optioned twice, once by someone whose wife obviously knew two of the creative forces behind the Oscar-winning film.

I contacted my attorney and his opinion was simple. I'd have to show that, via the Yorks, Stoppard and Zwick read my treatment and came up with their own version. This, we realized was probably impossible. Oddly enough, I had another treatment in Michael York's reading pile at the moment, again featuring Shakespeare. I faxed him and told him that I would like it back and to please not show it to anyone. He emailed me to say that he had shown it to no one, not to worry.

Much ado about nothing? Probably. Facing reality, I told myself that it was such an obvious idea to write about a fictitious "Dark Lady of the Sonnets" that someone would've done it sooner or later. Also, it could have been just another case of writers "tapping the ether" of imagination simultaneously, as Mark Twain did when writing *Pudd'n'head*

Film is more than the twentieth-century art. It's another part of the twentieth-century mind. It's the world seen from inside.

—**Don DeLillo**

Wilson. He was sued by an Australian writer who claimed that Twain knew about a book the Aussie had written. Twain proved that he could not have, and that settled it.

Still, when I read in January 2004 that Edward Zwick was being sued by a writer who felt cheated out of credits on *The Last Samurai,* I again wondered. But that wasn't enough to make me want to hire another detective with an eye toward a lawsuit. I simply didn't want the hassle, and I'd rather spend my time creating something new.

At the risk of offending everyone English, I still believe my story was more entertaining than *Shakespeare in Love* and that (gasp, blasphemy!) I'd write a better screenplay.

If you think my scenario is unusual, consider another one. When Mirko Betz's first screenplay was purchased by director/producer Roland Emmerich, an article appeared in *Daily Variety* in which Emmerich declared the script would be his next feature project.

So much for public pronouncements. Emmerich found another screenplay he liked more (*The Day After Tomorrow,* 2002), and put that one into production instead.

Meanwhile, Betz was established as a screenwriter. He got a manager he couldn't get prior to the sale, and agents now returned his phone calls. His next screenplay, titled *The Peaceful Warrior* began making the rounds. It was a fine script, which he paid me to evaluate, so I knew it intimately.

A few months go by. One day I read in *The Hollywood Reporter* that British director Ridley Scott planned to make *Kingdom of Heaven* (2005) for Twentieth Century Fox. The script revolved around a young peasant who becomes a knight, saves a kingdom, and falls in love with a princess during the Crusades. Pretty much the same plot as Betz's script. He was crestfallen, but didn't think he had been ripped off and planned no action. Like me, he believed that many stories were simply "out there" and could be written down by diverse writers at the same time. Don't believe us? Consider this. On January 14, 2004, I read the following at HollywoodReporter.com:

> Touchstone Pictures has picked up "Unique," an
> upcoming graphic novel from Platinum Studios, to
> serve as a directing vehicle for David Goyer . . . .
> "Unique" centers on Jon Geoffries, a man who dis-
> covers the Earth has a twin, a parallel world in
> another dimension. The worlds are closely linked,
> explaining such phenomena as déjà vu and love at
> first sight, with people having counterparts on both
> Earths.

The story was nearly identical to one I had been developing for some time, except that I had never in any way shared my story with anyone. My twin Earth was on the other side of the sun, but why quibble. The creators of "Unique" had a better idea than mine, as further description of the project revealed:

> However, a few are born "unique," with no doppel-
> gangers, and can travel between worlds. Geoffries
> is one such person and soon finds himself a target
> of enemies who want to exploit his connection.

Hey, I thought, *they have a better story.*

The people who are most likely to have ideas stolen by people in Hollywood are those who are the least connected. That's why you need to break in with a *great* screenplay, not just a good one. A great one will get you connected quickly.

There are only so many popular restaurants and popular clubs in Hollywood. There are a finite number of major studio and television networks. You tend to see the same people repeatedly. So if you know you'll run into people again, do you really want to steal from them and have them find out? Stealing from a stranger living outside of town? Hmmm . . . .

My client Ted Gasowski had been sending me scripts for years and his writing had continually improved. Finally, he wrote one that I told him was his graduation ticket and that he could sell. At the very least, I said, it would work as a "show script" that could get him work. Fired up, Ted entered a screenplay contest and won with his high-concept story. A synopsis was mailed out to various legitimate companies known by the contest organizer. He promptly began getting phone calls from producers and his script had heat.

Then, nothing. Ted asked me about the silence, and it wasn't long before I forwarded to him a mention of an almost identical story that had been sold as a pitch; no script was yet written. Ted contacted his entertainment attorney who said: "Wait and see." A few months went by, the sold pitch seem to fade from sight, and Ted got another phone call from a Hollywood pro who had another company interested in his script. Ted learned a lesson about keeping himself protected by not disseminating a very good high-concept idea too widely through the usual outlets for beginning screenwriters.

I continually advise writers to keep records that "prove access." That is, who's seen their work and when. I tell them to save not only emails, but the "headers" (full electronic details) of email exchanges, keep copies of printed letters, get confirmations of delivery, and try to submit work though an attorney, manager, or agent whenever possible.

Will they steal your idea? Who is "they"? The answer is nebulous because it can vary completely from one situation to another in Hollywood. I've generally found that the higher-end people, the folks who make the studio features, tend to be more likely to pay the money and take their chances. In 2004, a sequel to *Amityville Horror* (1979) was to be made by two different groups, both of whom thought they had the rights. Cool heads (including that of a producer friend who actually had a better claim) prevailed.

The groups joined forces, and the movie moved forward with Miramax. Production and profits were more important than claims and posturing.

> *Hollywood money isn't money. It's congealed snow, melts in your hand, and there you are.*
>
> **—Dorothy Parker**

Roadside Assistance

There are a lot of ideas floating around Hollywood at any one time. It helps to have people who know who is busy with what, and most people think they need a Hollywood agent to handle that. So what kind of person is a Hollywood agent? It's often a person who works twelve to fourteen hours a day, seven days a week. That agent you want didn't take a vacation last year and has burned out two treadmills. Oh sure, he is making $100,000+ in the agency he works for, but if his clients with credits don't pay more than that in commissions, the agent will be gone. Can you explain to me again why this agent should pay attention to you?

Most screenwriters I know think their works should be made into movies, and all that stands between them and riches is (a) finding an agent who isn't an idiot; (b) getting past the gatekeepers; (c) the use of agents/managers to the real person who can make a decision; (d) some great stroke of luck.

Here's the real story.

Most agents are not idiots if they manage to stay in business. They do, however, tend to favor the same kind of writing/writers so if you don't write the kind of thing they like, you shouldn't even be talking to them. As long as I've been giving Hollywood advice, I've suggested that beginning writers find a manager to help them navigate the town. Managers find agents for writers and make introductions to producers. The only way a manager can mess you up is by doing things like attaching themselves to your property as a producer to make more money when they're really not needed, and thus possibly kill the project.

It takes a concentrated flow of attention to achieve something worthwhile, and if you let that stream get polluted (with other people's bad ideas) or diluted (from a busted channel of concentration), there goes your project. In just about every instance I can think of, when I've had a great idea or gone out with a project that reached fruition, almost instantly negatives (side distractions) popped up. When I've been in production on something, even a play, as soon as you think things are going great, some big thing will pop up that threatens to kill the whole production. When you get over that seemingly insurmountable hurdle, keeping the rest of the show on track isn't nearly as hard.

As I've studied a phenomena called the Elliott Wave (see www.elliottwave.com) and learned about the natural flows and ups and downs of life, I've learned to expect a big drop-off (the second downward wave in a five-wave upward-moving positive Elliott Wave trend) once a project is underway. I've also seen it happen in a career, with the second script of Mirko Betz as mentioned above. (Some people call this type of thing "the sophomore jinx.")

The problem with lots of agents is they simply don't have the time to nurture you through the natural ups and downs of a writing career. At least most of them don't. A good manager, on the other hand, can shape and guide your career in highly positive ways.

As of this writing, I don't have an agent because I don't have anything new to show. I have a management company, The Gotham Group, which is one of the preeminent management and production companies in the business. To give you an idea of what a top manager goes through, I spoke to Peter McHugh at Gotham about how that company works. Peter is a Dartmouth Grad (1993, History and Religion double major, Cum Laude). He worked as Assistant Director of Admissions for Dartmouth College before packing up the bags, driving cross-country, and starting as a trainee in the Creative Artists Agency mailroom. From there he moved to Michael Ovitz's Aritsts Management Group (AMG), where he was promoted to manager. When AMG dissolved, Peter spun off with The Gotham Group.

Skip: *When The Gotham Group takes on a new writer or content creator, what goes into the decision to sign that person?*

Peter: We are a management/production company. We represent creators—whether they are writers, directors, artists, producers, authors, or game designers. In reviewing potential clients, we look at the body of work they've created. We get a sense of the stories they have yet to tell, and where they want their careers to go. We rarely take on new clients. We, as a group, have to believe in a new client as a whole. It's a tough business and we believe that you will have the greatest success if you're managed by a team of representatives. If we believe in someone's creative abilities, if we respond to the stories they've told and want to tell, we'll meet with a potential client so that he or she can get a better sense of who we are and he or she can get a better sense of us. If we feel we can help the creator meet his creative and financial goals we will move forward together, relentless in achieving those goals. This is an industry of "Nos"—to work tirelessly for someone, you have to believe in him or her despite the "Nos" and do all you can to move others to a "Yes."

Skip: *How does Gotham assess the current Hollywood marketability of a property?*

Peter: We're in the trenches 24/7. Our job is to know the media marketplace, whether in film, television, gaming, or publishing. The buyers come to respect our opinion—they know we see a lot of material. They also know that we have a sense of what works and what doesn't. We let them know when we believe in a person or a property and they listen. Our reputation is on the line.

We listen to the buyers' needs. We strategize with our clients to find the right buyers and shape the clients' projects so that they better fit the buyer's needs. The buyers also know that our clients can execute the ideas they are presenting. Keep in mind, someone may have a great idea, but remember . . . it's all in the execution, and the ability to execute comes with experience.

We'll let our clients know about the right timing for a project. We'll also inform a client if we think something is a "tough sell." Time is one of a creator's greatest assets, and if we think his or her time is better spent elsewhere, we'll let him or her know.

That said, if there's an idea both we and the client think is a

gem, no matter how tough the sell we will be unstoppable in setting up the project. Most sales are uphill battles . . . and those are
the battles we like to fight!

Skip: *Once someone is a client, how much regular interaction do you
have?*

Peter: It depends on the client, their needs. If we've placed someone
on an overall deal, we'll have less interaction than someone
who's aggressively trying to find the next opportunity.

Skip: *On average, how many calls would you say you make during a
day?*

Peter: Two hundred fifty.

Skip: *How about emails, faxes, and letters?*

Peter: Too many. Most written correspondence is via email. I get about
two hundred emails a day.

Skip: *How much reading do you do in an average week? How much of
it is covered for you first?*

Peter: I read almost everything. I'm a voracious reader. If the material
is written by a client, I definitely read it. For potential clients,
we circulate material. If we like what we initially read, we'll read
more.

Skip: *How much time do you spend networking and attending events
to work the room?*

Peter: The career is 24/7. Social and business intertwine—breakfasts,
lunches, dinners, social events.

Skip: *How long will you and/or other people at Gotham stay with any
one project before you think you can't move it?*

Peter: If we believe in a project, we never give up. How long is a lifetime?

Skip: *How long will you try to sell for a client before you have to part
company because it's no longer financially feasible?*

Peter: We're loyal to our clients and our clients are loyal to us. There
are good times and bad times. We stick with them, and as a
result we have a reputation for our clients sticking with us.

Skip: *Do you also try to see that your clients have a separate agent?*
Lawyer? If so, why?

Peter: Some of our clients have just us. Some also have a lawyer, agent,
business manager, and publicist. Typically, as a client's career
grows both financially and creatively, the team surrounding the
client grows as well.

Skip: *What type of current and future buzz properties do you see Hol-*
lywood wanting?

Peter: If we're talking movies—Hollywood is always looking for the big
idea. Think of the one sheet, the one liner. Sounds cliché, but it's
the name of the game, especially if someone is trying to break in.

If it seems like a top management company is as busy as an
agency and might not have time for a beginner, you're right. Most
writers get their agent or manager by a personal referral from another
client or someone with whom the agency or management company does
business.

You can always check the Writers Guild Signatory Agents and
Agencies list for contacts. It's better than it used to be and some agents
on it will actually talk to you. See www.wga.org/agency/AgencyList.asp
for agents in twenty-five states and the District of Columbia. The agencies represent film, television, and interactive writers.

Then there's always the do-it-yourself method. No manager, no
lawyer, no agent—just good writing and smart marketing. Let's see how
that's done, courtesy of one of the most successful independent screenwriters in Hollywood.

Building Your Own Highway

Some writers don't let anything stop them. Generally, the people who
make it fall into that category. William C. Martell is that kind of screenwriter. Seventeen of his screenplays have been produced. He has had

three HBO World Premiere movies, two movies for Showtime Films, and a couple CineMax Premieres. His USA Network thriller *Hard Evidence* (1995) was "video pick of the week" in more than two dozen newspapers, was a Blockbuster-featured new release, and beat the Julia Roberts film *Something to Talk About* (1995) in video rentals when both debuted the same week. He is the west coast editor of *Scr(i)pt* magazine and was the only non-nominated screenwriter mentioned on "Siskel & Ebert's If We Picked The Winners" Oscar show in 1997. *Washington Post* reviewer David Nuttycombe said, "William C. Martell is the Robert Towne of made-for-cable movies." Bill's book, *The Secrets of Action Screenwriting*, has received rave reviews and his Web site www.ScriptSecrets.net was chosen as the best site for screenwriters by *Entertainment Today*. He lives in Studio City, California.

Skip: *You've sold your scripts yourself. How did it work out that way?*

Bill: Every single one of my seventeen produced scripts and the handful that haven't made it to the screen were sold without an agent. I have nothing against agents. I've had agents and managers before, but none of them have ever sold anything for me. They have other clients, other priorities, and seem less motivated to make a sale for me than I am. No one is ever going to be more interested in my career than I am.

I had an agent once that lost me deals. I bumped into the vice president of development for this start-up production company in a hotel. They had just finished their first film, a co-production with a Swedish company; a low-budget horror film starring John Saxon that was getting a limited theatrical release. I pitched one of my scripts, he loved it, and said, "Have it messengered to my office Monday morning." So I told my agent to messenger it over. A couple of weeks later I called to find out what happened, and he told me he hadn't sent it, yet. He was busy with other clients. I asked him to send it right away—before they forget about it.

Two weeks later their little horror film came out and was a huge hit. I called my agent and asked about the script, and he *still* hadn't sent it. I don't know if he ever sent it. The little horror film was *Nightmare on Elm Street* (1984) and the company was New Line. If I had known he wasn't going to send my script, I would have put a copy in the mail myself!

Another factor is that Groucho Marx thing: I wouldn't want any agent who would take me as a client. I want the agent who wants David Koepp! I want the agent who will open doors I can't open on my own.

Skip: *The nightmare agent . . . . So how did you sell your first script?*

Bill: I didn't go to film school, I was too poor for that. I went to a (free) community college. There was a film appreciation class where they showed movies and you wrote reports about them. Every semester you had to make a three-minute movie on Super-8mm. I ended up making a twenty-minute parody of all of the films they made us watch. It opened with my dying words, *Citizen Kane*–style, and the search for their meaning passed through take-offs on a dozen classic films . . . ending with a silly punchline. Compared to the other films, it was *Citizen Kane*.

They would bring in the past success stories from the class to be judges: a guy who made instructional videos, a guy who made exploitation films for drive-ins, and notorious pornographers The Mitchell Brothers. My film, being in focus, was the highlight of the night and led to my first film job—which was *not* directing porn for The Mitchell Brothers nor carrying equipment for the guy making instructional films. I ended up working on a drive-in movie. We aren't talking Hollywood films, we're talking backyard films. Paul made these kung fu movies in my hometown starring no one you've ever heard of. I gave Paul one of my scripts. He read it and asked if I wanted to work on his next kung fu film. Not as a writer. As a laborer, for no pay. I worked on a drive-in exploitation movie called *Weapons of Death* (1981). I was easy to get along with and said funny things on the set, so a year later Paul called me for his next film. This time he needed someone to do a page-one rewrite on a script called *The Falcon's Claw*. They had already cast the film, secured the locations, and were ready to shoot . . . when they realized the script sucked. They gave me two weeks to rewrite it, using the exact same cast and locations. I threw out everything (including the title) and started from scratch. *Ninja Busters* (1984) was my first paid job, done in my hometown, all due to this guy who went to the same community college that I did.

But drive-ins were dying and they changed the tax laws. No one was making low-budget films any more, and I had to get a job in a warehouse. I drove a forklift for ten years before selling my next script, to a company on the Paramount lot.

Skip: *How did you get your script to Paramount without an agent?*

Bill: By accident. I met this actress in my hometown, flirted with her, gave her a copy of one of my scripts, and told her there was "a role in this script that's perfect for you." My plan had nothing to do with selling the script—I had the hots for the actress. She moved to Los Angeles and was cast in some really low-budget horror film where she takes off her top and gets killed by the monster (I don't think her character even had a name). She gave my script to the line producer and told him the lead role was perfect for her. She was going to use my script to get work! But that wasn't the *producer*, it was the guy who orders equipment and manages the set. He read it and really liked it and passed it up to his best connection (he was trying to get work), who passed it to his best connection, and a couple of years later I get a call from a company on the Paramount lot wanting to buy my script. I have no idea how it got there. They flew me to LA, bought the script for about two years' worth of warehouse wages, and then never made the film.

So people passed that script around because they liked it. If you have a great script, it does all of the work for you. You just have to get it into somebody's hands.

Skip: *What happened once you moved to Los Angeles?*

Bill: Instead of using that sale to find an agent, I had an attorney negotiate the contract. Paramount never made *Courting Death,* and whatever heat I had dissipated. When my money began running out, I needed to sell another script and realized I'd spent two years writing and no time making connections. So I began querying and cold-calling producers. I targeted producers who made films like the scripts I wrote (thrillers and action) and actually made the scripts they bought. This was the early '90s, and the cable revolution was upon us. Every week there was a new cable channel, and every cable channel needed movies. USA Network needed movies, Lifetime needed movies, HBO needed movies, Showtime needed movies. Unlike the studios, cable networks actually had to film the scripts they bought. If HBO didn't film my script, they'd have to run a test pattern between 9:00 p.m. and 11:00 p.m. on the airdate.

Next thing you know, I'm writing movies for USA Network (*Hard Evidence,* 1995), HBO (*Virtual Combat,* 1996; *Crash Dive,* 1996; *Steel Sharks,* 1996), Showtime (*Black Thunder,* 1997), and CineMax Original Movies (*Treacherous,* 1994; *Night Hunter,* 1995). Many of these films were made by studios. *Treacherous* was made by Twentieth Century Fox and *Hard Evidence* was made by Warner Bros. for cable networks.

Cable movies were kind of like the Wild West at the time; nobody cared if you had an agent, they only cared if the script was any good. If a homeless guy had a good script, they'd buy it. I think that's true even now. If you have a great script it will open doors for you in Hollywood. Your script creates the connections. During the '90s I probably turned down three times as many jobs as I accepted. I prefer to write my own stories rather than script producer's ideas, so I focused on companies that allowed me to pitch ideas based on their needs. That way I could tell my story and still have it be exactly what they wanted.

Since moving to Los Angeles, everything I've sold has come from a query letter or a phone call or me figuring out how to track down some producer. Every sale is breaking in all over again. Even though some companies know me, many more have never read one of my scripts and I have to query or cold call. I get meetings with companies I have never worked with before, all from queries and cold calls.

You don't need to have relatives in the business, you don't even have to know anyone in the business . . . you just have to *get to know* someone in the business. And you don't have to know anyone important. I pitched a script over the phone once to an office temp who asked to read it himself. He then used my script to become a permanent development guy at the company he was temping for. Oh, and my script sold as a side effect of his promotion.

Your best connections might be the people around you— people you already know! Do you know someone who wants to direct movies? That person may be the next Spielberg. My advice to anyone who doesn't have an agent is not to let that get in the way of their career. Query or call producers yourself. Agents don't need new clients, but producers need new scripts. I think it's easier to sell a script than it is to find an agent. Just get your scripts out there!

Skip: *You seem to have an encyclopedic knowledge of old films and have written about using such movies as templates for new scripts. Is this something you advise new writers to do—study old movies and imitate them?*

Bill: I think it's important to study films and scripts, not to copy them, but to learn from them. If you want to be a novelist, you've probably read hundreds of novels. But I meet people who want to be screenwriters who have never read a screenplay. You need to read a big stack of scripts before you sit down to write one, so that you can think in that format. Most of the questions new writers ask on my message boards could easily be answered just by reading a stack of scripts. When I don't know how to do something, I flip through a bunch of scripts until I find the answer.

You also need to know how movie stories work. That comes from taking apart movies and seeing how they tick. The templates you're referring to are my "timelines"—I take a bunch of films in whatever genre I'm writing and do a modified "beat sheet" outline for each, noting what happens in the story and when (in the running time) it happens. This gives me a good overview of the genre. I know what the story expectations are, and how the genre is paced. You begin to see the patterns.

For my class on writing thrillers, I took a bunch of very different thriller films, broke them down, and compared them. I noticed that all of the films (from *Breakdown,* 1997, to *North by Northwest,* 1959 to *The Game,* 1997) had scenes between twenty and twenty-five minutes into each film where the protagonist goes to the authorities. The authorities then search for evidence of a crime, and not only find nothing—but they find that what the protagonist said is just plain wrong. They almost always arrest the protagonist! (They *do* convict Roger Thornhill of drunk driving.) So the next question is why? Why do dozens of very different thrillers all have this type of scene at almost the same time? The answers:

1. If the protagonist can go to the police, the story is over. So we need to get the police out of the story as soon as possible.
2. We also need to keep the police out—so the hero has to look crazy. We need a situation where the audience knows the protagonist won't be able to go to the authorities for the rest of the movie (though part of the pattern is that they do—with tragic results).

3. Thrillers separate the protagonist from society. The authorities represent society.

4. Thrillers throw the protagonist into a world of chaos, a world without order. Again—the authorities represent order.

A thriller needs the protagonist to be "on his own" for Act Two, so this type of scene usually takes place near the end of Act One . . . around page twenty or twenty-five.

The *reason* for the pattern is more important than the pattern. If you write a script by patterns you end up with a cookie-cutter script—we have the scenes but may not have the reasons behind the scenes. It ends up arbitrary instead, or organic to the story, the motivations of characters, and the effect on the audience. If you know the reason you can find a different way to do the scene. But to know the reason, you have to do the work yourself—you have to watch movies and really pay attention. You have to look at how stories are told, and why they work better when told one way than when told another. But, isn't that our job as writers?

Pacing is something else you learn by breaking down films this way. Most scripts from new writers just don't have enough story and enough things happening. If you are writing a chase thriller like *North by Northwest* or *The Bourne Identity* (2002) you need to make sure your story has similar pacing. If your script is slower paced than a forty-five year-old pre-MTV movie such as *North by Northwest,* you're in a heap o' trouble!

Skip: *When I first met you, you'd written a book, but weren't pushing it that much. Now you do seminars all over the place and seem to enjoy it quite a bit. Have you found that you're filling gaps about the craft of screenwriting that the traveling gurus who haven't actually written and sold screenplays leave out?*

Bill: My book, *Secrets of Action Screenwriting,* has a strange backstory. My friends kept giving me scripts to read, and many of them had the exact same problems. I got tired of typing up the same notes over and over again, so I created a little red booklet I gave to my friends with all of the basics. Now I could read a script and say, "Look at chapter three" or "Check out page seventeen." One of my friends said I should publish it, so I wrote an expanded version, which has sold really well. It was #11 on the Amazon screenwriting list the last time I looked, and it's the bestselling screenwriting book in the Sam French Bookstores here in Los Angeles. Professional screenwriters often recommend it.

My focus has always been on writing scripts, and suddenly people are lumping me in with all of these screenwriting gurus such as Syd Field and Robert McKee. I'm not really a teacher; I'm a guy who writes scripts for a living and wrote a book on screenwriting.

The Raindance Film Festival in London asked if I would be interested in teaching a screenwriting workshop. They offered to pay my way, put me up, pay me to teach the class, *and* buy my drinks. The warehouse employee side of me jumped at their offer to buy my beers. The class went well, and I began doing more classes and a few film festivals. It's all part of my master plan never to waste $10 on a movie with a bad script again. If I can pass on some of what I've learned as a professional writer to the next generation of writers, maybe the quality of films we see will improve.

Skip: *How do you see the current state of opportunities for beginning screenwriters?*

Bill: Well, the cable movie has been killed by hour-long original series such as *The Sopranos,* so those opportunities don't exist anymore. But others have taken their place. DVD sales make two to three times more money than the theatrical box office, so many studios have created direct-to-DVD divisions to make theatrical film sequels that were minor hits. Someone needs to write those movies. There are also DVD originals with $20 million stars such as Sylvester Stallone. It's a much bigger market than theatrical and different than the old VHS direct-to-video market because people don't rent the movies the way they rented VHS tapes, they buy them. All DVDs are "sell-through priced." People will *buy* a movie like *Wild Things 2* (2004) even though Kevin Bacon isn't in it.

It's too early to tell whether DVD will be a place for new writers to get on-the-job experience the way cable movies and direct-to-video was in the '80s and '90s, but more jobs for screenwriters are always a good thing.

As far as studio films are concerned, it's the same as it ever was. It's difficult to break in, but everyone is looking for a great script. The frustrating part of writing studio films is that they seldom get made. About four years ago I stopped writing cable movies—I had too many meetings on big theatrical projects. When one of my scripts would go out wide to fifty studio-based producers, I'd end up with forty-eight meetings . . . and those meetings led to other meetings and stacks of scripts or novels or magazine stories to read and "pitch my take on." Not a single film came out of any of this . . . all phantom credits!

A couple of years ago I adapted a *New York Times* bestselling thriller novel for a studio-based producer . . . and that project was shelved when the star did another film. The same year I wrote an action film for MGM that was shelved when both the star and director moved on to another project. I was paid, the movies weren't made. It was very frustrating to do some good work and have nothing to show from it but a paycheck. So much so, that I decided to produce a couple of my own scripts as DVD originals just to get something on the screen again. It's also self-defense against the sausage grinder of development.

One of the things many new writers don't understand when they think they can write something better than that big Hollywood movie is that anybody can. Hollywood buys a great script, then has it rewritten into crap. The reason why indie films are always up for Oscars is that indie films don't go through the sausage machine. Even on my cable flicks, where they're only spending $3 million, I get notes from the producer, the director, the star, the development executive, the foreign sales guy, the marketing department, the product placement guys, and the video distributor. Most of them are not creative types, and have no idea how stories work—but I have to do rewrites based on their notes! The system is designed to turn filet mignon into hot dogs!

Skip: *If you were starting your career today, would you go about it any differently?*

Bill: A million ways! I would have signed with an agency after selling *Courting Death* even though I didn't seem to need one at the time. I would have started producing my own films much earlier, and I would have realized the importance of having a high-concept script before I turned out all of those scripts with mundane ideas. Heck, I made a million mistakes to get to where I am now. I learned from most of them (and there are things I'm still learning). I began writing scripts years before Syd Field wrote his book.

There were no screenwriting books, no Web sites with information, no magazines, nothing! I had to learn by trial and error (and a whole bunch of error). It would be nice to start out back then with what I know now, but I don't own a time machine.

Skip: *If you were to isolate the main thing beginners are doing wrong, what would it be?*

Bill: First-time writers often forget that film is a mass-audience medium. The average film will be seen by six to eight hundred million people worldwide. A story that will only be of interest to the writer's friends and family isn't going to work as a screenplay. There are too many self-indulgent scripts out there. This doesn't mean that a script can't be personal—it *must* be something that the writer cares about or it will be lifeless on the page—but it can't be a story that *only* the writer cares about. The key is to find a story that you are deeply passionate about, that those six to eight hundred million people will also be passionate about. When I spend my $10 on Friday night I want to leave my troubles behind and be transported into another world. I want to laugh or cry or sit on the edge of my seat in suspense. I want to be entertained. I always tell writers to write the same kind of movies they pay to see every week—those movies that they are part of the audience for.

Another problem is not having a story. Too many scripts are just a collection of incidents or subplots that concern the same character. They meander all over the place. A story needs a central conflict (the Greek "Unity of Event"). I don't spend a great deal of time talking about screenplay structure when I teach my classes, but I do focus on the importance of the central conflict. Many scripts from new writers are just a collection of events, not a story.

Story is conflict. Either your protagonist has a goal and the antagonist stands directly in the way, or your antagonist has a goal and the protagonist stands directly in his way. Then the entire script is about the struggle to achieve that goal.

By the way—in most stories, regardless of genre, the antagonist's goal is what kicks off the story. In *My Best Friend's Wedding* (1997), it's Cameron Diaz (the nicest antagonist in film history) who creates the story when she becomes engaged to Dermot Mulroney. Without Cameron Diaz there is no wedding for Julia Roberts to break up. Most new writers don't give enough thought to their antagonist and their plan. The antagonist is more important than the protagonist!

A script also needs to be as exciting to read as the movie is to see. People say that a script is the blueprint for the movie, but it's really more than that. When a producer reads your script, it *is* the movie. A script is submitted "naked." You don't have the charm of Tom Cruise or the cinematography of James Wong Howe or the music of Jerry Goldsmith to make it work. All we have is our writing! We need to use our writing skills to create the movie in the mind of the reader.

And Hollywood is run by the readers—kids fresh out of college who are paid $35 to $40 to read a script and write a four-page critique. The studio will use that coverage to decide if they want to buy the script or not. Los Angeles is an expensive place to live, so these kids may have to read as many as five scripts a day in order to pay their rent. Your script isn't automatically given their attention, it has to earn it. They are going to skim through a dull script and give it bad coverage. Is that fair? Hey, a boring script isn't a good script! If the script can't make one person care, how can anyone expect it to make those six to eight hundred million people worldwide care? We are writers. Our job is to use words to involve the reader. A script that is exciting to read is going to be the high point of that reader's day. He's going to recommend the script, plus tell all of his friends about the great script he just read. Next thing you know, people are passing your script around town and it ends up on the desk of some big studio producer who calls you when you're on your way to your warehouse job because they want to fly you to Los Angeles and buy your script. That is how screenwriter's careers are made! It all starts with a great script, and the script makes the connections for you.

Hopefully, you'll write that great script and successfully market it the way people like myself and Bill Martell have advised in this book. Or you might come up with a better way to do it yourself. Meanwhile, some listings follow of people who might decide that property of yours should be on the screen, people who will do whatever they can to get it there and make you famous, maybe even rich.

Thanks for reading the book and . . .

Good Luck!

CHAPTER

12

Hollywood

Market Place

The studio of Mos Eisner . . . You'll never find a more wretched hive of scum and villainy. So be careful, we're going in without an agent.

—"Slappy Wanna Nappy" (cartoon character) in Animaniacs (1993)

There is no "studio of Mos Eisner." The phrase above is a play on the imaginary spaceport "Mos Eisley" from *Star Wars* mixed with the last name of Michael Eisner, the head of Disney. Eisner's former partner, Jeffrey Katzenberg, helped move Disney back into Hollywood prominence before he left to become one of the founders of DreamWorks, the company that produced *Animaniacs*. (DreamWorks was originally DreamWorks SKG, the S and G representing Katzenberg's partners Steven Spielberg and David Geffen.)

With me so far? Such changes, which I follow every day as a Hollywood participant, help illustrate the impossible dilemma I face each time I write one of these books. The Hollywood landscape shifts as regularly as the earthquake patterns in the San Andreas Fault running underneath Los Angeles. That is to say, people move around, companies move around, people come and go, and companies go out of business. So how can anyone hope to publish a book months in advance and hope the listings will stay correct?

On the following pages you will find such listings of people who might option your property, help you shape it, help you sell it, or all of the above. These are folks I believe have a strong possibility of being where I say they are and who I say they are as printed. If you discover otherwise, please email me via my Web site, www.skippress.com, and I'll try to help you sort it out.

Before we get to the listings, allow me to qualify the situation just a little more. There exists a Hollywood "Catch 22." (See the book or movie of the same name for clarification if you're not familiar with the term, or look it up on www.imdb.com.) You usually need an agent for most big producers to take you seriously, but agents want writers with a track record. Here's how to handle that:

a. Don't worry about big producers; smaller ones are much more likely to take your call and read your work without representation;

b. Find a manager who will tout your worth; the manager might find an agent for you, or produce your work;

c. Make a sale; the good agents will then find you.

The day I discovered that agents would talk to an unproven writer if I had a director or producer of note interested in my property, I understood Hollywood. *Agents make a living by selling.* Agents cannot by California law produce movies. So they want people who are already making money, or have a commercial property that is a lot easier to sell than other types.

When you contact producers, if they like the sound of what you're selling, they generally say, "Have your agent send it over." They might let you sign a release, but that can some times be legally chancy. So if you're not represented, you can call an agent and say, "So-and-so wants to see my script." That can get you an agent for that transaction. It's called hip-pocketing. The same situation could arise if someone the agent currently represents refers you. Either way, the agent figures your work has been pre-screened. They might read what they hip-pocket, but don't be surprised if they don't.

Of course, I've also been signed by an agent simply because he read my script and liked it and so can you. On the WGA agents list (www.wga.org/agency/AgencyList.asp) you'll find a breakdown of how agents consider writers: (a) New Writers OK; (b) References Required; (c) Letter of Inquiry Required; and (d) No Unsolicited Material. You won't find such detail when dealing with most producers.

Writers provide the gas in the Hollywood bus, but producers drive it. It's been that way ever since the studio system changed to a more independent structure. Many of them now also serve as managers, which means you get the benefit of their years of experience for free, and they take the time to groom you as a writer. You would be hard pressed to find an agent who would do that today.

And what if you want to break into television? The hottest person in television is the writer/producer known as a showrunner, so if you want to write for television try to find a showrunner who will help you get started.

Producers in all fields are hustlers and entrepreneurs. I've consistently found working producers to be very engaging people. Good producers are ready to share information and willing to hear from writers anywhere in the world. The only things I hear them gripe about are bad material, writers who do not know the basics of screenwriting, and impatient people who find it hard to wait for a response to a submission.

Thoughts from a Major Agency

Despite my ongoing belief that you should contact producers directly before worrying about an agent, the fact is that people at major agencies *will* pay attention to any writer they think has talent and great earning capacity. That is why, in each book I write about selling to Hollywood, I am certain that the responses to questions below would be the same if they came from other top agencies both inside and outside the U.S. Here are the questions, with answers distilled from several top agents:

Q: *At what point in his or her career should an aspiring screenwriter expect to get an agent at a major agency?*

A: At any point in your career. Signing with the right agency might be your one shot at the career break you need.

Q: *If you are able to sell a script on your own, or make a film on your own, why do you then need an agent?*

A: An agent will see you through the entire process of selling a script and getting it into production. A good agent provides career planning and connections, and gets writers to the next level of their careers. Agents stay on top of what writers are getting paid. If you're already making money as a writer, the commission you pay an agent is a good investment in your career, particularly if you get an agent who shares your passion.

Q: *Do you need an entertainment attorney as well as a good agent?*

A: It depends on the agency. If an agency is big enough, it has a business affairs department stuffed with entertainment attorneys, so you won't need an outside attorney for entertainment matters.

Q: *What are the components of a great, marketable script?*

A: That never changes: good characters and a good story, told in a fresh way.

Q: *Can a new writer get a script assignment via a great sample, or are those jobs reserved for seasoned writers? If so, how much does it pay?*

A: Yes, a new writer can, but it's tough. If a new writer gets a script assignment through our agency, they'll get Writers Guild scale plus 10 percent.

Q: *If a new writer only has a treatment, will you try to sell it?*

A: We only sell completed screenplays.

Q: *Is it easier to get started in TV or in film?*

A: It's actually possible to get a television staff writing position without a great script; the medium simply needs so many ideas. Some writers stimulate other writers. They're good in a room. So they make good story editors. Some are good at writing jokes, while others specialize in character development, or even in one character on a show. So day in, day out, getting started in television is easier if you live in L.A.

Q: *What route would you suggest for a beginning writer?*

A: It depends on your career goal, your beliefs, and your passion. Focus on what you picture yourself being. Do you want to be the next Joe Ezsterhas? Callie Khouri? Or is David E. Kelley your role model? Also, you can get typecast as a TV writer and have difficulty breaking into feature writing, although that transition is far less difficult than it used to be.

Q: *Do you see any current story trends that you feel will be sustained in the coming years?*

A: You'd have to ask someone at a smaller agency. We look for talented writers, not trends. You can read *Variety* for the box-office charts if you want to try to figure that out. They go back ten years or more. We look for good writers and good projects, period.

Contact Resources

For up-to-date contact information, I suggest the following sites. Their databases are constantly updated, used by professionals, and they offer free or low-cost trials.

Done Deal (www.scriptsales.com): This news resource for sales in the film industry also features interviews and other advice; the agency and production company listings have only basic information, but it's free.

Hollywood Creative Directory (www.hcdonline.com): Home of printed books and online databases that offer up-to-date information on production companies, television shows, and studio and network executives. It's cooperative with *The Hollywood Reporter* trade news magazine.

Internet Movie Database Professional (www.imdbpro.com): Listings for more than forty thousand people in Hollywood, eight thousand companies, and much more. As advertised, at $12.95 per month, it is "the lowest priced film and television resource available."

ShowBiz Data (www.showbizdata.com): This entertainment search engine features contacts and many other features including box-office revues, development news, and a free newsletter.

Studio System (www.studiosystem.com): Along with features in Hollywood and Studio Log, this site offers a vast array of helpful tools. Show biz trade news magazine *Variety*'s "The Vault" defaults to Studio System.

Who Represents . . . ? (www.whorepresents.com): No longer free, this database only covers agents and who they represent, nothing more.

Please do yourself a favor and use online databases to find the exact information you need. A week of free trials might get you in touch with people who can make your entire career. I've spent weeks of cumulative time over the years repeating this mantra to people who could have easily found the info they needed themselves without dashing off an email to me.

Web Site Producer Submissions

There are a number of sites on the Internet where you can find all sorts of producers looking for screenplays. The honest ones state up front what their credits are on Internet Movie Database or cite movie titles that you might recognize. Others only give you an email address, don't identify themselves by name, and might even ask you to email your screenplay for their "consideration."

Naturally, that could be suicide for your material, but many writers fall prey. Any time I would consider that type of approach, even if I had no credits, I would only do so via credible Web sites such as Howard Meibach's HollywoodLitSales (www.hollywoodlitsales.com). Meibach has a cooperating agreement with Sony-based production company Escape Artists (see separate listing below), "the people behind such films as *Antwone Fisher*, *A Knight's Tale*, *Forrest Gump*, *I Know What You Did Last Summer*, *Risky Business*, *Donnie Brasco*, and *Wild Things*." He has a full page about submitting material and explains in great detail how you can do so for that company as well as how to contact others if interested. This site gets thousands of submissions and thus will not allow more than five submissions per a thirty-day period from any one person. Meibach's site also offers good advice such as: "If you are unable to reduce the storyline to sixty words or less, you might want to rethink your story." You can choose between Narrow Submissions that never get posted to the site and Wide Submissions that other producers, agents, and companies can consider. There is also a "Scripts Wanted" page with ads from various companies. When I checked I found:

a. Brian Flinchbaugh, Tough Drive Entertainment, a start-up company, Christopher Yamamoto contact person, toughdriveentertainment @hotmail.com, looking for screenplays for intense dramas with approximate budget of $5,000,000;

b. Alex Stanford, Reid Media Group, ReidMedia@aol.com, looking for reality television material;

c. Michael G. Currie, Rushlight Entertainment with IMDb credit *Acrobats & Maniacs*, possible money up front, rushlight@sympatico.ca looking for co-productions and providing 50 percent of the financing for budgets over $3 million.

Does that give you some idea of the kinds of companies you can find on such sites? It can be all over the board. They're worth exploring, but remember to be cautious, and *never* send anyone anything substantial until you know quite a bit about who they are. You wouldn't buy a car that cost a year's salary without checking it out, would you? Then don't give away a screenplay that took you a year to write.

Open Source Hollywood

I'm working on revising a database of agents, managers, directors, and producers I've accumulated in over a decade. The idea is to use the "open source" model from the computer world (as Linus Torvalds did with the Linux operating system). I provide the core file (or "kernel" if you know computers) and it is added to and passed on from user to user. My file can then be added to and changed and freely passed on to others. I might use the Filemaker software (see www.filemaker.com) to do this, or I'll use Microsoft Word. Filemaker is an amazing database tool in use by a lot of Hollywood companies because of its flexibility and power, but tons of people use Word for word processing. I am open to your suggestions and contributions in this endeavor, which will first be developed through my "Skip's Hollywood Hangout" Yahoo! discussion group.

The cost of obtaining this file is nothing more than asking. Send me an email via my Web site.

The Listings

I know many of the people listed below, but don't be surprised if you call someone and mention my name and they say, "Who?" That's Hollywood, and I don't know everyone. Good luck selling—I hope you make a sale soon.

2929 Productions / 2929 Entertainment / Rysher Entertainment, 2425 Olympic Blvd., Suite 6040W, Santa Monica, CA 90404; Phone (310) 309-5200, Fax (310) 309-5716

Marc Butan, President of Production

Mark Cuban, President and Co-Founder

Todd Wagner, CEO and Co-Founder, twagner@2929entertainment.com

Kent Kubena, Production and Development Executive, (310) 309-5705, KKubena@2929productions.com

Couper Samuelson, Director of Development, csamuelson @2929productions.com

2929 Entertainment was created by Todd Wagner and Mark Cuban, an electronic business billionaire and the owner of the Dallas Mavericks basketball team. The companies are based in Los Angeles and Dallas. According to their Web site, "2929 owns 100 percent of Rysher Entertainment, Landmark Theaters, and Magnolia Pictures Distribution, and holds an interest in Lions Gate Entertainment." The company produces and finances movies through two production companies. 2929 Productions produces films in the $10–$30 million budget range and HDNet Films produces smaller-budget movies shot exclusively in high definition. 2929 Productions' first major film was *Godsend* (2004), a thriller co-produced with Lions Gate starring Robert De Niro, Greg Kinnear, and Rebecca Romijn-Stamos.

They're into everything, including novels. In March 2004 they optioned Mark Borrowcliffe's *Infidelity for First-Time Fathers*, about a man in his late thirties who impregnates both his fiancée and his college-age girlfriend.

By acquiring Rysher, 2929 gained syndication rights to such TV shows as *Hogan's Heroes, Lifestyles of the Rich and Famous,* and *Star Search.* They created a new version of *Star Search,* which completed its second season in 2004. Again, from their site: "Wagner and Cuban are also partnered in HDNet, the leading high-definition national television network co-founded by Cuban. HDNet's two 24/7 general entertainment networks, HDNet and HDNet Movies, are currently available on Adelphia Communications, Charter Communications, DIRECTV, DISH Network, Insight Communications, Time Warner Cable, and several other cable providers."

2929 is partnered on two films with Section Eight, Steven Soderbergh, and George Clooney's production company, and have huge aspirations. Their Web site explains in detail how to reach them.

Production and development exec Kent Kubena came to the company from director Dennis Duigan; prior to that he was at LivePlanet where he helped develop the "Project Greenlight" series. He epitomizes a young company with tons of money and no place to go but upward.

Contact: **Couper Samuelson** or **Kent Kubena** with a brief description of screenplay material. For submissions to HDNet Films, email hdnetfilms@opencityfilms.com

AEI-Atchity Entertainment Intl., c/o AEI Submissions, 9601 Wilshire Blvd., Box 1202, Beverly Hills, CA 90210; Phone (323) 932-0407, Web site www.aeionline.com

Ken Atchity, President
Chi-Li Wong, Vice President
Michael T. Kuciak, Associate Manager/Producer
Margaret O'Connor, Creative Executive-Books
Brenda Lui, Director of Development
Jennifer Pope, Story Editor

AEI-Atchity is a literary management and film production company with dozens of credits including books, films, television, video, and theater. See their Web site for extensive details. They accept scripts without referrals after an initial query. Prior to show business, Ken Atchity was a professor of comparative literature at Occidental College and has shown a taste for heroic and action properties with well-developed characters. Their most recent coup is a deal with Paramount to franchise *Ripley's Believe-It-Or-Not!* as a series of feature films along the lines of the "Indiana Jones" movies, in conjunction with Alphaville's Jim Jacks and Sean Daniels. AEI charges no fees other than sales commission, and refunds its commission when a film moves into production. They have downloadable releases and samples of treatments and other things on the site.

Contact: **Jennifer Pope** at submissions@aeionline.com

Alan Sacks Productions, Inc., 11684 Ventura Blvd., #809, Studio City, CA 91604; Phone (818) 752-6999, Fax (818) 752-6985, Email asacks@pacbell.net

Alan Sacks, Producer

Teena Portier, Assistant

Alan Sacks's eclectic resume includes *Welcome Back Kotter, Lizard Woman,* and *Cowboy Poetry Gathering* (a celebration of ten years of cowboy poets). He is the Chair of Media Arts at Los Angeles Valley College, where he develops full two-year programs to train students for jobs in the entertainment industry in broadcasting (radio and television), cinema, and new digital media. It's the best deal in town for learning digital filmmaking. Los Angeles Valley College is at 5800 Fulton Avenue, Van Nuys, CA 91401-4096; Phone (818) 781-1200. He looks for anything "totally cool" or "cutting edge." *The Color of Friendship,* a 2000 TV movie, was a multi-award winner, including the Emmy for Outstanding Children's Program. His most recent film was *Pixel Perfect* (2004). At the time of this publication he was producing a one-man stage show about comedian Lenny Bruce.

Contact: **Alan Sacks.** Query before sending a screenplay.

American Zoetrope, 916 Kearny Street, San Francisco, CA 94133; Phone (415) 788-7500, Fax (415) 989-7910, Web site www.zoetrope.com

Francis Ford Coppola, Writer/Director/Producer

Kim Aubry, Senior Vice President Post Production and Film Science

Howie Stein, Facility Manager

You might admire the work of Francis Ford Coppola in such films as *Bram Stoker's Dracula* (1992) or *The Godfather* movies, but this multi-award winner isn't going to buy a script from you via his Web site. It started out that way, but has since evolved into its own unique community. From the site:

> The Virtual Studio is a submission destination and collaboration tool for filmmakers—a community where artists can submit and workshop original work and where producers can make movies using built-in production tools. Membership is free. If you have questions that you would like answered before joining the site, please email us. Please note that messages sent to this address for the Coppola family or the production department will not be forwarded.

And further:

> By submitting work to the Virtual Studio, you are participating in a thriving workshop environment designed to help refine your craft. You'll receive invaluable feedback, collaborate and network with other artists, and market your services to potential buyers. All submissions will be made available to American Zoetrope and other member production companies, contingent only on your participation in the workshop. The cost is free and the benefits unlimited.

I've known writers who have sold their scripts in this manner, so it's worth checking out.

Contact: **Other writers and filmmakers** via the site.

Barracuda Productions, (address for submission if interested in your query), Los Angeles, CA; Phone (818) 749-3729, Email TVMovies@aol.com

Marc B. Lorber, Producer

Emmy-nominated producer Marc Lorber originally formed his company in 1994, but has also started or restarted TV divisions for companies such as Hallmark, Phoenix Pictures, and Carlton America (now Granada) to name a few. His development and production credits are diverse, ranging from *The Chris Isaak Show* for Showtime as well as two Emmy Award–winning family films for the same network, to CBS's miniseries, *Shake, Rattle & Roll* (1999), to action films for USA and Lifetime including *Rough Air* (2001), *Seconds to Spare* (2002), and *Danger Beneath the Sea* (2001), to comedies such as Oxygen's first original telefilm *A Tale of Two Wives.* Marc focuses on television miniseries, films, and one-hour series. At the time of this book, he had projects in development at networks ranging from Oxygen to Lifetime to TNT and ABC Family Channel.

Contact: **Marc Lorber** via email query only with a brief synopsis of finished scripts, books, and manuscripts, *not* ideas or pitches.

Barstu Productions, 10880 Wilshire Blvd., Suite 1500, Los Angeles, CA 90024; Phone (310) 234-5050, Fax (310) 200-2023, Email ViaMason@aol.com

Paul Mason, Producer

A graduate of Northwestern University, Paul Mason was twice awarded *Fame Magazine*'s Critic Award for writing and producing the best television detective series (*MacMillan and Wife*). He was nominated for the Emmy for best TV series (*Ironside*), a series that also won the first Image Award from the NAACP. From 1986 to 1990 he was President, Motion Pictures at Trans World Entertainment. Following that, as Senior Vice-President of Production at Viacom and Showtime from 1992 to 2002, Paul was responsible for $300 million in annual production. During his ten years at Viacom his actual results were within plus or minus one percent of his estimates. His other credits would fill a chapter. They include the TV series *Diagnosis Murder* (seven seasons), *Sabrina the Teenage Witch* (five seasons), and dozens of TV movies and pilots. His most current film is a sequel to *The Amityville Horror*. The book *Producing for Hollywood* by Paul Mason and Don Gold should be required reading for anyone trying to make a film.

Contact: **Paul Mason** with a quick pitch (logline) of what you have to sell.

The Bedford Falls Company, 409 Santa Monica Blvd., Santa Monica, CA 90401; Phone (310) 394-5022, Fax (310) 394-5825

Marshall Herkovitz, Producer/Writer

Edward Zwick, Executive Producer/Writer/Director

Richard Solomon, President

Joshua Gummersall, Creative Executive

Jason Novak, Creative Executive

Troy Putney, Creative Executive

Robin Budd, Head of Development

Ryan Coleman

David Passman

They first hit the big time with the long-running TV hit *thirtysomething,* and in 2001 secured an exclusive five-year, multimillion-dollar development deal with Touchstone Television, with whom they produced the ABC drama "Once and Again." Emmy-winning producers Marshall Herskovitz and Ed Zwick have done pretty well with feature films, too. Zwick directed *The Last Samurai* and other films, but don't count on him to concentrate on epics. You never know what they might like, such as a biopic on Chicago artist Henry Darger, a recluse who's had quite a story revolving around his fantasy-themed artwork. The producers are easy to deal with and open to hearing from new people.

Contact: **Robin Budd.** They prefer a phone call or a fax describing what you have to offer.

Benderspink, 6735 Yucca Street, Los Angeles, CA 90028; Phone (323) 856-5500, Fax (323) 856-5502, Email info@benderspink.com, Web site www.benderspink.com

Chris Bender, Producer/Manager

Charlie Gogolak, Manager, President of Production

Mason Novic, Literary Manager

Brian Spink, New Media Executive/Manager

J.C. Spink, Producer/Manager

Jake Weiner, Development Executive

A cutting-edge young company with hits behind them including the *American Pie* (1999, 2001, 2003) movies and *The Ring*, Benderspink offers hot manager/producers with a flair for comedy and hits. While at Zide Entertainment, Bender and Spink set up tons of projects before forming their own company. Benderspink accepts queries for screenplays, shorts, and feature films of all genres as well as new media projects. According to their site: "Our company's focus is breaking new talent and constantly discovering, creating, and developing unique material."

Contact: **Their Web site** for full details (note: you'll need the latest version of Macromedia Flash to view the site).

Bonny Dore Productions Inc./ Bonny Dore Management, 10940 Wilshire Boulevard, Suite 1600, Los Angeles, CA 90024; Phone (310) 443-4189, Fax (310) 443-4190, Email Bonnyinc@aol.com

Bonny Dore, Executive Producer, MOW's/Miniseries/Features/Series

Bonny Dore Productions Inc. has been in business since the mid-1980s. The company has a long list of award-winning movies of the week and miniseries for network and cable including *Sins* (1986), a seven-hour miniseries for CBS, *The Jill Ireland Story* (1991 MOW for NBC), *Captive* (1991 MOW for ABC), *Glory, Glory* (1998 six-hour miniseries for HBO), and *Sinking of the Rainbow Warrior* (a 1992 MOW for ABC). They have worked with such stars as Joan Collins, Timothy

Dalton, Jon Voight, Sam Neill, John Stamos, Chad Lowe, Richard Thomas, James Whitmore, Giancarlo Giannini, Joanna Kerns, and Ellen Greene among many others. The company looks for quality finished screenplays for independent feature films, and strong character-driven stories for cable/network movies of the week and miniseries. Additionally, the company has expanded into Bonny Dore Management, a second company that encompasses personal management of both literary talent and theatrical talent and is growing.

Boz Productions, 1632 N. Sierra Bonita Avenue, Los Angeles, CA 90046; Phone (323) 876-3232, Fax (213) 876-3231, Email bozenga@sbcglobal.net

> **Bo Zenga,** Writer/Director/Producer
> **Dan Wolf,** Director of Development

I've spoken on Hollywood panels with Bo Zenga and long admired him because he's such an amazing salesman. In 1997 he sold a *dozen* (!) pitches to major studios. His methods are aggressive and clever; he got Emilio Estevez on board his *Time Jumpers* then they took it to Tom Cruise, who signed on to an instant studio deal. (Estevez and Cruise were old friends, you see.) Then Cruise backed out, so Zenga almost immediately set the deal up with Dreamworks SKG. In February of 1999 he set up "Last Summer I Screamed Because Friday the 13th Fell on Halloween," which became Dimension Films' *Scary Movie* (2000), which took in more than $40 million at the box office the first weekend. More recently, he and writer Chuck Wilson sold *Soul Plane* (2004) to MGM. Bo is always flying high with something and has always been ready to hear new ideas.

> Contact: **Bo Zenga** or **Dan Wolf** with a query.

Butchers Run Films, 1041 North Formosa Ave., W. Hollywood, CA 90046; Phone (310) 246-4630, Fax (323) 850-2741

> **Robert Duvall,** Actor/Director/Producer
> **Rob Carliner,** Producer/Manager

Adam Prince, Director of Development

When he's not turning in fine performances in movies like *Secondhand Lions* (2003), Robert Duvall is dancing to the tune of his own music. Rob Carliner told me that to produce *The Apostle* (1997), Robert Duvall had to write a check for $4 million. He sold it to USA/October for $5 million and Duvall was nominated for an Oscar (the film won big at the Independent Spirit Awards). Duvall's *Assassination Tango* (2002), shot in New York and Argentina and backed by American Zoetrope and United Artists, was another fine low-budget film. Agents regularly call Rob Carliner to try to sign Duvall, who lives on a farm in Virginia and doesn't have a regular agent—since Duvall is agency-independent they can bypass packaging and call the director of the film. Director of Development Prince came on board after winning an award from USC and writing something Duvall and Carliner believed in. Their criteria for material is "as long as it's good"—can you impress them the way Prince did? Rob Carliner only reads three pages before he knows whether something is good or not. They like Westerns, totally different characters, something not seen before. They want a standard format script, no cute touches, and are *not* only looking for Robert Duvall star vehicles.

Contact: **Rob Carliner** or **Adam Prince.**

Contact: **Adam Prince** with queries.

Circle of Confusion Ltd., 575 Lexington Avenue, 4th Floor, New York, NY 10022 and 548 Washington Blvd., Culver City, CA 90232; Phone (212) 969-0653 (New York) and (310) 253-7777 (Los Angeles), Email queries@circleofconfusion.com, Web site www.circleofconfusion.com

Lawrence Mattis, Manager

David Alpert, Manager

David Engel, Manager of Development

A management company moving into production, Lawrence Mattis's company likes tough, New York–style science-fiction and horror writer/directors. They represent people such as the Wachowski brothers (*The Matrix*, 1999) and Jeff Monahan (writer/actor of *Tom Savini's Chill Factor*). Circle of Confusion's first feature, *Red* (2005), is about how a pack of thugs incurs the wrath of a man whose dog they killed.

Contact: **Email** is preferred. The Los Angeles number reaches David Alpert.

Deep River Productions, 100 N. Crescent Drive, Ste. 350, Beverly Hills, CA 90210; Phone (310) 432-1800, Fax (310) 432-1801

David Friendly, Producer

Marc Turtletaub, Producer

Julie Durk, Producer

Melissa Pontius, Director of Development

It's a small town. When I met Julie Durk she was head of development for Richard and Lauren Shuler-Donner, the company listed just below. It can also be a good town. The head of development for Deep River, "Missy" Pontius, is one of the more personable and friendly people I've ever met in Hollywood. This company does classy projects like the romantic comedy *Laws of Attraction* (2004) starring Pierce Brosnan and Julianne Moore (produced in conjunction with Brosnan's company, Irish Dreamtime). With an urban version of *The Honeymooners* TV series with Cedric the Entertainer and Mike Epps in the Ralph Kramden and Ed Norton roles, respectively, in the works, they also developed a Jackie Robinson biopic. In other words, if it's classy and interesting, it might have a home at Deep River. The last time I spoke with Ms. Pontius she told me they look for projects in these categories:

1. Romantic comedy;
2. Uplifting drama (*Chocolat* [2000], *Good Will Hunting* [1997], *Rain Man* [1988], and so forth);
3. Sweeping romance (doesn't need to be period); or
4. High-concept comedies (the kind you don't usually find in novels).

They generally don't care for thrillers or mysteries, and don't like anything dark, violent, or depressing.

Contact: **Melissa Pontius** at map@deepriverproductions.com for current needs.

The Donners' Company, 9465 Wilshire Blvd., #420, Beverly Hills, CA 90212; Phone (310) 777-4600, Fax (310) 777-4610

Richard Donner, Producer/Director

Lauren Shuler-Donner, Producer

Jack Leslie, President of Production

One of the most successful filmmakers in Hollywood, Richard Donner's credits include *Ladyhawke* (1985), *Lethal Weapon 1–4* (1987, 1989, 1992, 1998), *Maverick* (1994), *Lost Boys* (1987), *Superman* (1978), *Dave* (1993), *Conspiracy Theory* (1997), the *Free Willy* (1993, 1995, 1997) series, and Michael Crichton's *Timeline* (2003). If you don't know someone at Donner or have a well-known agent, your chances of selling them a property are slim. Nevertheless, they continue to be open to great new properties. Richard Donner is comfortable with action material that has a sense of humor, because basically he's like a big kid (pinball machines in his office last time I looked). In 1996, he joined forces with mega-producer of action films Joel Silver to form Decade Entertainment. Their most recent project is the live-action adaptation of the Japanese cartoon series *Speed Racer.* Lauren Shuler-Donner has similar tastes, with such projects as *Constantine* (2005), based on an adaptation of the DC-Vertigo comic book *Hellblazer;* it's a *Dirty Harry* (1971) set in the world of the occult.

Contact: **Jack Leslie** with a query letter via an agent.

Edwards Skerbelis Entertainment, 264 S. La Cienega Blvd., Ste. 1052, Beverly Hills, CA 90211; Phone (323) 466-3013, Fax (213) 467-1258, Email ESEntertainment@aol.com, Web site http://hometown.aol.com/rebelrona/esentertainment.html (will default to www.esentertainment.net once the site is fully built).

Rona Edwards, Producer

Monika Skerbelis, Producer

Rona Edwards's and Monika Skerbelis's class "Intro to Feature Film Development" at UCLA draws rave reviews, and their "15-Minute Pitch" seminar is equally popular. In their "day jobs" they produce and develop projects for feature film and television. Producer/manager Rona Edwards co-produced and/or executive produced *Out of Sync* (2000, VH1), *One Special Victory* (1991, NBC), *The Companion* (1994, USA/Sci-Fi Channel), *I Know What You Did* (1988, ABC), and for German television *Der Murder Meiner Mutter* (1999). She was VP of creative affairs for John Larroquette's Port Street Films, Michael Phillips Productions, and Brookfield Productions. She has had projects made and/or in development with many of the major networks and studios. In addition to teaching and producing, Monika Skerbelis is the festival and programming director for the Big Bear Lake International Film Festival. She was vice president of creative and executive story editor for Universal Pictures' story department for ten years, and prior to that was story editor for Twentieth Century Fox. She started out as an assistant in the story department for Paramount Pictures. This extensive knowledge of the studio system makes her a valuable producer.

Contact: **Either** of the principals.

Emmett/Furla Films, 1041 N. Formosa Ave., Mary Pickford Bldg. Ste. 101, Los Angeles, CA 90046; Phone (323) 850-2800, Fax (310) 659-9412

Randall Emmett, Co-President

George Furla, Co-President

Dal Walton, VP Development

Rosie Charbonneau, Assistant

The company has tough, even brutally hard-edged films to its credit including *Blind Horizon (2004)*, *Wonderland* (2003, the story of porn star John Holmes), and *Narc* (2002). At this writing they had an *Amityville Horror* sequel in the pipeline as well as other "troubled souls" projects such as *American Rain* (2006). One of their more interesting developments in recent years was the launch of digital production company Resolution Digital headed up by Raves.com founder Gavin Lloyd, who was a major player in the rave scene in Los Angeles. This is a good company for anyone with a well-written, gritty, or urban drama.

Contact: **Dal Walton** or dial extension 144 to learn about upcoming films.

Escape Artists, c/o Sony Pictures, 10202 West Washington Boulevard, Lean Building 333, Culver City, CA 90232; Phone (310) 244-8833, Fax (310) 244-2151, Email scheme: firstname_surname@spe.sony.com

David Alper, CEO & Partner

Todd Black, Producer

Chrissy Blumenthal, VP of Development (310) 244-8658

Jason Blumenthal, Producer (310) 244-8670

Mickey Guerin, Executive Assistant

Brian Morewitz, Senior Vice President

Steve Tisch, Producer (310) 841-4330

With collective credits *Risky Business* (1983), *I Know What You Did Last Summer* (1997), *Donnie Brasco* (1997), *Wild Things* (1998), *A Knight's Tale* (2001), and *Alex & Emma* (2003), it's hard to try to pin down what Escape Artists will do next. In recent years they've acquired diverse projects: *The Weatherman* (spec script secured in a bidding war); *Knowing* (supernatural thriller nabbed in turnaround from Columbia Pictures); and *Need* (Halle Berry vehicle bought by MGM about a New York therapist who discovers one of her patients is having an affair with her husband). When they produced *The Antwone Fisher Story* I was so impressed by how Todd Black went to bat for Mr. Fisher that I wrote him a fan letter. This is an imaginative company that takes chances on material and turns out always interesting movies. (See their cooperative agreement with HollywoodLitSales.com discussed above.)

Contact: **Chrissy Blumenthal** with a query or via HollywoodLitSales.com (see above in this chapter).

Esparza-Katz Entertainment, 3030 Andrita Street, Los Angeles, CA 90065; Phone (310) 281-3770, Fax (310) 281-3777

Moctesuma Esparza, Producer/Director, cocte@ix.netcom.com

Robert Katz, Producer, robertk@earthlink.net

Kimberly Myers, Producer

Luis Guerrero, Assistant, luisg@mayacinemas.com

Robert Katz and the award-winning writer/director/producer Moctesuma Esparza formed their company in 1984. Lately they've been on a heavy roll. After *The Milagro Beanfield War* (1988), which Robert Redford bought instead of a project of mine and their feature film *Selena* (1997), which made a star out of Jennifer Lopez, they became the premier company in Los Angeles for Hispanic-based projects. That doesn't mean that's all they do by any stretch. *Gettysburg* was one of TNT's biggest success stories, and they followed up with *Rough Riders* (1997) and *Gods and Generals* (2003) for Turner. They always have a ton of projects in the pipeline. Moctesuma Esparza said he wants to produce a "Salt of the Earth" remake that will gain a wider audience than the original did. The 1953 *Salt of the Earth* was the only movie blacklisted in the United States during Cold War retribution against left-leaning filmmakers. This fine company is open to anything that has "a great story, good writing, and compelling characters, done in a unique and different way."

Contact: **Anyone** listed above with a short description of what you have available. Describe full projects (no treatments) only.

Fast Carrier Pictures, 535 Hayden Avenue, First Floor, Culver City, CA 90232; Phone (310) 836-5018, Fax (310) 836-5012, Web site www.fastcarrier.com

Formerly based at Showtime, Fast Carrier Pictures is a motion picture and television production and development company founded in 1999 by former studio and network marketing executive Steven Jay Rubin. Rubin likes "popcorn films" that he classifies as "proven genre films that have worked over the decades because they appeal to wide audiences." Fast Carrier's first film for Showtime was *Bleacher Bums,* (2002) based on a popular, long-running stage play. They later developed a slate of World War II–themed projects. VP of Development Rory Aylward is a Slamdance Award winner. Their current focus is outdoor/nature films, low-budget horror, and thrillers that can be shot mostly at a single location.

Contact: **Steve Rubin** at steve@fastcarrier.com or send story pitches to **Rory Aylward** at fastcarriervp@aol.com

Gallagher Literary Management, 8160 Manitoba Street, Ste. 309, Los Angeles, CA 90293; Phone (310) 822-2070, Email DealmakerX@aol.com, Web site www.robgallagher.freeservers.com

Rob Gallagher, Manager/Producer

Jim Fernald, VP Development

Lanette Brown, Creative Exec

Kimberly Algeri, Creative Exec

Formerly a literary manager and head of literary for Cyd LeVin & Associates and head of literary for Messina-Baker Management, Gallagher has agented for Major Clients Agency and APA, as well as serving as VP of acquisitions and development for Ivy Entertainment. Prior to show biz, he was a military intelligence agent in Europe during the Cold War. He works with "a select list of talented and prolific screenwriters and directors" and knows tons of development executives. He has many associates who provide development notes and is looking for original and high-concept completed scripts to sell and/or produce. Gallagher prides himself in his unorthodox "guerrilla warfare" methods of finding material before it reaches Hollywood, which he has done primarily by using the Internet. Pitch only completed specs to him in *only* the following format via his email address *only* (no attachments): Title, Genre; Author, Phone number; logline; fifty-word synopsis; Similar films. He will only reply to pitches he is interested in, within a week.

Contact: All pitches must be made via **Web site only.**

The Goatsingers, 177 West Broadway, 2nd Fl. New York, NY 10013; Phone (212) 966-3045, Fax (212) 966-4362

Harvey Keitel, Partner

Peggy Gormley, Partner

Dennis O'Sullivan, Assistant

While Harvey Keitel's company has seemed somewhat inactive in recent years, I generally appreciate Keitel's performance and his help in getting new writer/directors started. The company has had various "first-look deals" with companies that allow them to develop and produce the "art house fare" that Keitel favors. The last time I wrote a book like this they were planning an adaptation of William Shakespeare's *The Merchant of Venice,* but it never got off the ground. So don't get your hopes up, but you might want to work with him.

Contact: **Peggy Gormley** and tell her what you have.

Grammnet Productions, 5555 Melrose Ave., Lucy Bungalow Suite 206, Los Angeles, CA 90038; Phone (323) 956-5547, Fax (323) 862-1774

Kelsey Grammer, CEO/Actor/Producer

Steve Stark, President

Joanne Asquith Weiss, Senior VP

Jessica Hochman Cassale, Director of Development

Mark Ganshirt, VP Development, TV

Karyn Lamb, Director of Development, TV

Sadly, *Frasier,* the smartest sitcom on network television, is no more, except in syndication. Housed at Paramount Studios, this is a company I hope has just as much success in films, and not because I've known company president Steve Stark since the days he worked with TV producer Al Burton on *Charles in Charge.* They look for smart, fresh material and if it comes from unknown writers, that's fine. In May 2004, they gave recent USC graduate Kara Holden her first sale when they bought *Inner Bitch,* a broad female-driven comedy along the lines of *Liar Liar.* Other projects in development at the time of the *Variety* article mentioning the sale were *Honeymoon from Hell, If You Only Knew,* and *Case of the Halloween Hangman.* If you had to categorize the type of feature projects they pick up, you might say it's something Frasier would love, but wouldn't admit he even liked. TV can be a different story; in 2003 they sold four projects to three networks, with drama scripts at ABC, NBC, and the Sci-Fi Channel. It's basically just a good solid company looking for quality, clever material. You might need an agent to get through to them.

Contact: **Director of Development** as appropriate.

The It Company, 528 Palisades Dr., #133, Pacific Palisades, CA 90272; Phone (323) 363-1734, Web site www.theitco.com

Sheree Guitar, Partner/Founder

John Broker, Partner/Founder

This management/production company grew out of Sheree Guitar's Writer Workshop by combining Sheree Guitar's writing with John Broker's business and sales acumen. Their students and clients include the writers of the animated Disney feature *Brother Bear* (2003) and they have placed clients on TV shows such as *Malcolm in the Middle* and *That's So Raven.* Given Guitar's expertise in teaching writers how the business works, this could be a good place for a beginner to start. According to their Web site: "We will treat writers with respect, dignity, and with the occasional free meal." Long-term clients and friends of mine have told me they practice what they preach. Although they place TV staff writers and will consider independent-type scripts, their primary focus is on high-concept studio pictures.

Contact: **Sheree Guitar** at Sheree@theitco.com or **John Broker** at John@theitco.com.

Leslie Kallen Literary/Media Management, 15303 Ventura Blvd., #90, Sherman Oaks, CA 91403; Phone (800) 755-2785, (818) 906-2785, Fax (818) 906-8931, Email kallengroup@earthlink.net, Web site: www.lesliekallen.com

Leslie B. Kallen, Agent

Leslie Kallen loves new writers, and she's done well by them, with several award-winners on her roster. Alone and in conjunction with UCLA professor Richard Walter, she has delivered seminars throughout North America. She is signatory with the WGA and runs a successful boutique agency. Always looking for "a great story, well-told," she looks for television films and feature films. She doesn't want one-hour episodic or sitcom scripts, poetry, or children's novels. Her partner in New York is Frank Weimann of The Literary Group International.

Contact: All inquiries should go to **Leslie Kallen.**

Metropolitan Talent Agency, 4526 Wilshire Blvd., Los Angeles, CA 90010; Phone (323) 857-4500, Fax 323-857-4599, Email (main) mta@mta.com

Christopher Barrett, President

David Boxerbaum, Literary Agent (dboxerbaum@mta.com)

Dino Carlaftes, Head/Agent, Literary

Barry Murphy, Literary Coordinator

Chris Barrett's "boutique" agency is better known for talent representation, but Metropolitan agents have sold scripts like *The Pearl* (2001), *Ronin* (1998), and *The Stars Fell on Henrietta* (1995). They are not afraid to take on other undiscovered writers who have excellent material, but this can fluctuate wildly from year to year, just like Hollywood. James Bradley and Ron Powers's book *Flags of Our Fathers: Heroes of Iwo Jima,* represented in conjunction with Hornfischer Literary, went for a huge amount of money to DreamWorks. Their personnel are industry veterans; for example, David Boxerbaum was a creative executive at RKO Films before joining the agency.

Contact: **Agents** listed above for current needs.

Mr. Mudd, 5225 Wilshire Blvd., Ste. 604, Los Angeles, CA 90036; Phone (323) 932-5656, Fax (323) 932-5666

John Malkovich, Producer/Director/Actor

Russell Smith, Producer

Lianne Halfon, Producer

Shannon Clark, Creative Associate

The last time I listed this company in a book, that book ended up on national television in an AMC cable channel special called "Malkovich's Mail." Hey, with such success, how can I leave them out of this one? Besides, John Malcovich is one of the most talented actors of our time, so maybe some screenwriter will get lucky, and he'll actually develop one of their properties. Is it true that more than forty tons of screenplay pitch letters are dropped into the Hollywood mail slots each year as the one-hour documentary claimed? Who knows, but some of the lucky screenwriters featured saw Malkovich act out scenes from their scripts. I've enjoyed just about everything John Malkovich has been involved in, including his directorial debut, *The Dancer Upstairs* (2002). If you're of like mind and can live with the fact that they develop almost everything in-house, give them a try.

Contact: **Shannon Clark** via a short fax describing your project; if she's interested she'll let you know.

Permut Presentations Inc., 9150 Wilshire Blvd., Ste. 247, Beverly Hills, CA 90212; Phone (310) 248-2792, Fax (310) 248-2797

David Permut, President/Producer

Steven Longi, VP Production

Daniel T. Mitchell, Development

David Permut is Mr. High-Concept Producer, but he's also eclectic. Who else would come up with a comedy version of the crime drama *Dragnet* or make a movie about a cop and a criminal who switch faces (*Face/Off*, 1997), or attempt a biopic about Sammy Davis Jr. (who led a pretty freaky life)? It's hard to keep up with all the things Permut and the affable Steve Longi have in development, but I generally always see the movies the company turns out. Permut and Longi are two of my favorite people in the business; one is all Hollywood and the other is all story and business. I'll let you find out which one. If you have a story about the crazy life of a comedian, they probably already beat you to it, with biopics about Sam Kinison and Rodney Dangerfield in the works. The last time I checked, they were also developing a movie from C.D. Payne's novel *Youth in Revolt,* about a precocious fourteen-year-old trying to lose his virginity. If you sell them something, let me know—David still owes me a script read.

Contact: **Steve Longi** or **Daniel Mitchell.**

Lynn Pleshette Agency, 2700 N. Beachwood Drive, Los Angeles, CA 90068; Phone (213) 465-0428, Fax (213) 465-6073

Lynn Pleshette, Owner

Michael Cendejas, Agent

Lynn Pleshette is one of the classier agents in Los Angeles and has trained several people who have moved on to great success elsewhere as agents. She believes that any talented screenwriter will get ahead because there is such a dearth of good scripts. Headquartered in beautiful Beachwood Canyon, she is interested in features and TV movies, and also sells book rights like Staton Rabin's unpublished young adult historical novel *Betsy and the Emperor.* Rabin's novel was classy material, as was the Pleshette sale *The Truman Show* (1998) and Scott Smith's novel *The Ruins* (sold to Ben Stiller and Stuart Cornfeld's Red Hour Films in a seven-figure deal). Pleshette represents a small, but quality group of writers; if she takes you on Hollywood will probably like you.

Contact: **Story Department** with a query. They only respond by phone if interested.

PMA Literary & Film Management, Inc., 45 West 21st Street, Sixth Floor, New York, NY 10010; Phone (212) 929-1222, Fax (212) 206-0238, (packages to PO Box 1817, Old Chelsea Station, New York, NY 10011), Email info@pmalitfilm.com, queries to pmalitfilm@aol.com, Web site www.pmalitfilm.com

Peter Miller, President

Scott Hoffman, Associate

Lisa Silverman, Associate

Nathan Rice, Associate

Greg Takoudes, Associate

Betty Ferm, Associate

A firm with a presence on both the east and west coasts and worldwide literary connections, PMA has sold a number of TV movies and actively looks for new writers. The author of *Get Published! Get Produced!* Miller does seminars for writers and is such a schmoozer he has actually sold treatments for writers. Always with an eye toward Hollywood, Miller started a sister corporation, Millennium Lion, as a production entity to coordinate "the submission of all potential film properties to television networks, studios, and film production companies. This company actively seeks production arrangements for projects to be produced in partnership or in association with Peter Miller, who functions primarily as an executive producer." That attachment might be seen as cumbersome at some studios, but maybe not. Miller will certainly be aggressive for you if he signs you.

Contact: Query **anyone** mentioned above by mail, fax, or email; I suggest you read over the Web site's extensive information.

The Ruddy Morgan Organization, Inc., 9300 Wilshire Boulevard, Ste. 508, Beverly Hills, CA 90212; Phone (310) 271-7698, Fax (310) 278-9978, Email ruddymorgan@earthlink.net

Al Ruddy, Producer

André Morgan, Producer

Mary Aymar, Creative Affairs

This major production company has a long track record in feature films and a large presence in network television. André Morgan also manages Hong Kong directors, a situation which sprang from their relationship with Raymond Chow's Golden Harvest (Hong Kong's biggest production company). Ruddy and Morgan won the Academy Award for Best Picture (*The Godfather*), two Golden Globes, and Italy's

"David of Donatello" award. They were partners in the Chuck Norris series *Walker, Texas Ranger.* Supposedly they are planning on making the long-awaited *Atlas Shrugged,* from the novel by Ayn Rand, but they were telling me that the last time I wrote a book like this one. Despite their serious projects, this is also a company that likes the lighter side. Projects in the pipeline include *Cloud Nine,* about a has-been coach (Burt Reynolds) who launches a women's volleyball team for strippers, and a film from the novel *Swish Hitters,* about two East Hampton antique dealers who become Mob hit-men. They're also involved in the Clint Eastwood film *Rope Burns,* written by Paul Haggis, one of their co-creators on *Walker, Texas Ranger.* So take your pick and give them your best shot; they could make you famous.

Contact: Try **Mary Aymar** first, but the last time I spoke with **André Morgan** he told me he is open to queries and that I could call anyone at the office.

Stefanie Epstein Productions, Inc., 427 N. Canon Dr., Suite 206, Beverly Hills, CA 90210; Phone (310) 385-0300, Fax (310) 385-0302
> **Stefanie Epstein,** Producer
> **Jason Murtaugh,** Development Executive

With TV movie credits like *A Boyfriend for Christmas* (2004), *Audrey's Rain* (2003), and *Abduction of Innocence* (1996), Stefanie Epstein Productions offers a beginner with good material a good place to pitch. Assistant Jason Murtaugh is on the ball, sharp, and very easy to speak with (according to my inside source).

Contact: **Stefanie Epstein** at Seproductions@aol.com or **Jason Murtaugh** at jamurts@aol.com.

Terence Michael Productions, Inc., 421 Waterview Street, Playa Del Rey, CA 90293; Phone (310) 823-3432, Fax (310) 861-9093, Email tm@terencemichael.com, Web site www.terencemichael.com
> **Terence Michael,** Producer/Chairman
> **Jeanne Trepanier,** Director of Development

Terence Michael Productions was formed in 1991 to produce independent films that are distributed by the studios. Since then they have produced more than twenty feature films and three TV shows. Their focus has always been directors. They look for interesting, unique directors with an odd or new perspective on life or situation to work with. Most of their projects have been comedies (including five films with New York writer/director Eric Schaeffer including Sony's *If Lucy Fell* [1996], MGM's *Fall* [1997], and Universal/Focus Features *Never Again* [2001], but they are open to just about any genre. Terence Michael was partnered with writer/producer Richard Finney for a slate of six films (The Lions Gate franchise of *100 Girls* [2000], and *100 Women* [2002], as well as two TV movies—Disney Channel's *Perfect Little Angels* [1998] and Lifetime's *The Pact*, [2002]. The company's next wave will be highly commercial, studio-driven products that can be made for a price and attract an artistic director.

Contact: **Terence Michael.** Always email first. He says: "I personally read every single one, even though I can't answer them all. If there's something that catches my eye, I'll request it and read it. It can be a book, an article, or script. No mere ideas. That alone won't help."

Union Entertainment LLC, 1337 Ocean Avenue, Ste. B, Santa Monica, CA 90401; Phone [310] 395-1040, Fax (310) 395-1065, Web site www.unionent.com

Richard Leibowitz, President, Union Games—rich@union-ent.com

Sean O'Keefe, President, Union Films—sean@unionent.com

There is perhaps no other company in Hollywood like Union. They simultaneously develop feature films, television, and video games, and have relationships all over Hollywood with top people. They also represent video game talent (which is how I met them) and work with the top people in that business. Richard Leibowitz started in the business as an entertainment attorney at Paramount before becoming VP of International Business and Legal Affairs at Rysher Entertainment. He has founded two video game agencies and knows everything about that business. Sean O'Keefe started with Neal Moritz at Original Films and worked on films like *I Know What You Did Last Summer*. He then became Vice-President of Production at Artists Production Group, the film division of Michael Ovitz's Artists Management Group, where he worked with top-flight directors including John McTiernan and Martin Scorsese. O'Keefe's most recent production was *Godsend* starring Robert DeNiro. They look for anything cutting-edge and interesting. A tour of their Web site will give you an education in what this unique company is all about.

Contact: **Either principal** with a short query.

Vanguard Films, 1230 La Collina Drive, Beverly Hills, CA 90210; Phone (310) 888-8020, Fax (310) 888-8012, Email mail@vanguardfilms.com, Web site www.vanguardfilms.com

John Williams, CEO, Vanguard Films & Animation

Neil Braun, President

Robert Moreland, Creative Executive

Back in the day when I used to work myself to death to send out a free email newsletter to my readers, I asked the producer of *Shrek* (2001) via email if he'd mind doing an email interview with me. No problem, he said, and answered the questions right away. With such classy credits as *Seven Years in Tibet* (1997) and such comedies as *The Tuxedo* (2002), I think of this company in terms of "movies I love to see." The Disney-based company develops projects such as the Roald Dahl classic illustrated children's book *The Twits*, so they might not take time for an unknown project, but you never can tell. Williams discovered *Shrek* as a small book his young son was reading.

Contact: **Robert Moreland** with a short query.

Zide/Perry Entertainment, 9100 Wilshire Blvd., 615 East Tower, Beverly Hills, CA 90212; (310) 887-2999, Fax (310) 887-2995, Email (general) inzide@inzide.com, Web site www.inzide.com (note: Web site was down as of this writing)

Jennie Frankel, Manager

Warren Zide, Manager/Producer

This management/production company has the *American Pie* and *Final Destination* (2000, 2003, 2006) movies to their credit, as well as other popular fare like *The Big Hit* (1998). They look for "very commercial material" and often get healthy six-figure advances for writers. For example, Paramount paid $600,000 against $1 million for an untitled twenty-seven-page thriller treatment from Chap Taylor about a jewel thief whose wife is taken hostage. The Web site covers their submission guidelines and more; I hope it is back up by the time you read this. Zide's production company, **Matinee Pictures,** develops projects like *Soul Calibur,* about a battle over a sword that can slice open the gates of hell and destroy the world.

Contact: **Jennie Frankel** or **Warren Zide. Zinkler Films,** 9000 Sunset Blvd. Ste. 1101, W. Hollywood, CA, 90069; Phone (310) 285-1840, Fax (310) 285-0440, Email info@zinklerfilms.com, Web site www.zinklerfilms.com

Jessica Russell, Producer

Arrika Russell, Producer

An actress and casting director, Jessica Russell starred as herself in a "making of" video about her short subject *A Sight for Sore Eyes* (2003). She also has a background in commercial real estate. Her 2004 feature *All American Game* followed on the heels of the films *Wisegirls* (2002), and *Boys Klub* (2001). She produces with her sister, Arrika. While it might appear they are only interested in chick flicks, their Web site will tell you otherwise and provide a lot more details about the company.

Index

Index

Index

ABOUT THE AUTHOR

Skip Press is the author of *The Complete Idiot's Guide to Screenwriting* and *How to Write What You Want & Sell What You Write*, among many other books. He has taught at UCLA and the Academy of Art College, and his online screenwriting course is available in almost 900 colleges and universities around the world. Press has appeared as a featured speaker at writers' conferences across the United States and regularly serves on entertainment industry panels. He lives in Southern California. For more information, visit his website at www.skippress.com.